UNDERSTANDING AND MANAGING
Sales and Use Tax

Sixth Edition

Robert J. Fields

CCH INCORPORATED
Chicago
A WoltersKluwer Company

EDITORIAL STAFF

Book Production Coordinator: Jeri Ann Stucka

Book Production: Marilyn J. Alvarado

ISBN: 0-8080-1115-4

4025 W. Peterson Ave.
Chicago, IL 60646-6085
1 800 248 3248
http://tax.cchgroup.com

Acknowledgments

Confidence may be defined as "faith or belief in, or reliance upon." This book is the product of such confidences: my confidence in others, their confidence in me and the resulting confidence I had in myself. Thank you to a host of tax professionals at PricewaterhouseCoopers LLP who have continued to push me to higher levels of achievement and knowledge in the tax environment. Thank you to those at CCH INCORPORATED for your sponsorship and assistance. You have collectively continued to express your faith in a book that is now over 13 years old, in its sixth edition, and still enjoying extraordinary readership and acceptance in the sales tax industry. And thank you, Karen, for your continuing understanding, friendship and love, and to Aaron and Shannah, my remarkable children, without whose encouragement and love this project would have been less exciting.

About the Author

Robert J. Fields is the Director of Technology for the State and Local Tax practice in the firm of PricewaterhouseCoopers LLP (since June 2002). Previously, Bob managed the national State and Local Tax Data Management Function at Arthur Andersen LLP. Prior to joining Andersen in September 1997, Bob was the president and chief executive officer of Fields & Associates, a sales/use tax consulting company he founded in 1973. In his work as a sales tax consultant, Fields has established a large following of major U.S. and international corporations that rely on this creative approach to sales tax issues and services.

Fields holds a Bachelor of Arts from the University of the Pacific and a Masters of Business Administration from Pepperdine University. He is professionally active in the Institute for Professionals in Taxation (IPT), in which he has earned the designation of Certified Member of the Institute (sales tax). He has been an instructor for the IPT at its beginning and intermediate annual Sales Tax Schools since their inception and is also a regular guest lecturer in a variety of other sales tax programs nationally.

Preface

This book is about the practical applications of sales and use tax and contains basic concepts that form the foundation for a working tax consciousness. The tax practitioner should find this book serving as a tool chest containing logically organized information or as a reference book to help formulate the appropriate questions. This work is not intended to serve as a recipe or how-to book.

This is not a book about rational laws, though I attempt to be rational in my presentation. My effort will not seek to value a tax as good or bad, although I shall try to help you understand and cope with what is tasteful or distasteful. No specific state or industry has received a concentrated focus, although I shall look at examples for clarification of concepts.

Do not regard this work as a synopsis of any **CCH** INCORPORATED sales and use tax subscription service, although it may lead one to the appropriate source for the answer to a vexing question.

Prior editions of this book have included many CCH INCORPORATED charts for quick reference. My editors and I have agreed that there is material risk in providing such date-sensitive information. Accordingly, I encourage your subscription to the CCH INCORPORATED on-line services that include the charts previously included as well as others, all maintained on a current basis.

As you read this book, you may recognize where both answers and questions can be found. I have tried to provide a tool to understanding, an instrument of discovery. Ask today what might cause you to question tomorrow.

You can help with your own sticky-tab notes for rapid reference and focused attention. Together we will build a bridge to understanding the practical issues surrounding sales and use taxation. Take care in your reading of the rules and definitions we offer. They will apply in most cases, but there are likely exceptions that may or may not be noted. And finally, engage your imagination when reading and working with sales and use tax. What is possible may not be obvious, and what is obvious is probably possible.

January 2004

Robert J. Fields

Introduction

In an attempt to offer the tax professional guidance supported by a simple analysis of sales and use tax concepts, this book is divided into two sections:

Section I—Concepts of Sales and Use Tax

Section II—Management of the Sales and Use Tax Function

Section I begins with a discussion of the book and its audience and concludes with a discussion of taxes in general. Chapter II contains a very important chart explaining how sales taxes differ. No tax professional can claim to understand sales tax without being conversant with and knowledgeable about the different types of sales tax. Local sales and use taxes are also covered in this chapter, as are a variety of quasi-sales taxes. Chapter III looks at the tax that complements the sales tax—the use tax.

Chapters IV and V take both the sales and use taxes and separately discuss how the taxes are measured, i.e., the transactions or values included in or excluded from the tax liability. The discussion of use tax is particularly significant to manufacturers and consumers. Failure to accrue and pay use tax, the purchaser's liability, often results in substantial tax assessments. Measuring one's tax liability would be easy were it not for the myriad exemptions and exclusions available to both sellers and purchasers. Chapter VI addresses this topic.

Chapter VII is concerned with the compliance audit activity, including some basic statistical sampling and a discussion of the hearing and appeal process. A discussion of the governmental administration of the sales/use tax function at the individual state level is found in Chapter VIII, followed by a short review of the latest activities in the multistate arena (Chapter IX). Section I concludes with a review of nexus and Commerce Clause issues (Chapter X), terms having constitutional ramifications that are extremely important to the tax professional.

Section II begins with an overview of the activities of tax department management, proposing several questions that are answered in other chapters. A section on process mapping is included in Chapter XI. Chapter XII talks about registration, an issue of increasing interest in today's mail-order world. Chapter XIII contains important tax insurance information—exemption documentation and forms. Chapter XIV has been regarded by many as the most valuable single chapter for the tax professional, offering nine easy-to-follow rules for handling those dreaded audits. Chapters XV through XVIII cover topics of general interest for those looking to increase the sophistication and productivity of their tax departments. Included in these chapters is a discussion of automation tools, particularly new web-based versus system-based applications. Chapter XVI covers the major elements of the typical tax return and discusses return preparation. The final portion of the chapter introduces the concepts of electronic funds transfer (EFT) and electronic date interchange (EDI). As increasing numbers of jurisdictions require taxpayer compliance via EFT and/or EDI, tax professionals will require a greater facility in understanding and implementing these programs. The much-ignored issue of record retention (Chapter XIX) often receives too little attention too late.

The last four chapters offer the reader an opportunity to play with some real-life situations. Chapter XX was developed in response to clients who offered their questions in return for some written answers. A question concerning procurement cards is included in this chapter. The voice of experience is powerful in this chapter. Chapter XXI covers some random issues that cause even the most seasoned tax veterans frustration. Chapter XXII takes a look into the environments and issues of six industries: retail, manufacturing, construction, telecommunications, leasing, and services. Each industry is discussed in light of its sales, purchases, special tax accounting questions and Constitutional issues. Chapter XXIII addresses the world of electronic commerce, the Internet, and the efforts by many states to simplify sales and use tax, a noble and frustrating effort. And Chapter XXIV plays with a live situation—is this book taxable? While a reader may not be a publisher or bookseller, this chapter probes very real issues in many tax environments. Specifically, certain issues discussed in Chapter XXII resurface in this chapter as real examples

In this sixth edition, I have added material throughout the book, beyond the changes identified here. Unfortunately, commenting on each change would give the reader of an earlier edition an excuse not to read this entire edition. Reading this book again is recommended as a refresher course and, hopefully, a chance to relish something newly learned or to enjoy an old idea remembered.

Finally, the Glossary provides the reader with a snapshot of the terms found throughout the book. Some of the terms may have special meaning in sales/use tax and should be properly used and understood. This book will not make its reader into an experienced tax professional, but it will have paid for itself with the ideas that may be gleaned throughout these pages.

LIST OF ILLUSTRATIONS AND CHARTS

TABLE OF CONTENTS

Chapter XXIII—Electronic Commerce, E-Business, and Other Mysteries of Cyberspace

Chapter XXIV—Is This Book Taxable?

Chapter I
Understanding Taxes in General

¶101 A Well-Spring of Opportunity

Much has been said about taxes and tax theory in the years since the colonists asserted their will and told King George to drink the Boston Harbor. The world now includes taxes assessed on a remarkable variety of transactions and activities including (but certainly not limited to) income, franchise, property, business license, value-added, sales, use, excise, occupations, payroll, etc. In our recent past political history, new terms have been coined to say "tax" without using the "t" word, such as revenue enhancer. Regardless of the type of tax being discussed, taxes have as much similarity as they have uniqueness.

#/ An individual's success in managing or administering as a tax practitioner is first a matter of being able to read and understand the body of law encompassing the tax in question. Interestingly, there is not a great deal of magic in understanding a tax law, statute, code or ordinance. While a legal degree is not a prerequisite, one must be able to discern key terms and phrases, sections, paragraphs and definitions that are the "genetic" code that distinguishes one tax from another. Once these characteristics have been recognized, it is the practitioner's task to build a working vocabulary to employ in decoding the tax genetics.

Is there any reason why a tax practitioner with average intelligence cannot become a sales and use tax expert? Is there special training given to law students that enables an individual with a law degree to comprehend tax codes? Is a tax consultant schooled in tax terminology and application? Is a certified public accountant instructed in the fine points of reading regulatory volumes? The answer to all of these questions is "no."

Perhaps the single common training that gives these "experts" their skill is in the school of hard-knocks and daily involvement. The individual who continually challenges his mentor, be it a senior tax partner, legislative aide, consulting supervisor, etc., will be the next person to possess the elusive knowledge. For trained experts, tax knowledge goes beyond theoretical understanding. Tax expertise is enhanced by the zeal to achieve profit through the use of knowledge.

Accordingly, the individual who first understands the body of law should seek experience in its practical application to gain functional expertise. Proceeding in reverse is slightly more challenging though certainly more common. Trained practitioners who become true experts are ones who take time to go deeper than the activity of transporting numbers, completing returns, designing elaborate data processing systems and performing all of the acts of compliance. It is because proceeding in reverse works (i.e., doing and experiencing, then learning) that there is a large audience for this book. That audience of tax professionals may include:

(1) legislators, who, with the help of aides and under the influence of special interests, carve out the tax laws;

(2) administrators, collectors and agents, who are charged with interpreting the tax law by writing regulations, collecting taxes and auditing taxpayers (but who are often products of their own imperfect training and systems);

(3) academicians, who study taxes and how they work, their similarities and differences (without ever experiencing taxes in a practical sense);

(4) statisticians and econometricians, who analyze and weigh the impacts of taxes upon taxpayers, build elaborate tables evidencing how much of what type of tax is collected, study and purport to understand how tax and fiscal policy impact the big economic picture (and who often ignore the real costs of the schemes, largely out of lack of experience);

(5) practitioners, who run the day-to-day departments of companies, collect and report taxes, plan and act out the world of tax matters (and who may not understand who really owes the tax);

(6) attorneys, who defend the tax laws or those upon whom they are "unjustly" imposed (with little regard for whose ox got gored);

(7) out-source providers (in increasing numbers), who handle the processing of returns for their clients, essentially doing what their clients say without typically questioning the inputs;

(8) accountants and preparers, who prepare, review, or amend returns, prepared by themselves or others (and who have technical skill but may lack practical experience); and

(9) consultants, who work with the tax laws and tax collectors for the benefit of their clients (and who often unknowingly leave the biggest problems behind).

And unless pushed beyond his or her own immediate concerns, there is often little relationship between an individual's professional standing in the tax community and his or her ability to view taxes any more broadly than the job dictates. This book is intended to benefit these people as well.

Simply, taxes are created by deliberative bodies to raise revenue. Businesses and individuals are taxed directly or indirectly and remit monies to political subdivisions governed by these same deliberative bodies. Commercial "helpers" (accountants, attorneys and consultants) are enchanted and smitten with the entrepreneurial urge to find business opportunities in the confusion of others. Thus is created a world full of possibilities. This book will guide the reader through that world.

¶102 Commonality Among All Taxes

Taxes are "imposed or levied" upon something, someone, some activity, or some value. In every tax code, ordinance, law or statute there is, typically, a phrase, section, or paragraph that sets out the imposition or levy. However, to get to that phrase, most laws provide working definitions. For example, how can a law "impose a tax on the sale of tangible personal property at retail" without first defining all of the terms. In this one short phrase of 12 words, there are at least seven words requiring very specific definitions: impose, tax, sale, tangible, personal, property, and retail. For all of the sales tax laws currently on the books in 45 states and the District of Columbia, no two sets of definitions are identical, although they are often loosely copied.

Deliberative bodies do not have the time or the personnel to directly administer the taxes they impose. Therefore, every law prescribes that these tasks be assigned to an administrative body authorized to act in some fashion. This provision may be part of the specific law or set aside in a code section of its own applying to all taxes imposed by the jurisdiction. When will the tax be due? If it is late, is there a penalty? How long must the records be kept? What transactions, either by definition, interpretation or implication, are not subject to tax and how do you prove this condition? And the list goes on. However, to make it easier for the reader, charts are included that demonstrate, state-by-state, where one would find the issues common to all states.

Finally, when a tax collector and taxpayer are in disagreement about the meaning, intent or requirements of the tax law, the courts are the prescribed arbiters of last resort. The order of administrative and judicial remedies (see Chapter VII) provides the rules that guarantee due process. Again, while the remedies are always present in the state statute, they might not be found in the specific tax code section under scrutiny.

To put it another way, state legislatures, state assemblies and, with increasing commonness, local jurisdictions, and, in some cases, the general public through the initiative process, vote on and pass laws that establish taxes and empower administrative or regulatory bodies to interpret these laws on a day-to-day basis. These state agencies are known as Tax Commissions, Departments of Revenue, Departments of Taxation, Boards of Equalization, etc. The interpretive writings are called rules, regulations, guidelines, etc. There are legal officers, tax counsel, administrative law judges, etc., who, by issuing findings, annotations, and opinions, make fine distinctions.

The overall structure of sales and use taxes is not unlike that found among other taxes, be they federal, state or local. The names of the deliberative bodies may be similar, the administrative agencies have designated responsibilities, the staffs of these organizations function in similar fashion, and taxpayers collect and/or pay the taxes so levied and imposed. As we look at the singular world of sales and use tax, we will become more aware of the similarities and the differences between the taxes, state to state.

Chapter II
Sales Taxes

¶201 Introduction

#2   Sales taxes, in the form we recognize today, were first adopted in the 1930s. Which state was first to adopt a sales tax and the precise form of that early tax code is of limited value to all but tax historians. What we do know is that 45 states and the District of Columbia now have a tax that is classified as a sales tax. In fact, some of these states have several taxes that are collectively called sales taxes, even though they are really distinct and separate, one from the other. Later I will talk about sales or transaction taxes imposed at the local level.

Rates and Basis

#3   All sales taxes have rates that generally continued to rise since their establishment. Rising tax rates are one of the two elements that cause revenues to increase. More recently, jurisdictions have also played with the base, the set of transactions that are used to define what will be taxed. Tangible personal property is consistently used to define the base. Now we are seeing the definition of the base include services, licenses or software (right to use), amusements, telecommunications services, etc. When determining what is taxed, it is often necessary to read more then the statute. Jurisdictions are playing with the base administratively as well as statutorily. So, the word is, "don't just read the word. Look behind the word to where the meaning may be hidden and interpretive." Audit assessments of sales tax are mostly a function of omitting tax due to improper interpretation of the words both in and outside of the statute, and less so because of someone uses an incorrect rate.

The five states without a sales tax (at the state level) are Alaska, Delaware, New Hampshire, Montana, and Oregon. Each of these states has fought or avoided the imposition of sales tax by having a revenue base from other taxes or income sources strong enough to handle the state's fiscal needs. Periodically, at least one of these five states offers its citizenry a plebiscite on the sales tax issue.

New Hampshire was such a fatality in the war against the "t" word. But in lieu of a sales tax it imposed an excise tax at the rate of five percent on telecommunications services in 1990. While some might argue that an excise tax is not a sales tax, this author feels the intent is there—to extend the grasp of government taxation through the imposition of a tax based on receipts, regardless of whether it is measured by the sale or use of the telecommunications services.

In 1990, voters in Montana, second of the five holdout states without a sales tax, went to the polls to consider an imaginative in-lieu tax, a "trade charge." The trade charge did not pass. The cunning state residents would not be fooled. They recognized the trade charge for what it really was, a sales tax wolf in a carefully crafted sheepskin.

In another attempt to solve a growing financial crisis, Oregon voters in 1992 went to the polls to vote on a tax initiative establishing that state's first sales tax at a rate of 5%. The need for the tax arose after the same electorate, only one year earlier, passed an initiative limiting state and local property taxes. It came as little surprise to most observers that the Oregon sales tax initiative was soundly defeated.

In November 1994, the same Oregon electorate went to the polls to consider doing away with all taxes and adopting a two-percent "trade levy." Not quite a sales tax and something more akin to a gross receipts tax or a value-added tax, this initiative failed as well. For Oregon voters, the issue of changing the tax structure is associated with the very high property tax (over 2% of valuation) that partially makes up for the absence of a sales tax. Being so close to California on one border and Washington on the other border, Oregonians can view two of the highest combined sales tax rates in the nation very close to home.

Increasing a sales tax can also be accomplished by merely expanding the definition of one of the following terms: imposition, taxable service, engaged (in business), etc. These are good ways to increase the base. Examples of how states define these terms are discussed throughout the balance of this book.

As a result of the statutory creativity exhibited by states like Montana, one of the sales tax practitioner's concerns must be the recognition and comprehension of differences between the various sales taxes. Failure to recognize and understand these differences can result in sizable and unnecessary assessments. This becomes clear as one addresses the pivotal concept of "imposition."

There are four clearly distinguishable types of sales tax imposed by the various states. How they are labeled is of no importance relative to how they are structured. But, for identification purposes in this book, we will label the four tax types as follows: privilege tax, consumer levy, transaction tax and gross receipts tax. There are, in addition, less common taxes administered by the same state agencies called business and occupations taxes, business license taxes, etc. These are discussed later in this chapter.

Before discussing these four tax types, one should recognize the three characteristics that are distinguishing features of these four types of sales tax:

(1) *Shifting* refers to the extent to which the tax burden must be transferred from the party required to collect the tax to the party who must suffer the tax cost. Reference to shifting herein is a statement that shifting is mandatory. When shifting is mandatory, the tax burden moves from the tax collector to the customer or consumer.[1]

---

[1] States have been careful in selecting between the use of the terms customer or purchaser and consumer or user. The customer or purchaser may not be the end consumer or user, as is the case with resales. Therefore, the choice of the term consumer or user gives credence to the fact that the tax expense is ultimately borne by the final consumer or user, measured by the final cost or price. Purchasers or customers may purchase for resale. Throughout this book, these terms have been used interchangeably unless a topic was specific to a given term.

Shifting can be required in states where the seller must collect the tax from the consumer because the consumer is legally liable for the tax. Alternatively, in most seller privilege states, the seller may attempt to recover the tax expense or reimbursement from the consumer. The actual tax itself is not recoverable from the consumer. The tax

(2) *Absorption* refers to the extent to which the seller or tax collector is able to pay the tax out of his or her own pocket without having to be reimbursed or passing the tax on to the purchaser or consumer. Reference to absorption herein is a statement that the state allows the seller to absorb the tax. Absorption is a competitive tool of price negotiation.

(3) *Separation* refers to the requirement in the law that the tax be identified as a distinctive line item on an invoice, sales ticket, sales receipt, etc. Some states allow tax to be advertised as being included in the selling price, provided that that condition is noted. Reference to separation herein is a statement that the state requires the tax be separately stated. Tax inclusion is a modified form of separation.[2]

Beyond these issues is the increasingly focused matter of being "engaged in (the) business." Again, we have a concept that is almost always defined in the introductory sections of the tax law. "Engaged" commonly means having a place of activity within the state from which sales are made. However, "being engaged in (the) business" has much to do with a requirement to be licensed or certified for the right to transact business, use the courts and enjoy the commercial marketplace in which a business earns its profit. This issue is discussed in greater detail in Chapter X.

¶202 The Privilege Tax

The imposition section of a "privilege" tax statute typically contains the following phraseology:

> There shall be imposed, upon each person for the privilege of engaging in the business of selling tangible personal property and taxable services at retail, a tax measured by the gross proceeds (receipts) therefrom.

In simple terms, the seller is liable for the tax measured by his taxable sales. The variations on this privilege tax theme are found in the key terms: shifting, absorption and separation. Notably, the tax law may or may not require that the tax be shifted to the purchaser. Even if shifting is required, with the privilege tax, the seller remains liable until the tax is paid. The law may state that the tax may be absorbed by the seller, leaving the seller the option of using the tax as an inducement to motivate the purchaser. Used in this fashion, the tax becomes a persuasive (particularly when the rate is high) negotiating point. Finally, separate statement of the tax is not commonly required with a privilege tax, as the tax is the liability of the seller.

(Footnote Continued)

liability cannot be shifted by law, only via contract. This distinction might seem absurd; however, getting a consumer to produce a check for tax reimbursement not covered by contract may be impossible.

[2] The term separation is also used by states to indicate a requirement that the tax account in the seller's records is a clearly identifiable account. That is, amounts attributable to taxes are isolated in the seller's books and records of sales. This is an issue in a state that requires the seller to collect the tax from the customer where the tax becomes a debt of the customer to the seller, recovery of which is enforceable under contract law.

Problem

Question: Who is liable for the tax? Both the seller and the purchaser are located in State A. The purchaser orders taxable tangible personal property from the seller. The seller delivers the property to the purchaser by any method.

Answer: The seller is liable for the tax and, in the seller's failure to add tax to the purchaser's invoice, the seller remains liable.

With a privilege tax, one should be mindful that the compliance audit of the seller is truly that, an audit to confirm that tax was paid to the state measured by the taxpayer's (seller's) gross taxable receipts, regardless of whether the seller enjoyed the good fortune of receiving reimbursement for that tax payment or expense. Viewed differently, with a privilege tax, only the seller is liable under the statute in a sales tax transaction, not the purchaser. The purchaser may become obligated to the seller to reimburse the seller's tax expense, but that is a contractual issue between seller and purchaser. In a privilege tax state, for a retail purchase, the buyer generally has no statutory standing before the tax courts. The buyer, however, does have a contractual standing relative to an agreement with the seller or the opportunity to claim a refund for the tax paid should the property be resold prior to any use other than demonstration or display of the property. Finally, with the privilege tax, it is often said that if the tax is not stated, it is understood to be included in the selling price of the property subject to tax. This would be true in the absence of contractual language to the contrary.

¶203 The Consumer Levy

The imposition section of a "consumer" levy or excise statute typically contains the following phraseology:

> There shall be imposed, upon each sale at retail at the rate of XX% of the sales price, a tax collected by the retailer from the consumer.

In contrast to the privilege tax, the consumer levy is clearly imposed on the purchaser with the seller serving as the trustee or agent of the state in collecting the tax. The seller may not absorb the tax and, in fact, is always required to separately state the tax on the purchaser's invoice. The consumer levy often emphasizes the burden on the buyer by stating that the tax must be paid to the seller at the time it is billed.

Problem

Question: Who is liable for the tax? Both the seller and the purchaser are located in State A. The purchaser orders taxable tangible personal property from the seller. The seller delivers the property to the purchaser by any method.

Answer: The purchaser is liable for the tax and, in the seller's failure to add tax to the purchaser's invoice, the purchaser remains liable.

Perhaps the most common form of sales tax in the United States, the consumer levy leaves the seller the least amount of latitude in using the tax for competitive purposes. Since the tax must be stated and added to the purchaser's invoice and typically remains a debt of the purchaser until paid to the state, all sellers must operate from a common framework of taxing each and every taxable sale, remitting the tax collected from the purchaser to the state. Because the incidence of the tax is on the purchaser, states imposing this type of tax often compensate the seller for being its agent in collecting the tax from the purchaser. This compensation is taken by the seller in the form of a small percentage deduction from the tax liability due during any given reporting period. The deduction is often called a "vendor discount."

¶204 The Transaction Tax

The imposition section of a "transaction" tax is borrowed from the imposition sections of both the privilege tax and the consumer levy. The transaction tax statute typically contains the following phraseology:

> A tax shall be imposed upon each transaction at retail at the rate of XX% of the sales price that shall be collected by the retailer from the purchaser.

The transaction tax is a tax that combines the payment responsibility of the privilege tax and the "debt to the seller" liability of the consumer levy. It is common for the transaction tax statute to contain a phrase indicating that the tax is the debt of the purchaser to the seller until paid.

Problem

Question: Who is liable for the tax? Both the seller and the purchaser are located in State A. The purchaser orders taxable tangible personal property from the seller. The seller delivers the property to the purchaser by any method.

Answer: The purchaser is liable for the tax imposed upon the transaction. In the seller's failure to add tax to the purchaser's invoice, the purchaser and the seller remain jointly liable.

The distinction between the two taxes, transaction and consumer levy, is in the liability for the tax. In the transaction tax, the liability for collection and payment of the tax is on the seller, with the purchaser being liable to the seller for the tax that the seller must collect and remit. With the consumer levy, the liability for the tax is on the consumer (or purchaser) to the state with the seller being the agent of the state for collection of the tax.

As with the consumer levy, the transaction tax is almost always shifted to the purchaser, cannot be absorbed, and is required to be separately stated on the customer's invoice. One might conclude that, while there are imposition differences, there is really no operational difference between the two types of taxes. This statement is not far from the truth. However, careful scrutiny of these types of taxes is required for protecting one's company from an unexpected tax liability or assessment. The key issues are:

(1) Upon whom or what is the tax imposed?

(2) Who is liable for the tax?

(3) After whom will the state come if the tax was not paid?

The following exhibit provides a quick view of the relationships between the three types of sales tax described above.

CONCEPTS COMMON TO TYPES OF SALES TAXES (GENERALLY)

TRANSACTION TAX imposed on transaction, sale or purchase	
engaged in business sells property/services at retail	shifting mandatory; no absorption; separation required
PRIVILEGE TAX shifting not allowed imposed on seller	CONSUMER TAX imposed on consumer

¶205 The Gross Receipts Tax

The imposition section of a "gross receipts" tax is borrowed almost entirely from the imposition section of the privilege tax. In fact, the two true gross receipts states, Hawaii and New Mexico, are really seller privilege states. As the number of services and sellers subject to tax increases, we are likely to see more states falling into the gross receipts category. While a number of states, particularly Arkansas, call their taxes "gross receipts" sales taxes, the taxes have a character more akin to a transaction tax.

The liability for a true gross receipts tax falls entirely on the seller with no requirement for shifting of the tax, absorption is allowed and the tax need not be separately stated on the customer's invoice or receipt. The gross receipts taxes are distinguished from nearly all other taxes by their all-pervasive nature. There are few exemptions or exclusions from taxable measure. Generally, tangible personal property and services are equally taxable.

A final important characteristic of the Hawaii gross receipts tax deserves mention. In all other seller privilege states and in New Mexico, the seller may seek reimbursement for the sales tax from the customer and report the taxable measure, excluding the tax itself, as the amount subject to tax. In Hawaii, the sales tax reimbursement collected from the customer is included in the taxable measure upon which the tax is computed. The effect of this provision is to impose a tax on tax. An example of this provision is depicted in Chapter XVI, ¶1602.

Recognizing these distinctions and taking these differences into consideration, the tax practitioner becomes equipped to structure elements of tax management. Understanding the differences in the imposition of the tax, state to state, will provide the practitioner important leverage that can and should be used in responding to audits by taxing jurisdictions.

For example, in a privilege tax state, an auditor cannot assess sales tax against the purchaser unless the purchaser has purchased otherwise taxable property for resale (or other exemption) by providing a resale (or exemption) certificate or resale purchase order to the seller. Alternatively, it is the task of the tax practitioner to determine if the assessment for sales tax not reported on taxable sales in a transaction tax or consumer levy state was possibly assessed against the purchaser in a separate audit resulting in duplicate collection of the tax on the same transaction. This situation is likely to occur where statistical sampling techniques are used in audits.

Considering the issue of sales tax from the purchaser's perspective also presents differing paths of action. With the privilege tax or gross receipts tax, the purchaser should never accrue and pay sales tax to the state. Furthermore, tax not billed by the seller should not be added to the purchase invoice by the purchaser, thereby voluntarily paying the tax to the seller. The purchaser cannot presume that the unbilled tax remitted to the seller will be construed as tax reimbursement rather than merely an overpayment. The seller's automated accounts receivable system probably has no method for handling any voluntary payment, other than to post it "on account," if the invoice does not include the amount being paid. That excess amount is not likely to find its way into the sales tax account, nor are states likely to give credit on an audit.

However, purchasers in consumer levy or transaction tax states should always accrue and remit directly to the state tax that is not billed by the vendor. As with seller privilege or gross receipts taxes, unbilled tax should not be voluntarily added to the purchase invoice and paid to the seller. In this latter situation, there is a likelihood that the seller may pay the tax under assessment separately, resulting in the state receiving the tax twice. The risk of not paying the tax to the state may result in a statistical sample assessment that unfairly taxes beyond the true liability of the taxpayer.

Consistent with this author's view of the importance of recognizing imposition and its three related conditions, the following state-by-state analysis is provided as an easy reference. The tax practitioner, until fully conversant in the distinctions in the states, should use this chart on a regular basis. As with any printed tax chart or table, one should recognize the timely nature of the material and the subjective interpretation of its preparer. The selection of terms used to categorize a state's tax type is based on the state's own code. The explanatory footnotes add clarification based on how a given state actually administers its tax. Taxing jurisdictions are known to change the way they interpret their laws in search of creative ways to assure themselves the greatest likelihood of capturing every last tax dollar. The following chart covers the issue of sales tax only, not use tax.

SALES TAX TYPES LEVIED BY STATE

State	Tax Type	Shifting is Mandatory	Absorption is Allowed	Separation is Required
Alabama	Seller Privilege[3]	Yes[4]	No[5]	Yes
Alaska	There is no state sales tax; however, five boroughs and 95 cities levy locally administered sales and use taxes with combined rates as high as 7%.			

---

[3] The sales tax in Alabama, though labeled a privilege or license tax, is deemed to be a tax on the retail consumer collected by the seller as a convenience to the state.

[4] Though the tax is imposed on the seller, it must be shifted to the retail consumer.

[5] Even advertising absorption is prohibited.

State	Tax Type	Shifting is Mandatory	Absorption is Allowed	Separation is Required
Arizona	Seller Privilege[6]	No	Yes	Optional[7]
Arkansas	Gross Receipts[8]	Yes	No	Yes
California	Seller Privilege	No	Yes	Optional
Colorado	Transaction[9]	Yes	No	Yes
Connecticut	Seller Privilege[10]	Yes	No	Optional[11]
Delaware	There is no state sales tax; however, there are various licenses, the fees for which are assessed based on the number of locations and a percentage of gross receipts. here is also a tax on rental receipts.			
DC	Seller Privilege[12]	Yes	No	Yes
Florida	Transaction[13]	Yes	No	Yes
Georgia	Transaction[14]	Yes	No	Yes
Hawaii	Seller Privilege[15]	No	Optional	Optional
Idaho	Transaction[16]	Yes	No	Yes
Illinois	Transaction[17]	Yes	No	Yes
Indiana	Transaction[18]	Yes	No	Yes

---

[6] With its seller privilege tax, the Arizona Department of Revenue has won its battle to impose tax on sales to the U.S. Government since the incidence of the tax is on the seller, not the purchaser.

[7] If the seller chooses to seek reimbursement for tax cost from the purchaser, any amount greater than the actual tax collected as tax reimbursement must be remitted to the state.

[8] Even though the tax is called a gross receipts tax, the regulations state that the tax is on the sale of property, not the property itself. This distinction makes the tax similar in operation to a transaction tax.

[9] The tax must be added to the seller's invoice and becomes a debt of the consumer or user as part of the total price.

[10] While this tax is labeled a seller privilege tax, the code states that, when added to the seller's invoice, it becomes a debt of the consumer to the retailer until paid. Once collected by the seller from the purchaser, the tax is deemed to be held in trust for the state.

[11] Tax may be advertised as included in the selling price. When so advertised, the words "tax included" or "tax incl." must be displayed. Regardless of the manner of invoicing or advertising, the tax must be separately identifiable in the seller's records.

[12] The District's sales tax is a transaction tax in operation and seller privilege tax in name. The tax is imposed on the seller; however, the reimbursement for the tax must be paid by the purchaser to the seller and is a debt of the purchaser in the same fashion as the underlying sale itself would be a debt.

[13] The Florida sales tax is a good example of a tax whose collection burden falls on the seller, even though the tax is imposed on the exercise of the selling privilege. The seller failing to collect the tax from the purchaser remains liable for the tax. Similarly, a purchaser may be assessed the tax unless able to prove the tax was paid to the seller.

[14] Georgia imposes its tax with a slightly different twist. The tax is imposed both on the seller and the purchaser and is measured by the retail selling price of taxable goods or services. The tax is also a debt of the purchaser to the seller until paid.

[15] Hawaii's tax is unique. It is labeled a seller privilege tax but is truly a gross receipts "excise" tax imposed on gross receipts including the tax reimbursement itself. See ¶1602 for additional information on this tax.

[16] Idaho's sales tax is imposed on the entire amount of a consumer's purchase at a given time. Contrary to most states, in Idaho the seller may keep (as compensation) tax collected under the bracket system in excess of the amount for which the seller is actually liable. See Glossary item (28) for the definition of bracket system.

[17] The Illinois Retailer's Occupations Tax is imposed upon sellers who reimburse themselves for the tax by collecting *use* tax from the purchasers. This is the only law containing such a provision. Furthermore, if the seller fails to collect the use tax, the state may do so directly.

[18] The "gross retail tax" is imposed on the transaction with the purchaser being liable for the tax. The seller is responsible for tax collection as an agent of the state.

State	Tax Type	Shifting is Mandatory	Absorption is Allowed	Separation is Required
Iowa	Transaction[19]	Yes	No	Optional[20]
Kansas	Transaction[21]	Yes	No	Yes
Kentucky	Seller Privilege[22]	Yes	No	Yes
Louisiana	Consumer Levy[23]	Yes	No	Yes
Maine	Consumer Levy[24]	Yes	No	Yes
Maryland	Consumer Levy[25]	Yes	No	Yes
Massachusetts	Transaction	Yes	No	Yes
Michigan	Seller Privilege[26]	Optional	Optional[27]	No
Minnesota	Transaction[28]	Yes	Yes[29]	Yes
Mississippi	Consumer Levy	Yes	No	Yes
Missouri	Seller Privilege[30]	Yes	No	Yes
Montana	There is no sales tax in Montana			
Nebraska	Consumer Levy	Yes	No	Yes
Nevada	Seller Privilege	Yes[31]	Optional[32]	No
New Hampshire	There is no general sales tax in New Hampshire; however, a tax is imposed on meals, rooms and telecommunications services.			

[19] Iowa's retail sales tax is imposed on retail sale transactions (listed in substantial detail in the code), collected by the retailer from the consumer/user, and is a debt of the purchaser to the seller until paid.

[20] The tax need not be separately stated when included; however, when included, a statement to that effect must be posted in advertising.

[21] While Section 79-3603 of the code indicates the tax is levied for the privilege of selling, Section 79-3604 places the liability for the tax on the consumer/user with the seller having the collection responsibility. The tax is a debt of the consumer or user to the seller until paid, with the state able to pursue either party for the tax (per the code).

[22] Kentucky's sales tax is imposed on the retailer, who is required to collect the tax from the purchaser. Failure to collect the tax from the purchaser does not relieve the seller of the liability for the tax. However, the tax *collected* is a debt of the retailer to the state.

[23] A Louisiana "dealer" (a purchaser or seller) is responsible for collecting the tax from the consumer or purchaser and remains liable for the tax if not collected. The tax is a debt of the purchaser to the seller until paid. There is also an advance tax on wholesale sales.

[24] Maine levies its taxes (sales and use) on the consumer but imposes the tax on the retail selling price of the property or taxable services sold, which must be collected by the seller.

[25] The Maryland sales tax is imposed on the retail sale with the purchaser being liable to the seller for payment of the tax as though it were part of the purchase price. The seller is the agent of the state, collecting and holding the tax in trust until remitted to the state.

[26] In Michigan, the seller may recover tax reimbursement from the purchaser; however, when so collected, it is deemed to be held in trust for the state to be paid over. The liability and imposition of the sales tax is clearly on the seller.

[27] A seller may not advertise that tax will not be part of the sales price, and the code does allow the seller to seek reimbursement for the tax due.

[28] The Minnesota regulations are explicit in stating that sales tax not collected from a purchaser by the seller can be collected from the seller directly as use tax even if the sale is in Minnesota.

[29] This transaction type sales tax is unusual in that it may be absorbed by the seller (effective 1990).

[30] Missouri has adopted the best (or worst, if you prefer) of both worlds, imposing the sales tax on the privilege of selling, requiring the seller to collect the tax from the purchaser, yet not relieving the seller of the tax liability if the seller does not pay the tax on a taxable purchase.

[31] The seller is required to shift the tax; however, failure to do so does not relieve the seller of the liability to pay the tax, nor does it place the burden of the tax on the consumer under the law. The law uses the phrase "insofar as it can be done" regarding the requirement to shift the tax to the consumer.

[32] There is no prohibition against absorption, but absorbing the tax by the seller may not be advertised.

State	Tax Type	Shifting is Mandatory	Absorption is Allowed	Separation is Required
New Jersey	Transaction	Yes	No	Optional[33]
New Mexico	Gross Receipts[34]	No	Yes	No
New York	Consumer Levy[35]	Yes	No	Yes
No. Carolina	Consumer Levy[36]	Yes	No	Yes
No. Dakota	Consumer Levy	Yes	No	Yes
Ohio	Consumer Levy[37]	Yes	No	Yes
Oklahoma	Consumer Levy	Yes	No	Optional[38]
Oregon	Oregon currently has no sales tax.			
Pennsylvania	Consumer Levy[39]	Yes	No	Yes
Rhode Island	Consumer Levy	Yes	No	Yes
So. Carolina	Seller Privilege	No	Yes	No
So. Dakota	Seller Privilege	No	Yes	No
Tennessee	Seller Privilege[40]	Yes[41]	Yes[42]	No
Texas	Transaction[43]	Yes	No	Yes
Utah	Consumer Levy[44]	Yes	No	Yes
Vermont	Consumer Levy[45]	Yes	No	Yes[46]
Virginia	Transaction[47]	Yes	No	Yes[48]
Washington	Consumer Levy[49]	Yes	No[50]	Yes

[33] The requirement of separation may be waived by the Director if it is determined that the burden on the taxpayer to do so would by excessive.

[34] New Mexico's gross receipts tax is a tax on the privilege of selling, imposed solely on the seller. However, if the tax reimbursement collected is greater than the computed tax due, the overage must be reported and remitted. Taxes not separately stated will be subject to the gross receipts tax.

[35] In New York, the seller, required to collect the tax from the purchaser, is considered an agent of the state and is liable for the tax to be collected. If the seller is unable to collect the tax, the consumer is held liable.

[36] Labeled a privilege tax, North Carolina's tax is really a consumer levy. The tax is imposed on the retailer who must collect it from the customer.

[37] While the Ohio tax is a typical consumer levy, the state has attempted to insure the tax collection and payment by having a comparable seller privilege (excise) tax imposed on the seller. Should the sales tax not be collected and remitted, the excise tax becomes due.

[38] A seller may not advertise the absorption of the tax; however, a sale can be made at a tax-included price. The burden to prove the tax was collected and remitted remains with the seller.

[39] The seller is liable for any tax it fails to collect or pay.

[40] The Tennessee seller is expected to collect the tax from the customer insofar as it is able to do so. The tax is clearly a seller liability. A small dealer tax collection "compensation" or vendor discount is allowed in Tennessee, an unusual situation in a seller privilege state.

[41] The tax is expected to be shifted.

[42] Absorption is discouraged as anti-competitive, but is allowed.

[43] The state may proceed against either the seller or purchaser for the tax not paid.

[44] Rule R865-19-2S-B states the tax is a transaction tax yet the purchaser is the taxpayer. The code at Sec. 59-12-103 states the tax is levied on the purchaser. The effect is the same.

[45] The seller is liable for the collection of the tax.

[46] Non-separation may be permitted with prior state approval.

[47] The Virginia sales tax is the liability of the seller who is required to collect the tax from the purchaser.

[48] Non-separation is allowed under special circumstances where the seller can demonstrate an undue burden of complying with the separation provision, e.g., restaurant menus. A statement that the tax is included could be acceptable.

[49] The state may proceed against the purchaser or seller for the tax.

[50] Absorption is not allowed; however, tax may be included in the selling price if the words "tax included," in the appropriate manner, are so noted on the invoice, sales ticket, etc.

State	Tax Type	Shifting is Mandatory	Absorption is Allowed	Separation is Required
W. Virginia	Consumer Levy[51]	Yes	No	Yes[52]
Wisconsin	Seller Privilege	Optional[53]	No	Yes
Wyoming	Consumer Levy[54]	Yes	No	Yes

The terms privilege, transaction, consumer levy and gross receipts used in distinguishing these four tax types may be inconsistent with the words used by the various states to title their codes or label their taxes. For example, Alabama's sales tax is called a gross receipts tax but is administered as a transaction tax. Connecticut and the District of Columbia both impose their taxes on the privilege of selling at retail, yet the taxes are administered as transactions taxes, based on this author's definitions.

\# 6 New Mexico calls its tax a seller privilege tax but administers it as a gross receipts tax. Hawaii calls its tax a general excise tax, imposes the tax as a seller privilege tax, and collects the tax as a true gross receipts tax, not even excluding the amount of the tax reimbursement collected from the customer from the taxable measure. For example, if the Hawaii state tax rate were 5% and a $100 sale were taxable, the seller would likely charge the customer $105.00. The amount represents $100 of taxable measure and $5.00 of tax reimbursement. The Hawaii tax is a privilege tax. However, when the retail reports taxable sales, the $5.00 in tax reimbursement collected from the customer is part of the taxable measure. The transaction is measured by the sale of $105.00, and the seller remits $5.25 in tax to the state.

Illinois has four different "occupation" taxes and matching consumer use taxes that, in combination, are essentially transaction taxes. As recently as 1990, Illinois had over 20 different sales or use taxes, each with its own name, imposition rules, and reporting forms (see a brief discussion of the occupation tax at ¶206). While Louisiana has a fairly typical consumer levy style tax on retail sales, it has an unusual provision that wholesalers and manufacturers must make an advance collection of the tax due. Nevada and Tennessee sales taxes are imposed on the retailer with shifting strongly encouraged. Viewed another way, if the tax is not passed on to the customer, the retailer remains liable.

Accordingly, the designation of the type of tax in the chart above refers to the manner of administration or imposition as described above, not the actual term used by the state in its statute.

---

[51] The West Virginia sales tax is the liability of both the purchaser and the seller, the former for payment to the seller or state, the latter for collection from the purchaser and payment to the state. However, if the seller does not collect the tax, it is still liable for the tax.

[52] Non-separation may be allowed where there is industry-wide relief sought or where taxable and nontaxable transactions are present on a single invoice or receipt.

[53] Wisconsin "authorizes" the seller to shift the tax but does not require that it be shifted. The tax is imposed on the seller.

[54] In addition to the sales tax, there is an excise tax levied solely against the seller for sales under 25 cents. The regular sales tax is collected from the customer.

There are many other issues to consider in the study of a sales tax. However, from a practical sense, imposition is one of the most important. In following chapters we will look at the method used by states to determine the taxable measure for computing the sales tax, the different types of products or customers that may benefit from statutory exemptions, the elements of the sale that may be excluded from the tax computation, the matter of audits and appeals, and taxes complementary to the sales tax.

¶206 Other Taxes on Sales

There are various other taxes imposed on the sale, storage, use or other consumption of tangible personal property. These taxes are the states' methods of taxing other sources of sales.

• Occupation taxes (Illinois)

Occupation taxes are really sales taxes, by other names, collected as use taxes. The "retailers" occupation tax is basically a retail sales tax, imposed on retailers for making sales of tangible personal property. The "service" occupation tax is imposed on persons providing services on the transfer of tangible personal property as an incident of the service. The "automobile" renting occupation tax is imposed on persons in the business of renting automobiles for one year or less. Finally, there is a tax on hotel operators engaged in the business of renting rooms to transients in hotels or related facilities. In all four cases, the person so engaged in business is required to collect the tax as a use tax from the customer or user. Effective on January 1, 1990, Illinois installed a new series of taxes intended to make life easier and more manageable for business. One can hardly imagine that anyone would fight Illinois' efforts at simplification.

• Business and occupation taxes (Washington and West Virginia)

As a method of capturing a greater tax base, which may include transactions otherwise exempt from the state sales or use tax, states (and localities) impose business and occupation taxes (also known as B&O taxes) on those engaged in business in the state. The tax is typically on all transactions, whether or not otherwise taxable, and is not passed through to the customer in a separately stated manner. The rates tend to vary by type of business.

• Gross income tax (Indiana)

In a slightly different manner than the business and occupation tax, Indiana imposes a "gross income tax." This tax, at a lower rate than that prescribed by the state gross retail sales tax, captures revenue measured by gross income in two classes: general business transactions and utility transactions. The effect of such a tax is to direct the sales tax at gross retail sales and the income tax at a broader base of transactions, some of which may not be considered taxable under the gross retail sales tax.

• Excise taxes

Beyond the sales and use taxes themselves, and yet separate and distinct from franchise and income taxes, many states impose excise taxes on fuel, cigarettes, utility services, alcoholic beverages, motor vehicles, litter control, hotels, automobile rentals, etc. These taxes are often imposed at the manufacturer or wholesale level of commerce and, at the retail level, are virtually indistinguishable from the selling price to the purchaser. Except where the excise tax is an "in lieu" tax, the state's sales or use tax tends to be imposed on the excise tax, which is considered part of the gross receipts or sales.

• *Local taxes*

One of the most troublesome and time-consuming aspects of sales and use taxation is the problem of local taxes. We have already noted that, in the 46 major jurisdictions, no two taxes are the same. Differences are more apparent in looking at the local or minor taxes that, at present count, number more than 7,000 separate jurisdictions. Their names are as varied as the types of jurisdictions for which they are collected, covering every type of governmental unit from the city to the parish, from the refuse district to the school district, from the police jury to the fire commission. Rates may be as low as one-tenth of one percent (0.1% or 0.001) and as high as four percent.

As with other taxes, local tax laws (more commonly called ordinances) have definitions, imposition sections, enabling clauses, administrative oversight provisions, registration and reporting requirements, and non-compliance consequences. Local laws tend to be weak in the areas of taxpayer assistance and procedures, which afford maximum legal protection to business. The organizations responsible for tax administration are often understaffed, poorly financed, and weakly managed. They fall under the direct control of city councils, boards of aldermen, county supervisors, and a host of commissions, agencies, etc., and also elected bodies made up of part-time and volunteer members.

The one common thread found in these local taxes is that they are probably the result of state legislative action. Yet, despite their common birthplace, it is remarkable that the state tax code may bear little resemblance to its local offspring. Differences between state and local taxes are found in taxable (or exempt) products, purchasers or sellers, the imposition of the tax, and when the tax is a "sales" tax instead of a "use" tax. In short, the definitions for common terminology are different.

From a business standpoint, administration of local taxes can be a nightmare. It is not always easy to determine where a local jurisdiction begins and ends. A shopping center that straddles two adjacent local taxing authorities may present a business tenant with the difficulty of having one cash register in one authority and a second cash register in a second authority. Simple zip code distinctions are often not an adequate response to the local tax collecting/ reporting task.

One interesting point of contrast between state and local taxes is that the state tax is typically administered based on the ship-to location, whereas local taxes are most commonly determined based on the ship-from location. Further confusing the matter, the local tax may even be based on the local order acceptance, place of delivery, or origin of property shipment. Taxation of elec-

¶206

tronic commerce has huge implications in this area (see Chapter XXIII for a discussion on the taxation of electronic commerce). States are willing to cooperate on standardized tax provisions when the situs for the transaction is in doubt. However, the localities will fight tooth and nail to protect their taxes from a transaction when the situs is varied. They have much more to lose on a relative scale.

A final positive note in the discussion of local taxes is that most tax reporting for local jurisdictions is done on the state's own return. The number of "home rule" jurisdictions (localities that collect and administer their own tax) remains relatively small (less than 15 percent nationally). In Louisiana, where this is not the case, a taxpayer is responsible for reporting tax in more than 600 local jurisdictions, each of which can audit for its own tax. In the recent past, to the delight of taxpayers in Louisiana, the law was changed to standardize the tax return form for local tax reporting. The number of states with home rule jurisdictions is increasing, albeit slowly. Illinois and Minnesota now join Louisiana, Alabama, Alaska, Arizona, and Colorado with recognized home rule jurisdictions. Some states call their local taxes "home rule" taxes, e.g., Pennsylvania and North Dakota; however, these taxes are fully administered by the state, which means that both the reporting and auditing is contracted with the state. Some states contract collections but not auditing. In these cases, a taxpayer may be audited by the state, the locality, or in some cases, an auditor hired by the locality.

The two remaining issues of difficulty are the number of jurisdictions in which return and compliance forms must be filed and the inconsistency between the state and localities in their views of exemptions. It should be clear to any state with home rule taxing jurisdictions that centralization of payment, consistency of reporting and commonality of exemptions will increase the likelihood that taxpayers attempt to fully comply, because compliance becomes less of a chore.

Chapter III
Use Taxes and Other Taxes on Purchases

¶301 Introduction

In the prior chapter on sales tax, we recognized the concept of "being engaged in business." That is, a person or company is engaged in business in a jurisdiction when it has personnel, facilities, equipment, inventory, representatives, and, more recently, has presence through the act of deriving financial benefit or availing itself of the commercial marketplace of that jurisdiction.

There is an important distinction between a company "being engaged in business" and a sale being consummated in that jurisdiction. In other words, a company can have personnel, property (real and personal) and even business dealings within a jurisdiction with the sale not occurring in that jurisdiction. In such a situation, the property is shipped into the taxing jurisdiction from a point elsewhere with the seller having no control of the property within the destination jurisdiction.

As sales taxes were established to levy an excise on commerce within a state, the legislatures writing these laws were concerned that property brought into their states might escape sales taxation if the sales failed to occur within the state. Out of this concern grew the compensating or complementary tax known as the "use" tax. Every state having a sales tax has a use tax that, often in its own imposition section within the Code, levies a tax on "the storage, use or other consumption of tangible personal property not subject to sales tax or otherwise exempt from tax" brought into that state, or acquired in the state under nontaxable presumption. However, before considering the key assumptions concerning use taxes, it is important to understand what we mean by "use" in a tax context. "Storage" and "other consumption" are both discussed later in this chapter.

A tax definition of use is "the exercise of any right or power over property which may be incidental to ownership of that property." Three examples of use, in a tax context, might be:

(1) renting or leasing property (the ownership remains with the renter or lessor while the lessee exercises control over the property while the property is in the lessee's possession),

(2) licensing property (the ownership remains with the license holder while the use of the product, patent, copyright, etc., is exercised by the licensee), and

(3) using property brought in from out of state (the ownership may remain the same or change, but there is no exchange of money or consideration to complete the sale).[1]

There are many other examples of use that will become evident later in this chapter.

---

[1] A "sale" is defined fully in ¶404.

¶302   Key Assumptions of the Use Tax

• *Function of federal prohibition on the taxation of interstate sales by states*

There are some key assumptions in the concept of a use tax that deserve mention. First, the existence of a use tax is largely a function of the federal constitutional prohibition against states taxing transactions occurring outside their borders. Looked at in a more direct sense, the right to: (1) tax in all states simultaneously, or (2) regulate movement of property between states is reserved to the U.S. Congress, with the right to tax within a given state being limited to each state within its borders. Therefore, one may infer that the U.S. Congress alone may tax a sale in interstate commerce (see ¶903 for a discussion of pending federal tax legislation). While this is largely correct, a state may impose a tax on an aspect of an interstate commerce transaction, provided it does not run afoul of case law to the contrary.

• *Self-imposition of tax*

Second, as the purchaser's activities, i.e., purchases in interstate commerce, are often visible to the purchaser alone, the consumer's use tax is primarily a tax whose reporting responsibility falls on the purchaser as a self-imposed tax. While the use tax may be collected by the seller (in which case it may be referred to as seller's use tax) engaged in business in the destination state, the liability for the use tax is ultimately that of the purchaser.

If the purchaser is an individual, it is very likely that the tax may never be reported to the state in which the property will be used, as there is a lack of understanding or concern on the part of individuals to self-assess tax and little likelihood of the state assessing tax against the individual purchaser. For businesses, however, states have all established use tax reporting procedures which, although "voluntary," provide the purchaser the opportunity of self-assessment. Failure to honor the "voluntary" program of self-assessment will likely result in assessment plus interest and penalty under a tax compliance audit.

In recent years, states have focused more attention on the issue of minimizing use tax revenue losses resulting from the failure of small businesses (medical, legal and accounting practices and those businesses of other professionals) to self-assess and report use tax when making purchases from unlicensed out-of-state vendors. New Jersey has instituted a self-audit program intended to "encourage" such businesses to self-assess and report use tax. Inducements (the small carrot) might include abatement of penalties, reduced interest on unpaid taxes, or reduced statutes of limitation. Encouragement (the big stick) takes the form of non-abatement of penalties and threats of audits covering full statute of limitations periods for non-reporters.

We can safely anticipate continued growth of this type of tax policy throughout the nation. Remember, use tax statutes already provide for this imposition of tax. States have struggled with the difficulty of motivating compliance. Ohio went slightly further than New Jersey by addressing its program of self-auditing to a much broader range of taxpayers. Ohio began its managed audit foray by focusing on small taxpayers. The goal was simply to increase compliance at the small-taxpayer level. However, in recent years, Ohio and several other states have become enamored with the idea of self or managed audits. These programs are now being directed at large taxpayers as well as small ones. Statutes and regulatory policies are changing in state houses as this edition goes to press. Again, inducements to participate in such a program include both a carrot and a big stick—take your pick. See ¶1403 for a more thorough discussion of managed audits.

Again, as with sales taxes, the safest way for a purchaser to be certain that a tax liability has been satisfied is through direct payment of the tax to the state— not by adding the tax to the invoice of and remittance to the seller for the property purchased. An unlicensed seller may not have a method for remitting unsolicited use tax to the state for which it was paid and may have no interest in so doing. Payment of tax to an unlicensed seller does not extinguish a legitimate use tax liability.

• *State sales and use tax rate similarity*

Third, it is safe to assume that the state (not local) sales and use tax rates will be the same in a given state and that property or transactions not subject to sales tax are probably also not subject to use tax. However, the issue of taxable and nontaxable property requires specific evaluation, state by state. Attempts by states to have different rates for sales and use taxes, i.e., use tax rates greater than sales tax rates, have been overturned by the courts. When these situations occur, the challenge is often based on discrimination, i.e., the out-of-state seller has a greater burden than an in-state seller or the out-of-state purchase is subject to a greater rate than the in-state purchase. Localities can have various rates in a given state; however, different rates within a jurisdiction may be subject to legal scrutiny in the case of interstate protectionism. Not imposing a local use tax when a local sales tax is imposed does not typically create a problem. An excellent example of this situation is Maricopa County, AZ where there is a 6.3% combined state and local sales (transaction) tax and a state and city, but no county, use tax.

• *Sales or use tax only*

#¶ Fourth, generally a taxable transaction will be subject to sales tax or use tax, but not both. In other words, the distinct activity that is represented by a given transaction at a discrete moment in time causes the transaction to be subject to sales tax or use tax. If the discrete activity is the purchase of property, the physical location of the property at the time of the sale or the legal place of the sale based on the contract will determine whether the transaction is subject to sales or use tax. Use tax is due when the taxable property is sold beyond the borders of the jurisdiction in which it will be first used, stored or controlled by the purchaser, or when property purchased for a nontaxable purpose is used in a taxable manner. Following are some examples of transactions in which the type of tax is identified:

¶302

(1) Property is in the seller's possession in the state where the customer will receive control (seller's possession could mean delivered by the seller's truck, a salesperson, or from the seller's in-state facility)—sales tax;

(2) Property is shipped or carried into the state to the seller's personnel (installers or assemblers) in the customer's state, and is then delivered to the customer by any method—sales tax;

(3) Property is shipped from the seller's facility in the customer's state by any method—sales tax;

(4) Property is sent into the customer's state via a common carrier, and the seller never has possession of the property within the customer's state—use tax;

(5) Vendor-retained tooling is held in the vendor's state, even though the parts produced by the tool are shipped to a different state where the customer incorporates the parts into resale property—sales tax on the tooling (if taxable) in the vendors' state (if title to the tool transfers to the customer) or use tax in the vendor's state (if the ownership of the tool does not vest in the customer);

(6) Leased or rented property, title to which does not transfer to the customer—mostly regarded as use tax, although it may be regarded as sales tax when construed as a continuing sale.

In rare instances, a transaction seeming to be a single activity will be subject to both a sales tax in one state and a use tax in a second state. It is foolish to assume that payment of tax in one state means no tax is due in another state.

• *Impact of use tax*

Finally, and highly significant about use tax, is the impact of the use tax imposition section when studied with careful scrutiny. Use tax is a tax upon storage, use or other consumption of taxable tangible personal property not subject to sales tax. *Storage*, in this context, is when the purchaser holds or controls property brought in from out of state and, though not placing it in use promptly, does not intend to resell it or hold it for demonstration or display. This may constitute taxable storage.

Clearly, property brought in from out of state, which is used prior to its being resold, and is not otherwise exempt from tax, would meet the second criteria of use tax—that is, *use*.

¶303 Tax on Other Consumption

And then, there is *other consumption*. This concept typically serves as the tax grabber. Other consumption has grown to include (but is not limited to) and causes major assessments for:

(1) resale or exempt property self-consumed (e.g., inventory parts used in a company-funded research and development project, finished goods or inventory items given away as samples to induce sales, etc.);

(2) creation and use of self-constructed assets (e.g., a computer company building a computer for its own use);

(3) transfers or sales of property between divisions or subsidiaries of the same parent company (e.g., division A builds a machine and transfers it to division B who uses the machine in its office, or sales between subsidiaries A and B with the ultimate user subsidiary B not paying tax that could be the collection responsibility of subsidiary A or not remitting use tax, the responsibility of subsidiary B);

(4) rental of property that does not qualify as a continuing sale, i.e., a true lease (sometimes viewed as a sales tax issue when property is rented from in-state company);

(5) resale parts inventory used to repair customer property under warranty;[2] and

(6) property purchased under a direct pay permit that is not resold or used in an otherwise exempt manner for which the permit is held.

In the above six situations, the measure upon which the tax is imposed is not necessarily 100 percent of the value of the property. Depending upon the state, the taxable measure can be the material cost, inventory or standard cost, or fair rental value. It can also be the full retail or fair market value (see Chapter V for additional comment on measuring use tax). What is extremely important in relation to use tax liability on other consumption is that the tax liability be certain and that the timing of the liability be considered. Certainty and timing center on whether the state of property origination assesses use tax based on a financial entry or actually making constructive use of the property in question. For example, is the removal of resale property from inventory in state A subject to use tax when the accounting entry is made to credit inventory and debit fixed assets, or when the property is put to use in state B where the use tax would be due? Or perhaps, because the property will be exempt in state B, there is no use tax due at all.

There is little question that use tax is the most misunderstood of the taxes imposed on the sale or use of tangible personal property. In many cases, it is simply ignored until an audit levels the playing field. So, in the tradition of the television game show, Jeopardy, if "the answer is 'it is subject to use tax,' the question is:"

what was not subject to sales tax;

what is not exempt from sales tax;

what is used, stored or consumed in the state (generally);

what is purchased without tax but is used in manner not covered by exemption; and

what is taxable and brought into state from out of state.

---

[2] Allowed only on motor vehicles and trailers and agricultural machinery.

¶304 In Summary, Differentiating Sales and Use Tax

Generally, one can say that sales tax is a tax imposed upon the activities of a seller within, or on transactions originating and ending in, a state. Use tax is imposed on transactions of a purchaser originating outside of its state. However, the exceptions are many, as noted in this chapter. When the tax condition of property is changed, a tax may become due and payable. A major "gotcha" relates to property withdrawn by a taxpayer from tax-free inventory for taxable use. Another major "gotcha" is that an exempt sale in interstate commerce may become a taxable use within the destination state. Clearly, the strongest statement that can be made in differentiating these taxes is that only one or the other can apply at any taxable moment. The trick is determining the taxable moment and, therefore, which tax applies to the transaction.

Chapter IV
Measuring the Sales Tax

¶401 Introduction

In most professional fields, there are "terms of art" that have taken on special meaning and, if used outside of the context of that profession, would have a very different meaning. For example, the word "bounce" has a common meaning that conjures a vision of the motion exhibited when a rubber ball is thrown at the ground. While having only a vaguely similar interpretation, bounce, to the hairstyling profession, refers to the action hair exhibits soon after it has been set and sprayed. In a nightclub, the word bounce has an altogether different meaning.

The word "measure" is such a term of art in the practice of sales and use tax. It may be what most people do with a yard stick; however, in the sales tax profession, measure is the amount upon which the tax is based, i.e., the value that is multiplied by the tax rate to yield the tax due. While life would be simple for tax professionals if all tax statutes merely stated that the tax is based on total sales without any exception, there would be substantially less job security and much less training required for the tax professional in such a world. This book would be unnecessary. Fortunately, no statute is quite so simple.

#10   At this point, it will be helpful to explain the use of two more terms that will play a major role in our further discussion of sales and use tax. The terms are "exclusion" and "exemption" and are often used interchangeably. Throughout the balance of this book, we will refer to adjustments to taxable measure as *exclusions;* that is, amounts that are excluded from an otherwise taxable computation. On the other hand, the purchasers, types of transactions, or properties upon which tax is not imposed or does not apply are *exemptions.*

To view this distinction one way, this chapter is first about exclusions, the different parts of and modifications to a transaction that reduce taxable measure. Viewed another way, this chapter is about gross receipts, not the type of tax, but the total value of a seller's receipts upon which tax is based, and the logical corollary to this issue, the amounts not customarily considered part of gross receipts, the allowable deductions from and offsets to gross receipts. What receipts are typically parts of gross receipts?

• Gross receipts

To begin with, gross receipts are defined in almost every sales tax statute as the total receipts from all sales, or the total receipts from each and every transaction. One should note that in neither definition is the word "taxable" used. The reason that statutes typically do not qualify their definition of gross receipts with the word taxable is because the states want to have the seller report all receipts before making adjustments for deductions. By requiring the reporting of total receipts, the states gather: (1) sales data for general statistical purposes, (2) industry-specific data to facilitate comparison between similar industry taxpayers in audits for compliance (the use of a reasonableness test), and (3) taxpayer records in detail sufficient to represent a business' trends that also improves compliance audit reliability (for a single taxpayer from audit to audit).

The selling price, in total, of *tangible personal property* is generally the measure of gross receipts. States, in the definition section of their statutes, go to great lengths to define selling price. That definition is often all inclusive, followed by a series of exclusions from that definition. For example,

> the selling price shall include all amounts received by the seller without any deduction on account of . . . except that selling price shall not include amounts represented by . . . which shall be excluded from the selling price.

• *Taxable services*

Later in this chapter we will look at what many states view as the receipts that may be excluded from gross receipts. However, in an attempt to broaden the tax base for purposes of revenue enhancement, increasing numbers of states are further defining their gross receipts to include the selling price of taxable services. Note that here the word "taxable" is used because customarily sales taxes are imposed only on tangible personal property, and a service literally does not result in the transfer of tangible personal property.

There is little question that labor or fabrication costs, which are included in the selling price of manufactured property, are elements of the gross receipts. However, one of the most difficult issues to be addressed in defining gross receipts for taxpayers and jurisdictions alike involves determining the taxability of mixed transactions, i.e., transactions in which tangible personal property is bundled with exempt services. Because this issue offers so many opportunities for misinterpretation, an extensive discussion can be found in ¶2207. There we will venture into the world of the "true object test."

What are the various categories into which services are commonly grouped for tax purposes?

(1) Professional services: These services are provided by doctors, dentists, accountants, attorneys, consultants and other professionals (typically individual to individual or company) resulting in the transfer or application of knowledge or information by taking an action or presenting the information through a verbal or written medium.

(2) Personal services: These services are provided by individuals or companies to individuals on a personal but nonprofessional basis. Examples of personal services might include haircuts, manicures, house-cleaning, landscape maintenance, laundry and dry cleaning services, etc.

(3) Repair services: These services result in the restoration of damaged or broken property to its original operating condition—unlike assembly (the final steps in the manufacture or construction of property), fabrication (the creation of property from various components), conversion (changing what something does), and modification (changing the way something works). Assembly, fabrication, conversion and modifi-

¶401

cation are activities that are generally regarded as taxable services because they result in the creation of new or different property.

(4) Installation services: These services do not create new property, but merely render operable property usable at the site of the user. The fine distinction between assembly and installation must be recognized. States generally tax assembly, but may not tax installation.

(5) Business services: These services result in the movement of someone or something. Taken broadly, that which is moved could include property (freight carriers), financial instruments or money (banking), persons (transportation companies), electrical or telephone service (utilities), risk (insurance companies), ownership of real property (real estate companies), and entire companies (investment banking), etc.

Individual sales and use tax laws may place a different emphasis in defining any or all of these terms. Definitions are very state-specific depending on the legislative body's intent when framing its law.

In looking at ways states have attempted to increase revenue through changing legal definitions, we find two notable historical examples of broadening the definition of taxable gross receipts to include services. Florida made its effort in the late 1980s with a service tax that not only fully taxed in-state services, but also called for apportionment of service purchased out-of-state where the benefits derived from those services could be deemed to have been enjoyed in Florida. Similarly, services purchased in Florida but enjoyed out-of-state were apportioned to the extent they were enjoyed in Florida. This law was enacted and lasted for a brief six months before falling victim to widespread political pressure. In more recent years, additional states are using variations on this theme as a way to shore up inadequate governmental revenues suffered during the post-"dot-com" recession.

The second notable example, of how a state attempted to broaden its tax base through the redefinition of its statutory terminology, is Massachusetts. Effective September 1, 1990, Massachusetts planned to expand its definition of tangible personal property to include gas, electricity, and steam when not used in industrial processing or heating industrial plants. As with any tax-expansion legislation, one can see who in the state is powerful and who is powerless, and who votes and who has no election franchise. The law was also drafted to tax many services in general and, specifically, legal, accounting, bookkeeping, engineering and architectural services that met various aggregate dollar thresholds. The existing rate of 5 percent would apply in the case of services as well as to tangible personal property. However, legislative squabbling delayed the effective date of the law for nearly six months.

As with Florida, Massachusetts was able to activate the law long enough to collect its first dollar. The final Massachusetts tax battle found the telecommunications and energy taxes left in place, the general service taxes repealed retroactively for the two days they were operative, and a commitment from the

¶401

Department of Revenue not to assess the telecommunications tax for the period during which the tax was in limbo.

Other states, along with Florida and Massachusetts, have learned from these two experiences. Rather than making sweeping changes, laws are being changed by the piecemeal approach, a new taxable service here, another service there. States have learned that organizing and galvanizing opinion against a law change is much easier for "big business" to achieve than individuals. The advertising industry beat the Florida law change. The legal and accounting industries were instrumental in overturning the Massachusetts law. However, taxing personal services is easier because customers see little impact and the vendors required to collect the tax lack the organizational strength to fight a new law.

In the years since the Florida and Massachusetts forays into expanding the taxable base by changing definitions, the most popular areas of actual change have been,

(1) software (distinguishing between taxable and non-taxable software – often a distinction based on whether the software is customized or whether it was delivered on tangible media or via telecommunications or the Internet)

(2) utilities (distinguishing between non-personal use and non-manufacturing use – resulting in the taxation of utilities for business use of an administrative nature or personal use that exceeds one's normal life-sustaining requirements),

(3) amusements (admission to entertainment environments like movies, theatre, amusement parks, etc.), and

(4) the traditional area of personal services.

In the state that excludes labor and installation costs from gross receipts, an interesting question arises regarding whether labor or installation costs occur prior to or after the sale of property (which would change the tax treatment). One way to test this issue is by asking if the property being sold was fully assembled prior to delivery and was operative before shipment to the customer. If this is the case, one can presume the installation, if separately stated, was labor after the sale and may be excluded from gross receipts. All elements of pre-delivery final assembly would be included in gross receipts.

But, if the seller must perform the final assembly at the purchaser's facility, calling that labor "installation" and separately stating it does not mean it can be excluded from gross receipts. This can work to the tax benefit of the purchaser. In a state in which machinery and equipment is exempt from tax and installation is taxable, characterizing the installation as the final step in the assembly process may turn taxable installation into the exempt sale of machinery and equipment. Further, the separate sale of an installation kit used by the seller's personnel will also tend to demonstrate that the sale is not complete until the property is installed. And, in the case of capital equipment requiring that the purchaser "accept" the property once it has been demonstrated by the seller to operate as

¶401

promised, and where the purchaser withholds the final payment until acceptance, the issue of whether the sale has been completed may then be a matter of the title clause in the sales/purchase agreement. Alternatively, if the property in question is delivered to the seller at the purchaser's dock and there must be acceptance by the purchaser for final payment to occur, with title transferring at that point, the sale may not be consummated until these conditions, acceptance and final payment, have been met.

A much finer distinction in the definition of gross receipts being made in states that do not appear to tax services is how services are included in gross receipts to the degree that they are part of the sale of, or involve the transfer of title to or possession of, tangible personal property. For example, is the "repair" of equipment, by swapping a single broken component for a new or rebuilt component, a repair (labor) service or really the sale of a new part in exchange for money and the defective component?

A more difficult question involves the issue of whether the true purpose or object of a transaction is the property that is transferred in the sale or the intellectual content embodied in that property. Is an author's manuscript (which is clearly tangible personal property) really the embodiment of the author's ideas, which could be transferred verbally but are more easily transferred in written form? See ¶ 2207 for a more complete discussion on services.

• *Rental receipts*

While *rental of personal and often real property*, in general, is considered part of gross receipts, rental receipts may be taxed either at a different rate, or may be viewed as receipts subject to use tax. For purposes of rentals and leases of tangible personal property, one must also distinguish a true lease or rental transaction (where the lessor grants a limited use without passing title to the lessee) from a continuing sale (which is often more of a financed purchase), which typically has a buy-out option at the end of the lease term. See ¶ 2205 for a more complete discussion of leases and rentals. It is notable that real property is viewed differently than leases and rentals of tangible personal property. Motor vehicles are also viewed differently than other tangible personal property. In many state statutes, sales of motor vehicles are treated in a separate code section from tangible personal property. One can only guess why this is the case. Equipment rented with an operator is often treated differently than the same property rented without an operator.

• *Other types of receipts*

There are also *other types of receipts* that may be recognized as gross receipts but are required to be reported at a different rate and/or on a different return form. Examples of such receipts would include revenue from amusements, sales of food served in restaurants, sales of motor vehicles, air and water craft, rolling stock, etc. These are sometimes dealt with separately in statutes.

• *Other taxes*

There are numerous *other taxes* that are due and collected by a variety of jurisdictions for as many other reasons. Federal excise taxes are levied on petroleum and rubber products, luxury and sporting goods, tobacco and alcoholic products, telecommunications and transportation services, and special types of vehicles and accessories. States also levy similar excise taxes. Nearly all of these taxes are imposed prior to the sale of the property and normally may not be excluded from gross receipts.

And finally, perhaps the least frequently taxed gross receipts are those included in the selling price of *real property*. Some states have elected to include in gross receipts all or part of the selling price of new or original construction or, perhaps, only improvements to, repair of, or reconditioning of existing property (see Chapter XXII). See ¶2204 for a more complete discussion of contractors.

¶402 Receipts Typically Excluded from Gross Receipts

To the extent that state statutes vary, one from the next, a given state is as likely to include as exclude a given element of gross receipts. With the exception of tangible personal property—the receipts from the sale of which are considered taxable in every tax statute—anything else included in gross receipts, e.g., amounts represented in a selling price as labor or real property, could just as easily be excluded from gross receipts. Beyond this obvious consideration, the issue becomes more complex as states vary in their view of exclusions and in the way the exclusions are actually defined.

• *Separately stated transportation*

While not universal, it is common that the portion of gross receipts represented by charges for *separately stated transportation* (also known as delivery or freight charges) occurring after the sale are considered to be excluded from gross receipts. Alternatively, some states look to the property's FOB (free on board or freight on board) point to determine whether the transportation charges should be included in gross receipts. Generally, separately stated transportation or freight charges on FOB origin shipments are excluded from gross receipts while transportation or freight charges on FOB destination shipments are included in gross receipts.

An easy way to remember this is by recalling that title is customarily considered to transfer at the FOB point. Therefore, if the seller has title until the destination, the transportation is likely to be part of the selling price until the property is received by the customer and, therefore, the charges for the transportation are incurred prior to the completion of the sale—it is part of the selling price. The same logic follows in reverse for FOB origin sales. Because "handling" is normally an activity preceding the completion of the sale, it too is normally part of the selling price and is included in gross receipts. For this reason, when the phrase "shipping and handling" is present in a transaction, one can assume that the receipts from "shipping and handling" are likely to be included in taxable measure.

• *Optional warranty agreements*

It can generally be said that the amount associated with manufacturers' warranties not separately stated are considered included in the selling price of property and taxed or exempted consistent with the taxability treatment of the underlying property. Arguments in many states and state courts have looked at the issue of whether the parts or repairs provided under these warranties are considered in the measure of the original sales price and are not taxable when delivered, provided, installed, etc., by the seller pursuant to such warranties. Look to the specific state for the manner in which it taxes these parts.

Separate and apart from manufacturer-inclusive warranties is the issue of taxability of *optional warranty agreements,* which are purchased by the customers from the seller and sold independently from the property being protected thereby. An example would be the sale of a three-year extended warranty agreement by Magical Home Appliance Centers to its customer when that customer purchases a new television. The optional warranty covers all parts and labor to repair the television for the three-year period following the expiration of the manufacturer's warranty. There are several issues related to optional warranty agreements that may impact taxability:

— Is the separately stated warranty optional or mandatory?

— Does the warranty include parts and labor?

— Is the service provided under the warranty provided by the manufacturer, the seller, or a third party?

— When is the optional warranty agreement purchased?

• *Prompt payment discounts*

With regard to various types of discounts, one should first consider when the discount is taken, given, earned or allowed. A *prompt payment discount* is considered to be taken after the sale and in many states is viewed as not excluded from gross receipts. In other words, the seller reports the gross receipts without reflecting the amount the customer may deduct due to a prompt payment. However, other states allow the seller to adjust the gross receipts after the fact, reflecting the decreased amount of the compensation received on a prompt payment discounted sale.

• *Trade or quantity discounts on invoices*

In most states, the reduction in the selling price represented by the netting of a *trade or quantity discount* shown on the face of the invoice results in the gross receipts being reduced accordingly. However, if the discount is conditioned on some factor outside of or subsequent to the sale, e.g., total annual purchasing volume, these discounts may not be excluded from gross receipts. It should be noted that the measure subject to use tax, in the case of discounts given or taken, may exclude the amounts represented by the discounts. In other words, generally, the discount should be computed and deducted from the purchase price of out-of-state purchases subject to tax prior to computing the tax. This topic will be covered in greater detail in the following chapter.

¶402

• Coupons or script

#12　　*Coupons or script*, used to reduce the cash tendered by the customer for the goods purchased, are more often than not considered an invalid basis for reducing the taxable gross receipts. For example, the grocery store that takes a manufacturer's coupon from the customer in lieu of cash, and presents that coupon to the manufacturer for credit, cannot reduce the gross receipts by the value of the coupon. However, this may be a legitimate exclusion in some states.

• Premiums or promotions

Premiums or promotions (free gift with purchase, monetary rebates that may be claimed by customer submission of a proof of purchase with a receipt and application form, trading stamps, etc.) are all issues requiring reviews of specific statutes. However, generally, the tax due, if at all, tends to be use tax on the cost of the goods rather than sales tax based on the measure of the property given away free. Monetary rebates provided by the manufacturer do not reduce gross receipts. Trading stamps purchased by retailers do not impact gross receipts; however, stamp redemptions may result in reportable gross receipts.

• Rebates

Rebates, amounts that are returned to the customer from the seller or the manufacturer can rarely be excluded from gross receipts, i.e., the rebate given at the time of sale or upon the submission of a rebate form or request, will not reduce the taxable measure associated with the original sale. It may be possible to structure the relationship between a manufacturer, seller, and consumer in such as manner as to give the manufacturer the economic benefit from the rebate, but the sales tax implications are hard to impact.

• Trade-ins

Certainly, *trade-ins* are some of the most confusing adjustments to understand as their treatment does not follow logically from the activity and often is qualified as to the nature of the property in question. Many states do not allow trade-ins to be excluded from gross receipts. In other words, the seller must report tax measured by the selling price of the new property being sold rather than the selling price of the new property less the value of the trade-in. Other states allow the deduction of the trade-in value prior to computing the taxable measure, resulting in the gross receipts being reported on the net invoiced value. And some states, which allow the deduction of the trade-in value, will only allow for that deduction on property "of a like kind" being traded.

• Returns, restocking charges and repossessions

Returns, restocking charges and repossessions also are treated differently from state to state. Often a return of property that results in a full credit may be excluded from the reportable gross receipts in the period the property is returned to the seller. Therefore, while the gross receipts on the original sale may have been reported on one tax return, the reduction of current gross receipts may be reflected on a different return. However, it is not unusual for a state to qualify this provision by stating that, if the purchaser does not receive a full refund (a restocking charge is deducted from the value of the returned property credit), then the original sale remains reportable and the returned property credit may not be used to reduce gross receipts in a subsequent period.

A repossession is property confiscated by the seller (or lessor) because the purchaser (or lessee) failed to meet the conditions of sale (did not pay for the goods). In this situation, the gross receipts reported on the original sale remain reportable and the repossessed property, which will be resold or leased to another customer, will also be included in future gross receipts. Whether a credit on tax already paid on the original transaction is allowed is a state-by-state issue.

• *Interest or finance charges*

In most states the *interest or finance charges* separately stated either in the contract or agreement or on the invoice itself are excluded from gross receipts. Similarly, the sale of a portfolio of commercial finance contracts would not be included in gross receipts. In the absence of statutory language, this is one type of exclusion that is widely accepted and understood when fully documented. However, the interest or finance charges computed in a true lease are often entirely included in gross receipts if tax is reportable on the periodic lease revenue.

• *Bad-debt write-offs*

Finally, bad-debt write-offs, which may be excluded in the sales tax environment, are one of the most ignored areas of gross receipts adjustment. in the sales tax environment. It is easy to recognize when a sale has taken place, but it requires careful data tracking to note the point in time when a sale is actually written off as uncollectible. Many states require that the write-off be reflected in federal income tax reporting. An astute sales tax manager should regularly interact with the federal income tax manager to determine bad-debt write-off opportunities. The environment in which bad-debt write-offs tend to be most widely ignored is where the value associated with individual transactions is individually small. However, when aggregated, this value can be remarkably large and can easily justify an adjustment. It is important to remember that bad-debt can be simply the failure of someone to pay an invoice or a check or credit card being regarded as bad, i.e., insufficient funds (for a check) or invalid credit card.

The common treatment shows that a bad debt may be excluded from gross receipts with a reduction therefrom in the period that it is actually written off but must be re-included in gross receipts at the time it is recovered or collected. It is important to remember the importance of writing off bad debts for sales tax purposes against the sales tax liability, as the benefit is 100 percent of the originally reported tax, whereas sales tax written off against the federal income tax liability only results in the savings of the income tax on the sales tax.

¶402

¶403 Recording Gross Receipts

As with most of life, timing is very important in matters of sales tax. There are statutes of limitation, requirements for providing certificates timely, due dates for filing and points in time when a tax liability affixes to a seller's transaction. For purposes of reporting gross receipts and sales tax, nearly all states prescribe within their statutes whether tax reporting must be based on cash or accrual accounting rules. While some states allow a modified approach, all states require consistency in the chosen method.

• *Cash-basis accounting*

Where there is a choice, *cash-basis accounting* makes the most sense in the retail sales environment. The distinction between retail and other businesses is the fact that sales are not made or recognized until cash (including checks and credit card charge slips) is placed into the register or cash box. In retail (cash) businesses, cash and cash equivalents are the only obvious basis for computing sales. Such businesses are commonly required to report sales on a cash accounting basis.

• *Accrual-basis accounting*

Contrast this environment with businesses using *accrual-basis accounting* where sales are "booked," i.e., a sales order is written, a purchase order received, property shipped and credit extended by issuance of an invoice, which will be paid at some date in the future. In this environment, where the seller ships property and holds the stated or implied security interest in that property until it has been paid for, the sale, which is part of gross receipts, and the tax liability thereon must be recognized at the time the property is shipped and the credit extended. States allowing businesses to report taxable sales when an invoice is issued to a credit-worthy customer or when a finance agreement is executed require tax reporting on an accrual accounting basis.

¶404 Elements of a Sale

Perhaps the most important concept in sales taxation is the issue of what must exist to constitute a reportable sale. There is broad-based agreement on this issue with the differentiation being a matter of timing. First, there must be a *transfer of title, right to use, or control (possession)* in the case of property or the *completion of the service act* in the case of a service. One should be mindful of the fact that judgment as to the taxability of the property, customer or service is not an issue in defining the gross receipts that states require taxpayers to report.

Second, there must be *consideration*. Each state takes a slightly different view on what constitutes "consideration." Every state agrees that consideration may be in the form of money (coin and currency of the realm). Of course, we also understand that money includes credit and debit card receipts, checks drawn on financial institution deposits, money and postal orders, food stamps and travelers checks. Accrual basis accounting states also assert that credit extended to a customer is part of consideration received.

What is the issue of timing? Often, two parties enter an agreement where a deposit, earnest money, an advance or pre-payment is required by the seller to begin execution on a contract. The construction and sale of a large or custom piece of capital equipment often requires months of planning, marshalling of materials, assembling of components and testing of the ordered property before that property is ever shipped to the customer. The seller may hesitate to begin this process without a financial commitment from the customer. Is there a sale when the purchaser sends the seller funds as a deposit or pre-payment? Literally, without some transfer of title to property, a sale has not yet taken place, and the receipts should not be reported for sales or use tax purposes. Tax may become due at some future time. Until then, the transaction may have no tax consequences.

An unusual variation of the timing issue is found in progress payment contracts, in which a contractual clause transfers title to property to the purchaser on the basis of each progress payment, rather than on the delivery (by the seller) and receipt (by the purchaser) of property. The seller maintains possession of the property in question, though the title is vested in the purchaser. In this situation, the sales tax liability is incurred based on issuance of an invoice (accrual method) or receipt of funds (cash method). If the transaction will be subject to use tax, the payment date probably determines the tax reporting date. In any event, careful attention should be paid in audits to payment timing involving pre-payments and the like.

In addition to cash and amounts represented by credit sales, property given in exchange for property purchased is also viewed as consideration in many states. Barter sales or exchanges and trade-in transactions are viewed as consideration and move those transactions into the world of gross receipts. Forgiveness of debt is often viewed as a form of consideration. This consideration comes into play in the realm of mergers, acquisitions, divestitures and business restructuring (a group of activities collectively known as bulk transactions).

¶405 Bulk Sales Transactions and Other Creative Strategies

When less than some specified (by code) amount of a business changes control, there may be a taxable incident. The simplest such transaction involves a corporation divesting itself of a division. Here, transferring ownership of the tangible personal property may be taxed in principle to the extent of the capital assets and supplies on hand. The (resale) inventory can be resold without tax coming due as it may be viewed as a sale for resale. Alternatively, if the transaction is really only a reorganization in which the ownership remains the same and the business unit is contributed as capital in commencing a new corporation, the code may exempt the sale. By example, following are several transactions that merit precise scrutiny by a sales tax professional to protect a company from a potentially large and unexpected tax bill and to save the tax professional from serious embarrassment.

(1) A division is spun off to management or acquired by another concern.

(2) A company negotiates a sale of its assets only (plant, equipment and inventory) but will continue to hold its liabilities.

(3) A joint venture is formed with one party contributing cash and the other partner contributing technology, personnel and equipment.

(4) The rights to a patented process are sold, along with the tooling necessary to produce the licensed product.

(5) A company acquires assets of a company in return for assuming the debt of the company selling its assets.

(6) A new entity is created, or an operating unit is spun off, as a division from one entity to another.

In recent years, consultants and creative tax accountants have developed a couple of strategies that offer some unusual advantages to sellers and purchasers alike. Captive leasing and captive purchasing companies are two such ideas that have value in specific environments. When considering both of these options, one must ask the question, "Do I have a valid business purpose that favors the adoption of the strategy?" Taxing authorities do not look kindly on taxpayers who implement "tax avoidance" strategies lacking a sound business purpose. At ¶2104 is a more comprehensive discussion of both of these strategies.

Truly, in these types of transactions, the advice "Buyer Beware" is only half the story. The seller must also beware of a sales tax liability that may not flow through to the buyer. Bulk transactions, first and foremost, require thorough planning and careful thought. Employing some very creative strategies can make an otherwise taxable transaction partially or entirely exempt or simply change the place where or person who pays the tax. On a very different level, companies often create bulk transactions to change the taxability or reporting activities for related entities. Creating leasing companies or purchasing companies may offer tax savings or one-time cost-of-funds advantages. However, a valid business purpose should be at the center of such strategies or the uninitiated may lose the advantages anticipated. Do not try to implement exotic strategies for your company without help.

Chapter V
Measuring Use Tax

¶501 Introduction

As with sales tax, one must understand how to measure use tax liability. Excluding the seller collecting use tax, use tax liability is not a question of gross receipts, but a question of sales price, purchase price, or taxable measure. In the case of the registered use tax collector, the basis for the taxable measure upon which the use tax is computed and collected may not be gross receipts but rather some other defined value, i.e., what the purchaser(s) is(are) liable to pay on account of given transactions. In general, the same rules that govern gross receipts for sales tax also govern gross reportable receipts for use tax.

Setting aside the issue of use tax receipts in the case of the seller's use tax, one needs to recognize the basis for establishing use tax reportable measure for the purpose of self-assessing use tax. In nearly every state, there is a line on the regular sales tax return that asks for the value of purchases or self-consumed property subject to use tax, an amount that is self-assessed. However, virtually no return indicates the basis for properly arriving at this measure. Determining the measure of the tax due most often requires answering two questions:

(1) Has some action triggered a taxable moment; and

(2) What elements of the purchase price, if any, may be excluded from use tax measure?

¶502 Use Tax on Purchases

We will concern ourselves first with taxable property acquired by a purchaser. To begin with, the use tax on a purchase is measured by the sale or purchase price of the property. As with sales tax, one must consider both the statutory definitions of "purchase price" or "sales price" and the issue of timing in determining what is or is not considered part of use tax measure.

The use tax measure should not include amounts upon which sales tax has already been paid to the state in which the property will reside. And further, use tax measure, generally, need not include amounts upon which sales tax was already legally paid to another state. Because a given transaction at the same specific point in time can only be subject to either sales or use tax, due to the concept of tax reciprocity (another term of art), most states will give credit for sales tax legally required to be paid to an origin state to the extent that it is equal to or greater than the state use tax payable in the destination state. However, the *Exxon* case may be the harbinger of things to come in this area. Caution is required not to extend the assumption of reciprocity to states that do not offer it and certainly not to local taxes (whose jurisdictions possibly have no reciprocity provisions whatsoever).

Finally, use tax may not be due a state if the property, which is otherwise taxable, is (1) moving through the state on a bill of lading or shipping instructions evidencing that its intended destination is a third state or some point outside of the United States, or (2) being held for *sale* to another legal entity. In both instances, the purchaser may not use the property in any way, except to store it or repackage it for further shipment, prior to placing it back into the stream of commerce. This in transit exclusion from use tax is not found in all states, though it is evident in many. With the former instance, states require different forms of documentation to confirm the continuing stream of commerce. As to the latter instance, most states will allow the resale exemption to be applicable to such a transaction. That claim must be evidenced by commercial invoicing or other appropriate documentation. When computing the use tax measure, as with sales tax, remember *all other taxes* imposed on the seller prior to transferring title to the property, e.g., most state and federal excise taxes, are generally considered part of the taxable measure.

Conversely, separately stated *common carrier transportation charges* would be considered excluded from the use tax measure in most states where transportation is not taxable (and especially where it occurs after the sale). A very simple rule is followed concerning transportation on the seller's conveyance. If the seller's personnel or equipment delivers property into a state from out-of-state, the transaction is most likely a sales, not a use, tax transaction and should be considered accordingly. Seller possession of property in the destination state changes what would otherwise be a use tax transaction into a sales tax transaction.

Treatment of *trade discounts* extended in the body of the invoice would almost always be allowed, that is, excluded from the use tax measure. However, *volume or quantity discounts,* which are conditioned on many individual purchases and are earned after the sale, mostly do not result in the reduction of use tax measure. *Prompt payment discounts* may be deducted from taxable measure in states that look to the consideration tendered in exchange for the property delivered. And treatment of *trade-ins, services in conjunction with a sale (installation or handling), installment or finance charges, etc.,* will generally follow the provisions of the sales tax.

¶503 Use Tax on Self-Consumed Property Purchased Free of Tax

To capture tax from purchasers who convert property for their own use that was purchased under a resale or other exemption certificate (other than direct pay), states require that use tax be reported on the conversion of such property, which, had the identical property been purchased at retail, would have been otherwise subject to sales tax. In ¶303, we described several situations that typify these actions of conversion. Following are the four bases by which the use tax is measured in such conversions.

• Material cost

Material cost is only the value of raw materials contained in the converted property at purchased cost. For a manufacturer, this would be the cost of the actual materials purchased for resale from outside suppliers. Sub-assemblies and components built by the manufacturer are also taxed on the raw material values even though they may be carried on the books at standard cost, which probably includes the direct manufacturing labor. For wholesalers and retailers who purchase assembled property for resale, the use tax is measured solely by the cost of the property itself. Acquisitions from subsidiaries, affiliates or any related but separate corporations are truly acquisitions and must be treated as purchases.

• *Inventory or standard cost*

#16   *Inventory or standard cost* is the direct cost of placing the property into inventory. The difference between material and inventory cost is direct labor, inbound transportation, and all other elements which make up the cost "at standard," e.g., indirect materials consumed and charged to the product, manufacturing burden, overhead, etc. Whether a state, which uses this cost basis to measure use tax, would argue for the greater of inventory or standard cost must be looked at case by case.

• *Full retail or fair market value*

Full retail or fair market value is the price at which the property is sold to your customers. This measure of use tax is rarely found, but it is valid and must be *#17* used in those states that require this basis. Full retail value and fair market value are _not_ always the same measure and should be clearly understood when following this measurement basis.

• *Fair rental value*

Fair rental value is the rental value of the property in the open market. Several states do use this basis for measuring use tax liability. Unfortunately, the value may be determined somewhat subjectively, leaving much room for interpretation.

A variation on the above issue of self-consumed property involves the "transfer" of manufactured consumable goods from one division to another. For clarification purposes, transfers occur between divisions of the same parent; sales occur between subsidiaries of the same parent. The use of a sales invoice and the issuance of a remittance advice between divisions does not change a transfer into a sale. Conversely, the absence of a sales invoice covering movement of property between subsidiaries, e.g., a journal entry booked at the parent, does make a sale into a mere transfer. One must look at the substance of the transactions based on recognizing the relationship of the parties in the transaction.

> **example:** A vertically integrated manufacturer builds production line machinery and equipment (M&E) in Division A, which transfers the M&E to the production line in Division B. If Division A makes no commercial sales, all of the raw material for construction of M&E should be purchased tax-paid. When Division A consummates its transaction with Division B, Division B is required to accrue use tax for payment to the state where the (taxable) property will be used, and only if there is a greater tax rate in Division B's state or the taxable measure as defined is on a larger value than

that provided by Division A's state (where State B offers reciprocity for State A's tax).

Problem

Question: What tax planning strategy could be followed to maximize tax savings and flexibility with the above described inter divisional M&E construction and transfers?

Answer: Locate Division A in a state providing an M&E tax exemption that does not exempt only that M&E for use in manufacturing tangible personal property for sale in that state. In so doing, Division A may purchase all of its raw material and M&E components to be incorporated into the exempt M&E on a tax free basis. The use tax liability would only be recognized when the M&E was actually received in Division B's facility, and then only if that state taxed M&E used in production. Additionally, Division A should not pick up (physically) raw materials or other components in a state that does not exempt such purchases as the sales tax will apply at the point of delivery, not Division A's state where the same property would enjoy a tax exemption.

If Division A transfers M&E to other divisions and sells to related entities and unrelated commercial customers, all of the material for construction of the M&E may be purchased for resale. However, in this situation, Division A still has a use tax liability in its own state for M&E transferred to other divisions in or out of its state and Division B would have a use tax liability in its own state to the extent that its rate or taxable measure definition caused additional burden in Division B's state. Again, one must note that the concept of reciprocity is at issue and, in transfers between states without reciprocity, the use tax may be due in full in both states.

When Division A makes sales to related entities (subsidiaries or related corporations) or to unrelated commercial customers, normal rules of sales and use tax come into play. The related entity in State B, where Division A is not registered to collect use tax, must accrue and pay use tax in full in its home State B. In this case, it is irrelevant to look at the four bases for use taxation. The taxable measure will be computed using the principles discussed at ¶502.

¶504 Use Tax on Taxpayer-Owned Property Used in New State

When tax-paid property (usually a capital asset) is purchased in one state, used for a period of time and then transferred to another entity in another state for further use, there is a question as to whether there is an additional use tax payment due in the second state and, if so, how should it be measured? Generally, the first issue is whether the property is taxable or exempt in the second state. Clearly, a given asset may be taxable in one state but not in another, depending on how it is used, e.g., the M&E exemption.

Assuming the asset is taxable, the next issue is whether the transfer is a sale or merely a re-deployment of an asset within the same entity. If there is a sale between related entities, the consideration is the measure of the tax. Within the same parent, depreciation is usually taken into account in arriving at the taxable measure. If the asset is merely transferred between divisions, the net book value may be the measure of the tax. This type of transaction is relatively common and requires careful research to arrive at the correct measure. It should be noted that some states do not tax assets transferred from one state's division to another state's division that have been used in the first state for a specified period of time prior to use in the second state. The exclusion from paying tax in this situation granted by the state, often referred to as a use exclusion, might indicate that use of property out of state for more than a given number of days, months or years constituted an intent by the purchaser/owner to purchase and use said property out of state. This overcomes the presumption of an intent to purchase for use within the destination state. Accordingly, the state would not consider the purchase subject to its use tax.

¶505 Use Tax on Self-Consumed Property Purchased Under a Direct Pay Permit

Unlike property purchased for resale and self-consumed, property purchased under a direct pay authority (see Chapter VI for explanation of direct pay authority) that is self-consumed is measured by the material acquisition cost of the property. Tracking this value in a large manufacturing operation, where the purchasing, accounting and tax departments do not know at time of purchase or payment what specific item, unit, quantity, etc., will be self-consumed versus compounded or incorporated into finished resale inventory, is extremely difficult. For this reason, some states will allow direct pay permit holders to perform retrospective reviews of material consumption to establish ratios that, when applied to total purchases, fairly represent the cost of self-consumed property and material purchased free of tax under direct pay authority.

In recent years, a number of states have begun to enter into *managed compliance agreements* (also known as MCA) to taxpayers who participate in audits that establish taxability rates to be used on a going forward basis. The MCA is often the result of having the taxpayer participate in a *managed audit*, an audit performed by the taxpayer and overseen by the taxing authority. In lieu of entering into the MCA or reporting tax measured by individual transactions, some taxpayers are electing to develop this taxability reporting rate (executing a *rate study*) privately. Once established without formal state approval, the taxability rate is used as though the taxing authority has accepted the rate and the process that developed it. When a taxpayer performs a rate study without state participation, it is critical that one follows state mandated procedures (assuming they exist) for establishing the taxability reporting rate. Developing such a rate customarily employs random statistical sampling, a concept that is not yet universally recognized or, when recognized, consistently executed by taxing authorities.

In summary, the method of measuring use tax is no less involved, complex, and varied than the method of measuring sales tax and may be significantly more complex. The tax professional should be wary that use tax liabilities tend to lurk in many hidden places with the measure of the tax just as subtle. When one feels they have mastered measuring use tax for state tax purposes, they must be alert to local use tax issues, whose imposition and measure may bear no similarity to state provisions.

Chapter VI
Exemptions

¶601 Introduction

In Chapter IV we looked at a variety of transactions that reduce or are excluded from taxable measure. Their receipts are not included in taxable gross receipts. A term mentioned at that time, and a term often used interchangeably with "exclusions," is "exemptions." Again, for purposes of this book, exemptions describe and define the types of purchasers, transactions or property upon which tax is not imposed or does not apply. In both cases, the taxpayer reduces taxable measure by amounts represented by excluded measure and exempt sales.

There are those who would argue different definitions for the terms "exclusion" and "exemption." In any event, what is important is understanding how specific states use the terms, and states do have differing views. In this chapter I have taken what are labeled as exemptions and attempted to organize them. The classifications are not written into any law but are merely used for clarification.

Exemptions fall into two broad classifications, and then into logical groupings within those classifications. Externally derived exemptions find their origin in the direct or indirect influence of the legislative process. Either legislators are strongly encouraged to provide the specific exemption or their failure to create an exemption will be viewed as politically insensitive. Following are groups of externally derived exemptions to be discussed in this chapter.

Governmental exemptions include, or are allegedly based on, those specific prohibitions found in the U.S. Constitution, exemptions that are implicit extensions of that document, and exemptions relating to states and their local subdivisions. *Interest group or politico-economic* exemptions are adopted as a result of financial persuasion typically shepherded by lobbyists for major business associations and trade groups or special interest organizations. *Business/public benefit* exemptions are adopted to encourage new business to take up residence in a state, promote action by business or the public, or encourage the expansion of existing business. *Voluntary services* exemptions are provided to various nonprofit and beneficent organizations in return for the "good" deeds they perform. *Humane* exemptions cover the range of sales to and purchases by regular folks to make it through life.

The second classification of exemptions includes those that are primarily transaction-related. The nature of the transaction, rather than the products or parties to a purchase or sale, dictates these exemptions. Transaction exemptions flow logically out of the tax statute since they have much to do, as enumerated in the statutes, with the concept of the tax in which they are found. This second set of exemptions are characterized as being internally derived, that is, derived from within the statute or code itself rather than drawn based on external influences or based on who is involved externally. These exemptions are generic, often require specific claim forms, and include the familiar concepts of resale and direct pay. In contrast, the externally derived exemptions may often be asserted by the very nature of the transaction or the types of participating parties. Therefore, specific documentation may not be required.

There is a final type of transaction that does not require traditional certificates, must be well documented in the seller's file, and does not appear to fall clearly in either the externally or internally derived exemption groupings. The exemption accorded occasional sales is predicated on the fact that the seller makes a minimal number of sales annually.

It is often said that sales tax is a tax ruled by form rather than substance. When it comes to exemptions, particularly those characterized as internally derived, this statement exemplifies the tax. Taxing authorities look mostly at the form of the transaction when granting or accepting the exemption. When we consider that the underlying assumption in sales taxation is that a transaction is deemed to be taxable until evidence to the contrary is presented, the form, i.e., the way the transaction is documented, is exceedingly important. Simply saying that the customer is purchasing the property for resale doesn't hold much weight with an examining agent regardless of the absurdity of the view in the alternative. Accordingly, when documentation is required to avail oneself of an exemption, failure to acquire and maintain whatever is required or expected can be both foolish and costly to the taxpayer.

¶602 Externally Derived Exemptions

• Governmental exemptions

State governments are not empowered to pass taxes that are imposed directly on the federal government. Without exception, this is the case. Federally chartered institutions and instrumentalities and agencies of the federal government, such as the American Red Cross, the National Ski Patrol, some "federal" banks and savings and loans, and credit unions and farming/utility cooperatives receive tax benefits by riding on the federal shirt-tails. However, states that tax the privilege of selling may not provide an exemption on sales to certain federal instrumentalities and agencies or on federal real estate contracts. In such cases, the determination is that the federal government is not a party in interest.

Furthermore, states may not impose taxes on sales outside of their borders. This is why sales, but not purchases, in interstate commerce are universally exempt from sales tax. However, a purchase in interstate commerce is almost assuredly going to be subject to use tax.

Many states have considered the wording of the U.S. Constitution and inferred that taxing newspapers and (often) periodicals could be construed as an impediment to freedom of speech. One could argue that this exemption is a natural extension of the protection of freedom of speech. Some states also see taxing religious institutions as possibly limiting freedom of religion. Thus, sales to and by "legitimate" religious organizations and, in some cases, their ordained representatives, are often exempt. In all three cases (freedoms of speech, press and religion), recent challenges by taxpayers alleging protection under these inferred constitutional "rights" have been unsuccessful. Entities governed by the

Interstate Commerce Commission may enjoy special considerations since they carry both persons and property, for themselves and others, across state lines.

Finally, the state governments themselves are often exempt from sales and use tax, though there are exceptions. Where a tax statute exempts sales to and by the state, one often finds the phrase "and local jurisdictions and agencies of the state and its subdivisions." In some states, contractors performing services for these entities may receive the pass-through benefits of the governmental exemptions.

• *Interest groups and politico-economic exemptions*

It may be said that to know the powerful in the state is to read the exemptions in the sales tax laws. "Big" money has been successful in nearly every state and local jurisdiction in gaining preferential sales tax treatment. In agricultural and farming states, products and equipment used to produce food for human and animal consumption are typically not taxable. In natural resource states, companies in the business of drilling, mining and processing oil, gas, coal, bauxite, copper, etc., are often the recipients of special consideration associated with their equipment or processing supplies. In the financial communities, banks, savings and loans, and insurance companies may pay a special tax "in lieu" of the sales tax. Special treatment of this type occurs largely as a result of effective lobbying efforts.

In recent years, national lobbying organizations have taken up the banner for their members in the quest of tax exemptions. The printing industry has successfully fought for exemptions on printing mail-order catalogues. The rationale is allegedly competitive pricing (tax equalization between states), matching those states without sales taxes and foreign low-cost printers. The movie and record industries have successfully fought taxation on various aspects of producing original works or master recordings. Notably, the direct mail industry successfully overcame efforts by the Congress to establish a national mail-order sales tax standard, followed recently by the Supreme Court's upholding the 1967 *National Bellas Hess* nexus standard in the recent case of *Quill Corporation v. North Dakota* (112 SCt. 1904 (1992).

If we look at when interest group and politico-economic exemptions are increasing, we will find major activity during periods of both boom and bust. Activity occurs during periods of boom because state legislatures are flush with revenue and feel particularly charitable and responsive to interest group pressure. Activity occurs during periods of bust because state legislatures want to encourage development, expanded business activity, or other agendas best achieved using tax incentives. As one can imagine, the beneficiaries of these interest group and politico-economic exemptions would be on opposite sides of the fence (politically and economically). When a tax exemption is already available but the taxpayer has not taken advantage of the exemption, we refer to this as a credit. When the taxpayer or interested party negotiates a special exemption or tax holiday, we are normally talking of an incentive. Credits can be highly restrictive or very broadly applied. However, finding them often requires the skill of a private detective. They are often based on specific property or activities carried on within precisely defined geographical boundaries. State and local agencies often post credit information on their Internet web sites. Incentives tend to be highly selective and focused on individual companies to encourage development or expansion.

Some exemptions are available in the form of "credits and incentives", not always spelled out in the sales tax statute. When a tax exemption is available and the taxpayer must apply to take advantage of the exemption, we refer to this as a credit program. In these programs the tax must be paid followed by claiming the credit (refund). The sales tax credits provided under these programs, often but not always, are not directly refundable but instead are an off-set to some other tax, e.g., income tax, not sales tax. What happens when the taxpayer is in a net loss position for income taxes? The credit is available in the statute but not for the specific taxpayer, in reality.

An example of a direct tax credit is the Minnesota's capital purchases credit. Here the state requires that the taxpayer pay tax on qualified (potentially exempt) capital purchases and then submit a refund claim after the fact. The result is obvious. The state gets the benefit of the tax until the purchaser files its refund claim. What happens to the tax that some taxpayers fail to claim? What is the value of the claims not filed? Again, the state can claim to be supportive of business expansion – makes the legislature and governor look great – and the taxpayer is at fault for failure to tax advantage of this credit.

When the taxpayer or interested party negotiates a special exemption or tax holiday, we are normally talking of an incentive. Credits can be highly restrictive or very broadly applied. However, finding them often requires the skill of a private detective. They are often based on specific property or activities carried on within precisely defined geographical boundaries. State and local agencies often post credit information on their Internet web sites. Incentives tend to be highly selective and focused on individual companies to encourage development or expansion in disadvantaged geographical areas. The taxpayer must apply for the benefit associated with the incentive, be approved to receive the incentive, and then carefully tax advantage of the incentive during the term prescribed.

An example of a sales tax incentive would be a tax holiday provided to a company for locating a new plant in an economically disadvantaged neighborhood. The incentive might prescribe that the company notify its suppliers of targeted property that it is in a specific "zone" and that it is not obligated to pay sales tax on those purchases for a specified period of time.

• Business/public benefit exemptions

There is a fine line that separates interest groups and their politico-economic exemptions from those in the business/public benefit category. The latter group tends to flow from the top down, that is, the exemptions are government-initiated, rather than from the bottom up—those promoted by the ultimate beneficiaries of the exemption. The following are exemptions that are probably government-initiated:

¶602

(1) *Industrial development*—capital equipment and consumable materials exemptions;

(2) *Industrial expansion*—capital equipment exemption related to an increase in productivity;

(3) *New product development*—exemption for expenses associated with research and development;

(4) *Pollution control*—exemption for purchase and installation of pollution control equipment; and

(5) *Alternative energy sources*—exemption for retro-fitting old equipment with clean fuel motors, solar power, etc.

• Voluntary services exemptions

Nearly everyone has a feeling of concern or empathy for individuals burdened with sickness, artists contributing beauty through sensual presentations, educators furthering our wealth in knowledge, youth representing our society's future, veterans deserving thanks for serving our country, etc. Politicians are realistic in recognizing that a tax code that taxes purchases by agencies serving the altruistic elements and endeavors of our society may be viewed askance by the voting public. As a result, state sales tax statutes are populated with a range of voluntary services exemptions that may include, but are not limited to, sales to and by:

(1) health care facilities;

(2) educational institutions;

(3) parent-teacher organizations;

(4) public museums and galleries;

(5) historical facilities operated by voluntary groups;

(6) organizations for youth soccer, skiing, swimming, etc.; and

(7) veterans groups and other not-for-profit programs.

• Humane exemptions

There is a fine line between voluntary services and "humane" exemptions. The distinction is in the beneficiary of the exemption. Voluntary services exemptions tend to impact organizations, whereas humane exemptions are directed at individuals. People need food, clothing, shelter and good health. Humane exemptions tend to be product specific. The following products or tangible personal properties are often exempt from tax:

(1) food that is not prepared and is sold in bulk form to be prepared by the buyer (prepared food is considered a luxury item);

(2) clothing in general, clothing for children only, clothing valued at less than some designated amount, but not athletic gear or furs;

(3) prescription medicines but not over-the-counter medicines;

(4) medical products that sustain life, without which the individual is likely to expire (pacemakers, insulin syringes, etc.) or make life tolerable for those afflicted with medical inconveniences (ostomy products, crutches, wheelchairs, etc.);

(5) utilities for individual homes; and

(6) real property.

In more recent years, state legislatures have played around with these humane exemptions but they remain largely intact. The food issue has gone the limit, as exemplified by California's abortive attempt to tax only snack foods identical to exempt "bulk quantities of the same food" (the snack tax). This was tax clarification (or if you prefer, obfuscation) at its legislative best. The same deliberative body showed extraordinary generosity to consultants by passing statutes on medical products that would require a medical degree to understand. A medical device purchased by the same hospital used two different ways yields two taxable outcomes. Clothing worn on the gym floor may enjoy an exemption in Vermont that is not accorded a similar product worn on the street.

In recent years, to counter the impact of contiguous states offering broad clothing exemptions, states with common borders are providing periodic clothing exemption periods (like right before school commences in the fall). Finally, of this group of exemptions, real property is most likely exempt from tax for the statutory reason that it is not tangible personal property by statutory or common definition. The exemption accorded real property may be either a function of the size of the taxable base represented by real property sales or because real property taxes may be considered "in lieu of" taxes. However, in some states, sales of real property are subject to sales tax.

• *Periodical literature exemption*

One of the more misunderstood exemptions is associated with newspapers and periodicals. It is a widely held belief that this exemption is somehow associated with the first amendment to the U.S. Constitution that guarantees us freedom of speech, and that to tax a newspaper or magazine is to tax this freedom. In reality, this author opines that the periodical printing industry has a very substantial lobby that has convinced our state legislatures that taxing periodical literature is both bad tax and bad industry policy. Newspapers abound in every jurisdiction and have been sold and delivered for years by newspaper carriers, often very young, ill-equipped to collect and remit taxes. Magazines have been sold through subscriptions, which represent the first form of direct mail marketing. Magazines have recipients in every possible state and locality. What publisher in his right mind would want to administer sales taxes on sales through interstate commerce to every subscriber home? So, let's disabuse ourselves of the Constitutional myth and recognize powerful self-interest and successful lobbying efforts for what they really are.

• Occasional sales exemption

If everyone that sold a single item in a given year were required to register, collect and/or pay and remit tax, and report that sale, jurisdictions would be overwhelmed with the administrative task of tracking a multitude of sellers who are not really doing business. While the one transaction might involve the sale of something as small as a used infant crib or as large as an entire business, jurisdictions have chosen to focus on the regular activity of selling, rather than random singular sales, when requiring seller compliance. Accordingly, most states have set a threshold of three or more separate sales in a single 12-month period as the basis for which a seller shall be required to comply with the state's sales and use tax code. Considered as an exemption, tax is not reportable on gross receipts represented by only one or two sales annually. However, that does not necessarily render the purchaser exempt from sales or use tax on the same transaction.

As an aside, voluntary organizations holding bake sales, fund-raising auctions, food sales at Little League games, etc., either are concerned about, or entirely ignorant of, their responsibilities to taxing jurisdictions. Generally, a single sales event involving multiple individual sales is not an exempt occasional sale. In response to these situations, states have often either granted exemptions to these organizations, through the voluntary services exemptions discussed at ¶602, or they have established single-event permits. And finally, let's distinguish between the occasional sale and the bulk transfer sale. The former is described here. The bulk transfer is described at ¶405. It is the sale of some or all of a business. While this can also be construed in some situations as an occasional sale, it is unlikely that it will escape scrutiny as a bulk sale.

¶603 Internally Derived (Transaction) Exemptions

Internally derived exemptions flow naturally from the logic of the tax statute. Before discussing these exemptions, one should put them into the context of the earlier discussion presented on sales taxes. An exemption is claimed by a seller because it is passed through from the purchaser, either due to the nature of the purchaser or the purchase transaction. The acceptance of proper *written* documentation by the seller from the purchaser will allow the seller to record a sale as nontaxable. The sale must be reported, but as a nontaxable sale. Chapter XIII contains a discussion of documentation relevant to this issue.

• Resale exemption

The sales tax statutes in all states (and the District of Columbia) impose the sales tax on the final retail sale. However, in addition to imposing the sales tax on the final retail sale, Louisiana has an advance tax on non-retail sales, and Hawaii taxes wholesale sales at a lesser rate. Since only the final retail sale is taxable, purchases that are for resale, i.e., the purchaser will resell the property purchased prior to making first use thereof, except that it may be held for demonstration or display, are not subject to the retail sales tax. Once the seller has received either a resale certificate or resale purchase order (in those states that will accept an order only) from the purchaser, the subject sale may be considered exempt from tax.

A slightly different twist on the resale exemption relates to the sale of packaging material. In many states, packaging material that is sold with the finished product and becomes a part of the finished product is exempt from sales tax because it may be purchased for resale. Stated differently, there is no separate charge for the container, label, box, carton, etc., that is sold with its contents. There are, however, three issues that prevent one from making the assumption that all forms of packaging and shipping materials are exempt from tax (deemed to be resold with their contents).

The first issue is that the packaging material is consumed by and used for the benefit of the seller, not the purchaser. Material that might be included in this category would be pallets, strapping, mailing labels, bills of lading, etc. The second issue is that the material is reusable and is either returned to the seller or further consumed by the purchaser, e.g., for storing property, and not simply sold with its contents. Gas cylinders, pallets, crating, etc., are included in this group of items. The presence of pallets in both lists should be an indication that this is a messy problem area. The third issue relates to when the packaging material is applied to the finished product. If it is applied as a step in manufacturing, the packaging might be exempt. If it is applied after manufacturing has been completed, i.e., to place the product in storage prior to sale, the packaging might be taxable. The packaging should not be ignored or taken casually. It can represent significant tax savings or a major liability.

• *Direct pay exemption*

Several states provide for a direct pay authority, which is the second major type of transaction exemption. The direct pay provision simply grants the permit holder the right to acquire all property without payment of tax to the seller. Thereafter, the full responsibility is upon the purchaser to determine which purchases are taxable and which are not and to remit tax directly to the state on the taxable purchases. The direct pay permit holder is mostly remitting sales tax, not use tax. The underlying property would have been subject to sales tax. The tax being remitted is only use tax when property is actually brought in from out of state under the direct pay scenario. The direct pay concept was developed to meet the needs of manufacturers that acquire property both for processing into inventory for sale and also for fabrication of property used or consumed by the manufacturer itself.

Where direct pay authority runs into problems, and is rarely found, is in states that impose local taxes that are based on the ship-from or order (origin) location rather than the ship-to or delivery (destination) location. Simply, it is too difficult for the permit holder to determine the location that should receive the benefit of the local tax. Such is the case in California. There, the direct pay authority has been in existence in the code since 1987. To date, no one has elected to be a direct payer. The main reason could be that the local sales tax is imposed based on the place where the principle sales negotiation takes place. This means the purchaser must determine where the order was taken or placed with the seller, which can be very challenging if not impossible to do. In the late 1990s, California enacted a direct pay authority for use tax payers, educational or governmental organizations. In this case the cause for the change was the desire to attribute local taxes in specific jurisdictions rather than in county-wide pools.

Every state offering direct pay authority uses extreme care in granting such authority. Prospective permit holders must have both the financial solvency and the administrative capability to meet very demanding conditions provided under the authority. For example, because the authority cannot be used to enhance the purchaser's cash flow through the delay of tax payments, (though there might be such a one-time benefit), the permit holder must be able to accrue and pay the use tax promptly, and without the benefit of a payment (collection) discount. In some instances, the permit holder may also use purchase ratios to determine the reportable tax measure—a less precise, but often more reasonable, method of establishing a liability. This approach is becoming more widely accepted by jurisdictions. The concept is referred to as formula-based rate or rate-study reporting (see ¶ 1505 for a more complete description of this approach).

When a taxpayer employs one of these methods for reporting tax liabilities, states may enter into agreements (managed audit agreements, a/k/a MCA) with taxpayers to evidence a mutual understanding about the development of the rate(s). Such an agreement will often discuss the manner in which the rate(s) will be applied, how the rates will be audited, and the frequency with which the taxpayer will "true-up" or confirm the accuracy of the rate(s). Interestingly, these agreements are mostly non-binding because a state will rarely give up the right to perform a compliance audit. Again, as with the resale exemption, the permit holder must issue its unique permit number or certificate to a seller to relieve the seller of any tax collection liability.

In summary, when viewed graphically, it is easier for one to note the groupings of issues that impact upon taxable measure.

Many of the Significant Issues
to Consider in Measuring and Reporting Tax Liability

method of record keeping

CASH OR ACCRUAL
(later or now)

adjustments

PROMPT PAY DISCOUNT
TRADE-IN
BAD DEBT WRITE-OFF
COUPONS/SCRIPT
REPOSSESSIONS
OTHER TAXES

special charges

TRANSPORTATION
REPAIR LABOR
INSTALLATION LABOR
CONSTRUCTION REAL
PROPERTY
SHIPPING/HANDLING
FEDERAL EXCISE TAX

special customers

NONPROFIT HOSPITALS
SCHOOLS/UNIVERSITIES
STATE/LOCAL GOVERN-
MENTS
RELIGIOUS ORGANIZATIONS
COMMON CARRIERS
FEDERAL GOVERNMENT

special property

MEDICINES/DRUGS
NEWSPAPERS/PERIODICALS
UTILITIES
FARMING IMPLEMENTS
MINING/DRILLING EQUIP-
MENT
INDUSTRIAL EQUIPMENT
UNPREPARED FOOD

types of sales

RESALES
EXEMPT
OCCASIONAL
BULK
DIRECT PAY

Chapter VII

Audits, Hearings and Appeals

¶701 Introduction

Compliance audits performed by jurisdictions need not sap the strength and resources of a tax department, regardless of the department's size. Audit coordination and control are the key to audit survival, both financially and practically. As we address this issue, we will consider the customary four elements of most audits, the increased use of sampling, and the activities that follow an audit until it reaches its conclusion. Chapter XIV discusses the general matter of handling an audit (or auditor).

There is increased consistency among the states and the Multistate Tax Commission in their execution of compliance audits. States such as California, New York, Texas, Ohio, Illinois, Massachusetts, and Michigan have set standards and procedures that are being emulated widely. The meetings of the Federation of Tax Administrators, the association of jurisdictional representatives, have become an open forum for the exchange of such information. As with much of our society, information of all types is not nearly as secure and compartmentalized as it may have appeared in years gone by. Accordingly, today there are more similarities in audit activities and methodologies across jurisdictions.

¶702 Elements of the Sales/Use Tax Audit

There are four elements in most sales and use tax compliance audits: review of sales, review of purchases, reconciliation of the general ledger sales and use tax accounts, and analysis of journal voucher transactions. The review of sales may be divided into several sub-sets: trade sales over a given dollar threshold representing sales of large-ticket items, trade sales under that dollar threshold representing all other sales, bulk sales (sales of entire divisions, subsidiaries, assets or liabilities as a class, etc.), occasional sales (sales of property for which a permit was not held or sales made in a jurisdiction fewer than two or three times a year), and sales as a result of mergers or acquisitions.

• Review of sales

The review of sales is the auditor's method employed for verifying that all sales, for which a valid exemption (resale or otherwise) certificate is not evidenced, are taxed. That is, the tax has been paid to the jurisdiction for all nonexempt sales. While most statutes indicate that such exemption certificates must be provided timely by the purchaser (given at the time the order is placed), some jurisdictions will give the taxpayer additional time to locate proper certificates or other documentation not in the file at the time of the audit. States vary on their rules regarding the amount of additional time allowed to complete the certificate file, with some states allowing no additional time at all.

If sales documentation is not complete, there is a significant likelihood that the seller may end up bearing the tax burden for those sales that were not originally taxed, with little opportunity to recover the tax assessed. It always seems that the customers, for whom the sales order files are incomplete, are those customers who have since gone out of business. The time to properly document a sales transaction is at the time the order is taken. When a statistical sample and projection are used to determine the sales (or use) tax liability, attempting to recover the audited and assessed sales (or use) tax for those untaxed customers' transactions in the sample is often a waste of time—an act in futility.

In considering the sales tax assessment stemming from an audit, the taxpayer must recognize that the issue of shifting the tax, collected after the transaction is long completed, is a function of the tax statute and the type of tax imposed by the jurisdiction.

Where the tax is imposed on the seller, the ability of the seller to recover previously unbilled sales tax is a matter of contract law rather than tax law. If the purchaser did not agree (by contract, written or otherwise) to reimburse the seller for the sales tax due on a given transaction, the seller's ability to recover the tax is an issue of purchaser generosity. For non-seller privilege taxes, the seller should, and may be required to, attempt to recover the tax wherever possible for two reasons.

First, by billing the customer for tax, the seller will likely be notified by the customer if the questioned purchases have also been audited with taxes paid thereon by the customer. Second, if the customer has not been so assessed and if the tax is remitted to the seller, the seller becomes whole less any interest or penalty assessed in the audit, which may not be recoverable.

A liability disclosed by an audit of sales is often called either "taxable sales—measure understated" or "claimed exempt sales disallowed." The former type of assessment is the result of the taxpayer failing to capture transactions as being sales for reporting purposes. The issue is first to report all sales, and secondly, to identify those sales not subject to tax. Therefore, a seller may report sales of several million dollars and yet show no taxable sales. Such would likely be the case of a vendor in a federal government supply contract, a distributor of pharmaceutical products or a newspaper publisher. An auditor could also schedule "taxable sales—measure understated" where the seller excluded elements of the sales price or gross receipts in error. For example, was tax reported on the retail selling price with deductions for discounts, trade-ins, coupons, etc., in states not allowing those deductions?

The latter type of assessment could also result from the taxpayer properly reporting all sales but taking a deduction for sales that were allegedly exempt from tax or excluded from taxable measure. Were sales "in interstate commerce" deducted from taxable measure where the customer picked up the property in the origin state at the seller's dock or facility? Were the claimed sales for resale properly supported by timely and complete resale certificates? Were the sales, which are exempt as sales to holders of direct pay permits or governmental entities, properly documented? When the order entry department asked the customer if they were "exempt," was the answer yes, but for a tax other than sales tax and was the claimed exemption inappropriate?

Second, it is not uncommon for the audit to be finished well after a large portion of the next open audit period has passed. Customers may claim that requests for late reimbursement of taxes, not billed at the time of the sale, are statutorily tardy and they feel no obligation to reimburse the late billed sales tax. Or equally disconcerting, adjustments to the billing and tax procedures are not implemented until many months have passed in the next statutory period, perpetuating taxing errors that will either require manual attention or result in a subsequent assessment in the next audit (including a penalty). And while it may be possible to bill and collect sales tax late in a period considered open by the customer, interest and penalties may be imposed due to the extent of the timing difference between when the tax was correctly due and when it is paid.

• *Review of purchases*

Three types of taxable purchases are subject to sales or use tax that may be assessed under audit by a review of the taxpayer's paid invoices: (1) purchases delivered into the taxpayer's state from out of state on which the seller collected no tax; (2) purchases for which the taxpayer gave the seller an exemption certificate where that property was not used in the manner for which the exemption was taken (or other exemption was available); and (3) purchases in a nonseller privilege tax state where the seller failed to collect the tax at the time of sale. Of course, if the auditor is reviewing transactions for the state and the localities, the above three issues may also be viewed and assessed under local statutes and ordinances.

As with sales, auditors may well review large transactions in detail and the remaining smaller transactions by use of a sampling technique. It is for this reason that fixed asset or capital asset purchases are audited in 100-percent detail and most other purchases audited by sample testing. An auditor's findings in the review of purchases is called "taxable purchases subject to sales (or use) tax understated."

• *Reconciliation of the general ledger sales and use tax accounts*

A single-state taxpayer will make all tax entries to the general ledger sales and/or use tax liability account(s). Many of these entries are automatic, e.g., a sales tax liability is booked to the tax account when the sales invoice to the customer is prepared and booked to sales or a use tax liability is booked to the tax account when a purchase invoice is set up for payment of taxable property upon which tax is not charged. In other instances, activity in the tax account results from manual entries, e.g., a customer who failed to provide a resale certificate timely deducts the sales tax billed by the seller. The seller must debit the tax liability account and credit accounts receivable, after getting the proper documentation from the customer.

In the case of the multistate taxpayer, general ledger tax liability account entries may be made for all states (and lesser jurisdictions) individually. The auditor's reconciliation of the general ledger tax liability account in this situation requires careful scrutiny of each entry to be certain that amounts for other states are not adversely tainting the balances for the jurisdiction being reviewed by the auditor. A tax liability determined by an auditor in the reconciliation section of an audit might be called "unexplained taxable differences." Poor documentation of adjustments to the tax account is the single largest culprit causing large assessments due to "unexplained differences."

• *Analysis of journal voucher transactions*

Journal vouchers are used for a myriad of legitimate purposes, some of which directly impact the tax liability account and others that appear to have nothing to do with the tax area but yet are directly related. Six examples of these types of transactions are listed at ¶303, which deal with use tax. Often an auditor will schedule numerous "questioned" transactions and place the burden on the taxpayer to explain or clarify what otherwise appear to be transactions subject to tax. Difficulties occur when the taxpayer does not have a clear understanding of the various types of journal vouchers being prepared, often on a regular basis, and is unable to gain insight into this matter by viewing the journal vouchers individually.

While, in theory, it is not the responsibility of the tax department to instruct general ledger personnel in the fine points of journal entries, the tax manager who shows little interest and lacks persuasion in these endeavors will be overworked and embarrassed during the settlement of an audit. Complete written documentation explaining the purpose and effect of all journal entries should be gathered and bound for reference purposes. If not, as with most other tax audit issues, the large and unexplainable assessments may remain uncontestable since the "responsible" employee left the company six months prior to the commencement of the audit and cannot be located.

¶703 Sampling in Audits

There are two ways to perform an audit: (1) look at all documents and transactions in detail and assess on an actual basis; or (2) look at a sampling of documents and transactions and infer from that sample the condition prevalent in the entire universe from which the sample was drawn. If the number of transactions is relatively small and the size of each transaction significantly varied, a sample would be inappropriate. However, where there is a high degree of homogeneity in the population, a sample may be both a reasonable and desirable method of describing the condition of the entire population without looking at each and every unit therein.

• *Block sampling*

Sampling is not new to the world of compliance audits. For many years jurisdictions have used a very simple form of sample technique, the block sample, to make reasoned appraisals of a taxpayer's compliance. In a block sample, transactions during a given period of time are often selected for review, e.g., sales invoices from one month in each year or one year out of three or four in an audit period. Depending on the number of transactions, a "block" may be a small grouping of transactions, e.g., all of the cash register receipts in one month or all purchases in a calendar quarter.

Once the block period has been selected, the auditor will review each transaction in the period, identify the errors (hopefully under- and overpayments), and either create a ratio representing the errors in the sample population or simply compute (project) the tax assessment for the block sample period. Auditors using the latter method will then multiply the tax due in the sample period by the number of periods in the audit and present the assessment. By using this technique, the auditor fails to take into consideration the variations in business activity for the entire audit period. Using the former method, the auditor will apply the ratio of error to the audit period, extrapolating the liability for the audit. Block samples have the advantage of being relatively easy to perform, requiring little auditor training. The main problem with the block sample is that the block selected for the test may not be fairly representative of the business during the entire audit period and timing differences may not be recognized to the appropriate extent. One very important thing to remember about block sampling is that it cannot be proven statistically. One cannot state about a block sample that every item in the universe selected for the sample had exactly the same chance of being selected as every other item. Making such a statement should be the goal of an auditor and the taxpayer in considering the validity of the sample result.

With the increased use of "data processing audits," jurisdictions are asking taxpayers for direct jurisdictional access to taxpayer computers and archival data. Providing such access is not advised in most situations. A sharp auditor could search through data and develop possible avenues of assessment that might have been otherwise ignored. It is best to provide an auditor only what is requested. This may cause stress and an extra workload for a taxpayer's information services department or cause a delay in the audit, but it also keeps the audit(or) under control. On the other hand, asking for specific data requires that the taxpayer representative fully understand the information retained in the company's data processing files. Care must be given to correctly identify the significance of date, amount, account, and tax fields. Often, a field label in a record layout bears no resemblance to the data entered into the field by clerks using the system. Finally, it is necessary to confirm that all of the subject data was provided without repetition of any single record. This confirmation may appear self-evident, but really demands careful data analysis and scrutiny.

• *Random sampling*

A more precise and "scientific" sampling technique is the random statistical sample. While the block sample should withstand the rigors of statistical theory confirmation, the true statistical sample should be performed in full conformity with the rules of sampling. The sample population in a statistical (stat) sample using a nonrandom selection method might include (by example) every tenth invoice, every check ending 00 or some other identifiable selection criteria. In a random stat sample, a set of random numbers that identify a group of random elements in the universe will be generated.

The size of a sample population is suggested, using a statistical equation for determining the proper sample size. This allows one to infer that the sample population is comparable, in the characteristics being tested, to the universe as a whole to a given level and degree of precision. A sample population and its corresponding universe should be homogeneous. That is, the data contained in the sample population is similar in content to the data contained in the universe—sales for resale should be matched with sales for resale, not sales in interstate commerce. Homogeneity can be demonstrated with data defined by specific account(s), types of vendors or customers, types of transactions, etc. Therefore, in a sales test, one should be able to make the statement that the percentage of sales not taxed (the characteristic being tested) in the sample population will be similar to the percentage of sales not taxed in the universe of all transactions from which the sample was drawn.

Once the auditor has selected the sample population, reviewed each item for proper tax treatment, identified the errors and developed the error ratio (or percentage of error), that ratio should be applied to the total of all items in the corresponding universe. Statistical calculations should be used to determine if the errors are homogeneous and are appropriately extrapolated. Ultimately, the stat sample technique of auditing, if applied according to the rules of statistics to a universe of like transactions in type, size and frequency, represents a simple and sound method of establishing a taxpayer's liability (or credit).

There are three very important issues to keep in mind when confronted by an audit performed using statistical sampling.

(1) Every assessment error noted by the auditor is not equal to the tax on that single error but is equal to the tax represented by the extrapolation (multiplication) of that error in the entire audit universe. A one dollar error in taxable measure understated in a sales test may be worth an equal amount of tax.

(2) An error recorded on a single transaction in the sample population is, in statistical theory, representative of other similar errors not otherwise noted, per se. However, because that one error is only a sample of what one may assume would have been found in a complete review of all transactions, the only way to see where the errors in the overall universe fell is by looking at every item. This represents a formidable task if one intends to bill back tax not collected timely (in test of sales).

(3) An auditor testing specific data for underpayment of tax may ignore instances where tax may have been overpaid. For example, in a paid-bills test performed as a review of taxable general ledger and expense accounts only, there is an implied assumption that tax was never erroneously paid or accrued on nontaxable purchases or transactions. In such situations, the taxpayer will be required to review the allegedly nontaxable accounts on an actual basis unless the auditor agrees to a statistical sampling of these accounts as well. Most jurisdictions expect the taxpayer to schedule credits (overpayments).

In all sampling audits, there are many decisions that must be made by the auditor and the taxpayer that fully disclose the rules of the audit, e.g., the date

¶703

field to be used for defining the population unit to be evaluated, the manner of handling missing items, the method of handling transaction corrections either selected in the sample or not reviewed, etc. Perhaps the most important decisions are those related to the sampling process itself. No one sampling process covers all audit situations. Engaging a qualified statistics expert to guide or oversee a sampling audit is money well spent.

The following is a very simple example of a statistical sample test result and how it is applied to an audit universe to project an assessment. This example is called ratio estimation because one is applying a ratio of error to the universe.

Capital Computers manufactures and sells computers and repair parts; audit period 36 months; tax rate is 4%. The auditor has found a problem in the manner in which the taxpayer was taxing both the parts and the shipping and handling thereon. Both items are taxable.

Total dollars in sales under $5,000:	$10,000,000
Total invoices for sales under $5,000:	6,000
Average invoice in universe:	$1,666.67
Auditor looks at 500 invoices valued at:	$700,000
Average invoice in sample:	$1,400.00
30 errors total:	$36,000
Average error:	$1,200
Ratio of error to sample:	.0541285 or 5.41285 %
	(36,000/700,000)
Projected assessment measure:	$541,285
	(10,000,000 × .0541285)
Actual tax due:	$21,651.40
	($541,285 × .04)

Besides doing the statistical test on the acceptability of the findings and the appropriateness of the sample size to infer that the sample results fairly approximate the results to be found if the entire population were tested, one can "eyeball" the numbers for reasonableness. Specifically, the average amounts of the invoice in the universe, sample, and average error are reasonably close. All of these invoice amounts are also less than $5,000. If the disparity between invoice amounts had been great, or any of these three numbers had exceeded $5,000, then one could challenge the results of the sample. In this example, a $1.00 reduction in the errors in the sample produces a corresponding tax reduction of approximately 60 cents (21,651/36,000) or an effective tax rate of 60 percent. In the final analysis, a qualified statistician, or at least someone adequately versed in sampling statistics, should review statistical samples that produce results that do not appear reasonable.

There is a second common method of projecting errors. It involves projecting the erroneous difference that exists on every invoice rather than applying a ratio. This type of procedure, called "difference estimation," is used when there is a consistent error of a similar amount on each invoice.

Repair Division of Capital Computers bills shipping and handling charges on its invoices. However all shipping and handling charges were not taxed. The auditor is looking at a sample population that will be projected and sees that the issue of not billing tax on the underlying parts can be separated from Capital's failure to bill tax on shipping and handling.

Items in the sample population:	400
Shipping and handling amount on which tax was not charged:	$20.00
Number of invoices where the error was present:	200
Rate of error:	
(200/400)	50 %
Items in the universe:	25,000
Items in the universe on which shipping and handling was Not charged:	
(25,000 × .50)	12,500
Projected assessment:	
(12,500 × $20.00)	$250,000
Actual tax due:	
(250,000 × .04)	$10,000

• Stratification

#21 By separating the sales of repairs from the charges for shipping and handling, the auditor addresses the two types of errors. Sampling was appropriate but the auditor concluded that separation of the issues produced a more accurate result. Stratification is the separation of data in such a manner as to give it greater internal homogeneity to the universe being studied. In this case, maximum homogeneity was found by breaking issues within a universe. The most common forms of stratification are by values or issues. Additionally, by using specific stratification techniques, one can optimize sample sizes and thereby reduce the total number of transactions required for review to make a valid statistical inference.

For example, it is common to group elements by amount. By so doing, one might not be looking at a transaction for $50 in a population containing a $50,000 transaction. Can one say that there is as great a likelihood of finding the $50,000 item as there is finding the $50 item? Usually this is not the case. For this reason, strata are often groupings based on value, e.g., five strata $0.00 to $100, $100 to $1,000, $1,000 to $5,000, $5,000 to $10,000, and everything greater than $10,000. In this example, different size sample populations would be drawn from each stratified segment of the universe based on statistical criteria set for the audit or study. It may be easiest to stratify in the fashion described here; however, good stratification by value should consider the number of units and dollars in each strata as a percentage of the entire universe. There are a number of excellent software applications available "off-the-shelf" for doing random statistical sample auditing, including proper stratification. However, the user should be knowledgeable about statistics before using such a program.

In some situations, stratification should not be set solely by values. For example, a systematic error with a single vendor in a purchase test suggests that the specific vendor's invoices should be stratified and perhaps studied on a sample or actual basis. In the audit of Capital Computers shown above, the assessment issue related to shipping and handling was stratified from the same taxpayer's failure to tax part sales. If a single general ledger account was considered exempt in error, it is best to stratify the transactions in that account rather than projecting the errors for that account over all other accounts where exemptions were properly taxed.

How does one know the best way to stratify data in an audit? Take time to investigate the data before the auditor shows up at your company. There is nothing wrong with being able to recommend a proper sampling approach if it will ultimately insure greater accuracy. A taxpayer that is knowledgeable about their data may even be able to "steer" an auditor towards or away from areas of known credits or liabilities. If the auditor does not reject this guidance, the taxpayer has proven that nothing is as important as preparation.

Finally, at the conclusion of the sampling process, an effort should be made to quantify the accuracy of the findings. The statement of belief in the results of a random statistical sampling process will be given as a level of "confidence". A confidence statement, proven mathematically, might declare that "Our sample has a confidence level of 95%". This means that, were we to draw multiple samples of the same size, we would derive the same result 95% percent of the time. The second type of statement that is made concerning an audit talks about precision. The precision statement, in conjunction with the confidence statement, might declare that "Our sample has a confidence level of 95% with a precision of plus or minus 5%". This means that we could have an error in our result of plus or minus 5% of the result. If our result is a liability of $10,000, the true answer could fall between $9,500 and $10,500. Audits that use random statistical sampling that fail to identify the confidence and precision levels are lacking in a critical evaluative measurement of accuracy. This book will not discuss the method of mathematically proving a sampling result but the recipient of an audit using sampling should expect the computation to be completed and included in the audit package.

When sampling is used to determine a taxable rate, rather than an historical rate of error in reporting, a different evaluative statistical tool should be used. When establishing attributes, e.g., that transactions are or are not taxable, one sets the confidence and precision levels in order to determine sample size. When determining an error rate, one must first estimate the number or percentage of errors anticipated to be found at a given confidence or precision level to determine the sample size. However, once the error rate is actually determined, the sample size must be evaluated to gauge if enough sample items were reviewed to assure the desired confidence and precision.

¶704 Audit Findings (a/k/a Determination)

At various stages during the audit, the auditor may, but is not required to, present the taxpayer's representative with schedules that identify questioned or potentially assessable items. It is a good policy for the taxpayer to take every opportunity during an audit to address the audit questions. Waiting until the audit is completed before reviewing the audit findings will probably assure the taxpayer representative of long work days and growing interest assessments while trying to unravel the audit into manageable pieces. One who waits for the auditor to complete the entire audit before beginning to review the audit findings may not have the auditor on site to gain clarification of the audit schedules. As a whole, a compliance audit is the state's opinion of the manner(s) in which the taxpayer failed to comply with the state tax statutes and rules or regulations.

The audit findings or determination may contain several different sections requiring attention. The state audit guide or manual used by the auditor may even be available for purchase by taxpayers and provides an excellent road map through the auditor's work papers. This audit manual is an excellent tool to have in one's tax library. Following are the elements one might expect to see in audit findings (viewed from the bottom of the work papers to the cover sheet).

First, the results of the audit will be portrayed by issue and/or category of tax. One can expect to see lead schedules labeled "Sales: Exempt Measure Overstated," "Purchases: Taxable Measure Understated," "Inventory Withdrawals: Measure Understated," "Reconciliation of Tax Account: Unexplained Differences," etc. For each lead schedule there is likely to be a set of supporting schedules. Most states have established standardized schedule formats that the auditor is required to follow in presenting this information.

Second, notes or comments may be separate from the schedules themselves. The taxpayer is entitled to all of the documentation prepared during the audit. The notes or comments identify for the audit reviewer and the historical record how the audit was performed, what material was reviewed, and any discussions the auditor may have had with the taxpayer.

Third, the summary schedule often provides a breakdown of the assessment by taxing period to allow for computation of assessment or credit interest. The summary may also indicate the rate at which interest accrues while the assessment remains unpaid. Where the state auditor is authorized to assess local jurisdiction taxes, separate computations of these taxes will likely be present both in detail and summary. Interest and penalties will also be computed for the local taxes.

It should be noted that rates applicable to refunds may bear no similarity to those on deficiencies. See ¶ 2104 for a further discussion of this issue.

Generally, payment of an audit assessment (even if under protest) will stop the interest "meter" and will not normally compromise or weaken one's ability to win a protest. Interest rates on assessments are normally higher than the cost of commercial borrowing for most taxpayers. Accordingly, there should be an incentive to curtail the accrual of interest as soon as practical. Why give the state more money than is absolutely necessary?

Fourth, a transmittal in letter and/or invoice form will indicate the full amount of the state's bill (or credit) including interest and penalty.

This transmittal letter may also provide two other very important pieces of information: appeal procedures and response due dates or deadlines. Some states actually provide a separate document explaining the appeals process. Never should the taxpayer assume the state will be timely in providing appeal information.

• *Review process*

29 Once the audit has been reviewed by the taxpayer and the taxpayer and the auditor have either agreed to the findings, have reached settlement on unresolved issues, or have agreed to disagree as to the proposed forthcoming assessment, the auditor will turn the audit in for administrative review and billing. During the review process, the audit will be checked for arithmetical accuracy, statistical correctness (where necessary), statutory conformity and completeness. There will be narrative material that is part of the audit file but may never be shown to the taxpayer. That written material, along with all other matters related to the audit, should be requested by the taxpayer to form a complete record of the audit.

The local level administrative review should result in a "report" of the audit findings for final review by the taxpayer prior to the audit being submitted to the state offices for issuance of the final statement of tax assessment, notice of determination or tax billing. At this stage, it is common for the taxpayer to be given an opportunity to have an informal hearing with the auditor's supervisor or a higher level local agency official. The purpose for this hearing level is to resolve contested issues prior to "submitting the audit" for issuance of a tax bill. Most jurisdictions use the various informal and formal hearing levels to resolve issues out of court or to place in the record the facts and the taxpayer's position concerning disputed matters.

• *Appeals process*

The system of appeals available to the taxpayer is called the taxpayer's administrative remedies. These remedies are not always explained in the sales tax code, but will always be found somewhere in the jurisdiction's statutory verbiage.

The taxpayer who disagrees with an audit or contests a decision concerning a refund request is required to exhaust these remedies in a very specific sequence, moving from levels of lowest to highest authority. For example, the following are the steps in the appeals process in a state taxing jurisdiction:

Level 1: Discussion with the auditor

While this would not normally be considered an appeal level, it is possibly the most important level at which to seek audit reconsideration. The auditor is most familiar with the taxpayer's company and accounting procedures. If time is money, then resolving differences of opinion at this level offers the taxpayer the greatest chance to successfully plead its case.

Level 2: Informal hearing with an audit supervisor or senior local manager

Again, the local review process is often the most productive. The higher the level of appeal, the greater the likelihood that the jurisdiction will fight. Also, the local level may be more able to follow a path of "give and take."

Level 3: Formal hearing at the local level

At this level, tax jurisdiction management is encouraged to resolve audits instead of sending them to a state appeal level. Each succeeding appeal level places the payment of the assessment farther from the tax due date, usually meaning a larger percentage of interest to tax. Up to this level of appeal, discussions tend to be less legalistic and more fact-based. In some states the taxpayer and the state will present their dispute to a Dispute Resolution Officer. This individual can review the positions taken by both parties and reach a position that is binding in the case of the state but not the taxpayer.

Level 4: Hearing with a hearing officer or administrative law judge

At the state level, the taxpayer is now dealing with legal issues. The facts should be clearly disclosed and not in dispute. The result at this appeal level will be a decision of a hearing officer and a recommendation to the state tax board or commission to assess or request that the auditor redetermine the audit findings consistent with the decision of this official.

In an attempt to reduce the logjam of cases reaching the courts and give the appeal process an appearance of independence from the taxing board or commission, some states have established an office of administrative law comprised of attorneys acting as administrative law judges (ALJs). ALJs hear cases and, in a panel of one, hand down decisions and recommendations. Conclusions reached by ALJs are subject to appeal by either the taxpayer or the taxing authority. Importantly, these decisions can establish tax "case" law upon which others can rely.

Finally, in some states a board of tax appeals may exist to settle tax disputes on a "take it or leave it" basis. In other words, these boards are empowered to gather facts and testimony and hear a case under the provision that the decision reached will be binding on both the taxpayer and the taxing authority. A court appeal is prohibited following a decision by such a board. When using the pre-court appeals process, one must fully understand the implications of having a case heard in this type of forum.

Level 5: Hearing before the tax board or commission

This level of appeal is usually the last step before going into the courts. In some states with elected commissioners or board members, this may also be the last opportunity to exert political influence either by direct persuasion or massing industry support at the hearing level. Use of legal counsel in both levels 4 and 5 is not always required but may be advisable as the taxpayer's goal in these levels of appeal is to win. Time and resources will favor the state in remedies available through the courts.

Level 6: Trial or Superior Court

Often admission to the first level of court appeals requires the taxpayer to pay the assessment and sue for a refund. Some states have established this first level of appeal in the courts in a "tax" court. The wisdom behind such an appeal path is two-fold: keep tax cases out of the civil court system that is already glutted with cases and hear tax cases using judicial personnel familiar with the terminology, concepts and issues that normally surface in tax matters.

Level 7: State Appeal Court

By this point in the appeals process, one is either very convinced of the principle at issue or has very deep pockets and feels a principle is at stake worth litigating. The latter situation is often the case when an auditor determined against the taxpayer in a potentially precedent setting situation. The taxpayer sees the writing on the wall and finds those of like mind in the industry or in a similar situation to contribute to the legal war chest.

Level 8: State Supreme Court

Since the audit was completed, time elapsed to this level of appeal has probably been over two years. Legal counsel is very convinced that the matter not only has merit but the lower courts simply didn't understand the issue. Who is legal counsel attempting to persuade, the courts or the taxpayer?

Level 9: U.S. Supreme Court

This is the last stop but is rarely, if ever, used. Mostly, the state supreme courts decide sales and use tax issues that were not settled in lower courts. The U.S. Supreme Court rarely ever hears a state issue because the Court has limited jurisdiction. These state cases are often intrastate in nature lacking a challenge to federal law. However, when a case does get the highest court's attention, the side that wins here wins all the marbles and gets to go home with gloating rights for a few minutes at least. Costs to reach this level often exceed $100,000 in legal fees and expenses and thousands of hours.

Perhaps the single largest risk in going down the full appeals route, beside the chance that the jurisdiction will prevail, is that the taxpayer may not have adjusted the tax procedure that produced the original assessment. Months or years of continued errors during the protracted appeals process may represent a subsequent assessment larger than the originally contested assessment.

The decision to proceed down the appeals path, especially beyond the administrative appeal levels 1—5, requires knowledgeable counsel with experience specifically in sales/use tax matters, a legal issue that can be decided in the light of historical precedent rather than an emotional issue (its just not fair and I'm not going to take this decision without a fight) that lacks legal substance, the financial resources to pay the legal fees and expenses customarily attendant to appeal activities, and the time to shepherd the process from start to conclusion. In the absence of these conditions, a taxpayer is probably ill-advised to appeal an assessment into the courts. By the time a matter is elevated to the judicial level of the appeals process, there should be no more issues of fact, only matters of legal interpretation.

Before proceeding with a full-blown appeal, the taxpayer should contact other professional friends and acquaintances, particularly in similar lines of business, to determine if the issue has been previously decided for someone else or if other taxpayers will support, in time, effort and resources, the appeals process. Professional tax associations and business trade associations are an excellent source of contacts and networking opportunities. Among business competitors, sales and use tax issues rarely represent situations of competitive advantage or disadvantage. Gaining industry support in a litigated matter is often accomplished by having industry members prepare and submit *amicus* briefs. These are formal legal statements to the court, tribunal, or other judicial body hearing the matter that support the position taken by the taxpayer, either appealing an assessment or petitioning for some form of redress. Mostly, they are helpful but may not be persuasive.

¶704

• *Framing an appeal*

An appeal begins with fact gathering and ends with thorough preparation prior to presentation. Nothing, absolutely nothing, takes the place of thorough preparation before presenting an appeal. Most states allow the taxpayer to present a non-court appeal, though it may be helpful to have counsel assist in some of the legal arguments. In any event, be sure the issue and potential result will justify your time. If the appeal is important enough to argue, it should be given full attention and resources.

(1) Confirm all of the facts and state them clearly and concisely. Do not assume that information gleaned by the auditor and confirmed by a clerk is the truth. Be skeptical until all of the details are disclosed and every rock overturned.

(2) Understand and be able to argue the state's position. There is no better way to prepare for a debate than to become intimately familiar with your opponent's arguments. Is there a sound legal basis or an attempt being made to create law? Are the citations from statute current and/or do they represent the period covered by the audit being challenged? Is the state serious in its resolve to "go to the mat" or is this a case of "going through the motions?" Is the appeal an auditor's attempt to justify too many hours spent on an otherwise immaterial audit finding?

(3) Characterize each issue separately. If multiple issues are involved, number each issue and use exhibits where necessary. Make it easy for the hearing officer or ALJ to follow your thought process and presentation.

(4) Employ unrestrained imagination in developing and presenting arguments. Often a jurisdiction will develop their position without considering tangential concepts and issues. How has a state with a similar tax addressed the same issue? Did a competitor have the same appeal? Can a federal law take precedence? There is always room for interpretation.

(5) Present your arguments clearly and simply. Rely on statute, rules, regulations, annotations, prior decisions, case law, etc. Quote liberally and accurately from authoritative documents and sources.

(6) Summarize your position and state "the inevitable" conclusion that should be reached by anyone considering the issue. However, be certain not to belittle or offend the hearing officer or ALJ.

Ultimately, write out the presentation in a form that contains four distinctive sections: the facts, the issues, the arguments and the conclusions. The appeal hearing may be one's last chance to place all of the facts, evidence and arguments "on the table." The use of experts or submission of affidavits is often very persuasive and highly advisable. Be ready to leave copies of a presentation behind as a "reminder" of critical points and your thought process which might otherwise be forgotten. Pictures, charts, exhibits, physical evidence and the written word are powerful tools in any presentation. Also, show respect, courtesy and humility as you demonstrate your knowledge and grasp of the issue.

¶704

• *Litigation issues*

Finally, there is a disturbing trend in the courts that hear sales and use tax cases that merits further consideration when groping with the litigation issue. The taxpayer may be given the victory by the courts, but with prospective application only. The taxpayer wins the case, the satisfaction of knowing that the tax was imposed or collected and paid illegally, but the state gets to keep the taxes collected to date. Future tax savings or reduced compliance costs may be realized in such hollow victories. This is not an attractive legal outcome and it is occurring more frequently.

However, in the 1989-1990 U.S. Supreme Court session, two significant cases were decided concerning the taxpayer's right to retroactive relief (the jurisdiction's obligation to make the taxpayer whole for tax assessed and paid in error). The cases were *McKesson Corporation v. Division of Alcoholic Beverages and Tobacco*, 110 SCt 2238, 496 US 18 (1990), and *American Trucking Association, Inc. v. Maurice Smith, Director, Arkansas Highway and Transportation Department*, 110 SCt 2323 (1990).

In *McKesson*, the State of Florida was given two choices when the case was remanded (sent back) to the state by the U.S. Supreme Court: refund the tax to the taxpayer or retroactively assess all those who benefited from the discriminatory tax that was stricken. The Court did say that a pay-to-play (my words) provision deprives the taxpayer of property, a right protected under the Due Process Clause of the Fourteenth Amendment. In 1998, the U.S. Supreme Court further assured taxpayer's rights related to discriminatory taxes erroneously imposed in two Florida cases, *Newsweek, Inc. v. Florida Department of Revenue*, 118 SCt 904, 522 US 442 (1998); CCH FL St. Tax Rep., ¶203-318; *Dryden v. Madison County, Fla*, 118 SCt 1162, 522 US 1145 (1998); CCH FL St. Tax Rep., ¶203-366.

In *American Trucking Association*, the state of Arkansas had imposed a tax that was discriminatory under the Commerce Clause and had been effectively ruled unconstitutional by the Court earlier in the case of *American Trucking Association v. Schiener*, 483 US 266 (1987). Because the Court had held against a virtually identical tax in Pennyslvania, and Arkansas chose to ignore that decision, retroactive relief was to be granted to the date of *Schiener*. As a result of these two decisions, other cases in line for consideration are likely to be tested against these standards and the juxtaposed opinion rendered in *Chevron Oil Co. v. Huson*, 404 US 97 (1971). In *Chevron*, a three-part test was established under which a decision need be applied only prospectively, when it: (1) establishes a new legal principle; (2) will not be furthered by retrospective application; and (3) could produce substantial inequitable results if applied retroactively.

Chapter VIII
Governmental Administration of Sales/ Use Taxation

¶801 Introduction

In Chapter I, we explored elements of sales and use tax statutes that are common to all states, the District of Columbia, and lesser jurisdictions. All codes contain definitions, imposition treatment, enabling language, administrative oversight provisions, registration and reporting requirements, taxpayer assistance, noncompliance consequences, and procedures that "guarantee" taxpayers due process. Statutory form will vary from state to state, but basic concepts will always be present. The actual code is either the tax practitioner's road map to job security or a maze to guaranteed employment mortality. Understanding the way governments structure tax administration can be the compass in charting a path through the tax labyrinth resulting in payment of what is due and when it is due. The purpose of this chapter is to give to the tax administrative organization rational meaning for creative and tactical use by the practitioner.

¶802 Enabling Language

We have discussed basic definitions and imposition treatment earlier. The enabling provisions of the code are the way the deliberative (legislative) body places the statute into action. During the life of any code, social, economic and political forces will influence lawmakers into adding exemptions, offering clarification, removing ambiguity, etc., and each time there is similar enabling language. That language may merely indicate an effective date (where the change is understood to be in effect for an indeterminate period), or a starting and ending effective date (where the change will have limited life). Often the same enabling legislation will indicate how the tax administrative agency is to view the change. While there is almost always legislative intent explaining the basis for a tax law change, that intent is rarely spelled out in the statutory language. Changes in a statute may be piecemeal or omnibus in scope.

¶803 Administrative Oversight Provisions

Most codes are vague and nonspecific, containing information of a generic nature, thus leaving much to the taxpayer's imagination (if the taxpayer can even read and understand the language). For this reason, and because legislative bodies must assign oversight responsibilities to individuals (civil servants) whose tenure in office will offer greater continuity than that of elected officials, administrative and regulatory agencies are empowered to enact rules and regulations that give the public a more simplistic explanation of the law. Unfortunately, the effort to simplify is not always successful.

A rule having very specific meaning for one industry may be, at best, inappropriate, or, at worst, totally confusing or contradictory to the spirit of the law for a second industry. For example, a rule that gives clarity to the manufacture of large pieces of tooling or capital equipment may be confusing to the manufacturer of minute integrated circuits; a regulation that addresses the taxation of the printing industry may be inapplicable to the printing activities of the advertising and/or publishing industry.

Working with the law and the interpretive rules and regulations, the administrative agency carries out those tasks that keep all "persons" (having the common meaning of partnerships, corporations, and other business entities as well as individuals) equal before the law. These tasks include (but are not limited to):

(1) qualifying potential taxpayers to be certified as sellers and registering such qualified taxpayers;

(2) providing taxpayer assistance, including issuing rules and regulations;

(3) issuing and processing tax return forms, granting extensions of time in meeting various deadlines, and dispersing tax revenues as per the terms of the tax code;

(4) performing compliance verification audits, including the issuing of assessments;

(5) protecting the jurisdiction from fraudulent acts by taxpayers injurious to the jurisdiction and its constituents by compelling testimony and initiating court proceedings; and

(6) hearing and resolving legal tax issues prior to referring those matters to the judicial system for resolution.

In addition, the legislatures assign the agency a variety of other functions that are housekeeping in nature (record retention, internal management, intra- and intergovernmental relations, statistical compilation, etc.). Most of these activities are rarely viewed by taxpayers. Agencies may be structured along functional lines (i.e., types of activities such as compliance, registration, legal matters, etc.) or along lines related to types of tax collected (e.g., sales, fuel, "sin," property, etc.). The key executive of the agency is typically an appointee with all other employees being "hired" by the agency, commission, directors, etc.

The hierarchy within an agency finds managers or department directors supported by their various staff assistants. Unless the jurisdiction is small enough to have all activities centrally directed, regional or district offices with secondary management handle nearly all taxpayer contact (registration and compliance auditing). Legal, technical, data processing, and statistical units are centrally controlled. In field offices, taxpayer files are kept updated, audits are assigned to audit personnel, and registration and taxpayer assistance are provided.

In recent years, states have passed Taxpayer Bill of Rights legislation in an attempt to show an awareness that the taxpayer may require special assistance beyond the code and may deserve some amount of "customer service" from the taxing agency. Arizona, in August 1986, was the first state to institute such legislation. By mid-1991, 23 other states added their own bill of rights. Following

¶803

are some of the key characteristics of these provisions. It is important to note that the provisions may be tax specific or may contain concepts beyond those listed below.

(1) Creation of an ombudsman "impartial third party" to assist in helping the taxpayer through the bureaucratic morass;

(2) Evaluation of the employees of an agency is not based on enforcement quotas;

(3) Interviews may be recorded;

(4) Payment of assessments may be structured in installments;

(5) An agency may be sued;

(6) Attorney's fees may be awarded if the agency loses an appeal;

(7) Published procedural instructions are available; and

(8) Advice is available.

There are often important hidden tools in these provisions that can be highly beneficial to the taxpayer. It is never too late to take a minute and become familiar with the rights' provisions.

¶804 Registration and Reporting Requirements

Whether the sales tax is imposed on the seller, the sales transaction, the gross receipts or the consumer, all statutes explain who must register and when the tax collection, payment and reporting activity must be completed. In recent years, the issue of who must register has gained prominent attention in light of sizeable growth of the mail-order industry and the Internet. A seller may have its facilities located in one state, sell into all other states and claim protection (from the need to register and collect taxes) under the U.S. Constitution's commerce clause. See Chapter X for an in-depth discussion of registration and nexus.

States may locate potential registrants through the telephone book, other agency registrations (i.e., franchise tax, payroll tax, property tax, etc.), listings in building directories, attendance and exhibitor lists from trade shows, and "leads" from tax compliance audits. Once registered, the new taxpayer may be required to post a bond or surety deposit to "guarantee" payment of collected taxes and cooperation with the taxing jurisdiction. A full registration will ask for, among other data, the identity of the company officers—those individuals who will be deemed responsible for errors. The new taxpayer is given a seller's permit or certificate of authority with a unique number, an initial reporting frequency, minimal instruction in tax, and some generic literature that, to a new business, probably looks like instructions to assemble a "no tools required" child's "ready-to-use" gift written in a foreign language.

A variety of different types of registration are available. Single and multiple location registrations are for both sales and use tax activities and are provided to those entities having in-state business locations. Vendors having no in-state locations may be obligated or elect to collect the state use tax and could be registered for that purpose. Non-retailers may have use tax payment responsibilities only and would not report sales tax transactions. States providing exemptions to nonprofit organizations issue permits allowing the organization to purchase property for its own use without tax. Finally, the tax agencies (in those states so prescribing) will issue other types of special authority, e.g., direct pay, resale, wholesale dealer, etc., to qualified registrants. Most registrations are permanent and require little maintenance other than the regular completion of periodic returns.

Closely associated with the issue of reporting requirements is the issue of the tax calendar, i.e., when do state agencies require that specific events occur. It is interesting to note that the tax calendar is mostly an administrative, not legislative, issue. The legislature delegates to an administrative agency the responsibility for implementing the sales tax law, including the aspects of timing, e.g., when returns are due, when taxes are remitted, frequency of audits, amount of time available to be heard, etc. In times of budget shortfalls and fiscal chaos at the state and local level, it is not uncommon for agencies to modify reporting calendars to gain access to tax funds sooner than later. This is no small matter. Penalties that are associated with late reporting and payment of tax can be severe.

¶805 Noncompliance Consequences (Enforcement Provisions)

After the first contact made by a person to register as a seller, and the periodic communication in the form of tax return form receipt and submission, the most typical agency contact is the compliance audit performed by the taxing jurisdiction. These reviews have one purpose: to confirm that the tax liability reported and payments made to the jurisdiction by the taxpayer fairly represent the true obligations of the taxpayer under the code. Field audits on a regular three- or four-year cycle for large taxpayers, occasional randomly selected audits for smaller businesses, and desk audits for most other tax returns are the current standard in all states. The audit finding is then followed by a formal assessment, access to a series of remedies, and finally possible settlement of disputed findings through the judicial system. The taxpayer that fails to comply with a jurisdiction's laws may be subject to penalties, attachment of assets, seizure of property, loss of its authority or privilege to transact business, and imprisonment of its officers.

In the last 15 years, jurisdictions used more of a carrot and less of stick approach in addressing tax noncompliance. A number of states had extremely successful taxpayer incentives to find tax scofflaws. These programs are often referred to as amnesty programs. Under such a program, taxpayers can pay back taxes without being asked questions in return for avoiding penalties. Interest is not so quickly ignored. Hundreds of millions of unpaid taxes have been recovered in recent years through these amnesty programs. These programs have been successful with both transaction and income taxes at the state and local levels and have earned repeat status in some jurisdictions (seems to contradict the theory of the "one-time opportunity to come clean" idea of an amnesty). See additional comments on amnesties at ¶904.

¶806 Taxpayer Assistance

Tax statutes are not easy to understand, and the agencies responsible for their administration are charged with the task of assisting taxpayers in attaining complete compliance. Taxpayer assistance takes several forms. Certainly most common is the promulgation of rules and regulations that are supposed to "translate" the statutory language into words regular people can understand. This activity is not supposed to result in the agency taking license with the code, however; interpretation is often more like legislation than simplification or explanation.

Assistance also takes the form of "technical advice" or "opinions." Toll-free telephone advice is now becoming available. Verbal advice is unreliable, especially when considered as the basis for collecting taxes. Therefore, when a taxpayer requests (and in some cases, pays for) clarification in written form, the code may guarantee that such advice or opinions can be relied on for at least one audit cycle. And perhaps most disconcerting, advice that is the outgrowth of an audit one year may be, and often is, ignored by a subsequent auditor from the same jurisdiction in a follow-up audit.

Therefore, when requesting written advice, ask for the citation of authority upon which the advice is based. Advice in writing may not always be relied upon and may be severely qualified. When presuming that another's situation is identical to your own, be certain that the fact patterns are identical. Almost identical may not be good enough unless the issue is generic. For example, advice on the taxability of a particular raw material used in a proprietary process may be limited in applicability to the one requesting the opinion. Whether a human heart valve implant, purchased and implanted by doctors in their patients at hospitals, is taxable should not vary from hospital to hospital, but it will vary from state to state.

¶807 Due Process

Every code provides for a system of administrative and judicial remedies that are supposed to guarantee the taxpayer due process before the law. Two important considerations must be remembered in the context of due process. The remedies may not be spelled out in each separate tax code but are found in a separate code section dealing exclusively with taxpayer rights of appeal. Secondly, a taxpayer failing to follow the procedures provided, in both a timely manner and according to the order in which they are available, may lose the right to the due process otherwise provided. Whether the procedures are for refunds, appeal of assessments, gaining advice upon which the taxpayer may rely or gaining access to information, it is up to the person asserting his/her rights to follow the prescribed rules. For in failing to do so, access to protection may be denied. Use the correct forms, file your paperwork timely, mail everything certified, and watch your calendar.

¶807

• *Statute of limitations*

Finally, one of the more confusing concepts is the "statute of limitations." Each code provides a statute of limitations to indicate when the time has been reached to assess tax that was not paid. The statute of limitations also provides the time limit for claiming refunds of taxes paid in error.

There are two key elements to the statute of limitations: the length of time (or time limit) and commencing date of the statute of limitations. The length of the period is typically two, three or four years. Some states have different statutes of limitations for refunds than for assessments (a concept that begs a challenge in the courts as a refund is essentially a credit assessment). The commencing date or tolling date is the date of the oldest period open under the statute of limitations. The statute of limitations begins to toll either:

(1) on the date the company becomes qualified or should have registered to do business in the jurisdiction, or

(2) the beginning of the period in months or years indicated in the statute of limitations for a taxpayer that has been filing returns timely.

For example, a tax statute indicating "a three-year statute of limitations from the date the tax was due" means an assessment may be made or a refund claimed three years from the tax due date. Therefore, if taxes were due at the end of the year and the questioned transaction was in January 1997, and there was a three-year limitation period, the jurisdiction could assess tax on the questioned transaction as late as December 31, 2000. On the other hand, a tax statute indicating "a four-year statute of limitations from the date the return was due" means an assessment may be made on taxes not paid (or refund claimed on taxes overpaid) four years from the return due date. Therefore, if returns were due on the last day of the month following the end of a calendar quarter, yet taxes had to be prepaid on the last day of each month, a transaction in January 1997 would remain in an open statute of limitations period until April 30, 2001.

A good tool for the tax professional to develop is a customized statute of limitations chart. Such a chart will list all states (and to the extent desired, localities) in which one's company is (or should be) reporting taxes, the manner of calculating the statute of limitations (by quarters, by return submission dates, by semiannual or annual periods, etc.), the last period open to jurisdictional review, and the refund statute rules as well. Refund statutes do not always parallel assessment statutes. This chart should also contain some information on the rules associated with waiving the statute of limitations.

• *Exceptions*

There are two exceptions to the above examples. The first is caused by failing to file returns. The second is caused by signing a waiver of the limitations period. If a return that is due is not filed, the limitations period remains open until the return has been filed or an assessment made. Or, if the taxpayer signs a waiver (usually a special form) to extend the limitations period, the statute of limitations remains open to the extent prescribed by and agreed to in the waiver.

¶807

The waiver applies equally to both the taxpayer and the taxing jurisdiction. Waivers should be fully understood prior to being signed. They can be beneficial (keep a refund period from being outlawed) or detrimental (keep an assessment period available). However, denying an auditor a waiver may simply result in an arbitrary assessment (an assessment arrived at by making an arbitrary estimate of the tax that may be unpaid for a given period).

In rare instances, an auditor may show up on a taxpayer's doorstep at the end of the 11th hour before a statutory period expires. This offers the taxpayer a likely choice between signing the waiver or receiving an arbitrary assessment. A classic variation places the auditor at a branch or plant location where the manager in authority might not understand the situation and would act to "protect the assets of the company" by signing the waiver. It is an opinion shared by many veteran tax professionals that the courts do not look kindly on such last-minute attempts by jurisdictions. Advising management companywide to handle such urgent auditor requests by referral to the tax department becomes critical as the tax professional sees a statute on the verge of expiration.

The decision to "play the game by the rules" is a two-edged sword. Whatever power the statute has accorded the taxing agency, it has (should) also given equal protection to the taxpayer. The taxpayer is often injured due to ignorance of the law, regulations, and rules. The most potent antidote is knowledge.

Chapter IX

Multistate Tax Compacts and Creative Tax Harvesting Techniques

¶901 Introduction

For many years, residents of New Jersey made a practice of going into New York to buy expensive clothing, jewelry, cameras, etc., which the vendors would willingly ship across the border (river) on a common carrier. The customer from New Jersey would avoid the New York state and local sales taxes (the sale was a sale in interstate commerce) and evade the New Jersey use tax (the individual did not have a method of reporting the tax to the state nor was the New York vendor licensed to collect the New Jersey use tax). The shipping or handling charge was a small price the customer paid for significant tax savings. The net effect of the transaction was to cause both states to lose tax revenue and promote the business of an out-of-state vendor. More devious customers would convince their vendors to ship an empty box to New Jersey (resulting in a bill of lading) while the customer actually took possession of the property in New York.

New York residents similarly found that purchasing some clothing in New Jersey was a great money-saving opportunity because New York taxed clothing and New Jersey did not. In a stroke of creativity, the New York legislature decided to run a little experiment to see the extent to which their residents found tax savings a motivator to cross tunnels and bridges to buy clothing. During the week of January 18 -24, 1997 a temporary tax exemption was provided on sales of clothing in New York having a value of less than $500. It could hardly be considered surprising that the state enjoyed an increase in clothing sales of nearly $200 million with a loss of $16.5 million in taxes during that week. Additionally, the Department of Taxation and Finance performed a survey in conjunction with this special program and learned that:

- 63% said their clothing purchases were affected by the special exemption;
- 83% said they would increase their New York clothing spending if the exemption were made permanent;
- 44% said they would decrease their purchases in other states; and
- 51% said they use mail order shopping for clothing to avoid New York sales taxes.

Who said states could not use creativity in trying to look at their tax problems and issues?

The success of the first New York experiment was so gratifying to some-one(s) in (a) high place(s) that we are now looking at a tradition being born, son of New York clothing deal. New York repeated the experiment in the fall of 1998 and again in the winter of 1999 and continues to repeat the program annually. Further, the saying that "imitation is the highest form of flattery" may be right on the mark. Florida copied the New York clothing-sale model with a minor exception. The maximum purchase exempted in Florida is $50. Florida has also struggled with some other interesting issues similar to those experienced by California when it instituted its short-lived snack tax. Is sports apparel exempt? Can you separate a suit into pieces and make the pieces exempt where the suit would have been taxable? And the list goes on. Human creativity works wonders when it comes to entertaining tax policy makers and administrators.

The use tax itself was an attempt by the states to prevent artful in-state residents from depriving their home state of its sales tax. Where states are thorough in their performance of compliance audits, registered taxpayers are often caught for failing to self-assess the use tax. Self-assessment is needed in the absence of the out-of-state vendor collecting and then remitting the use tax to the destination state of the purchased property. However, the individual who is not registered to self-assess the use tax may certainly try to avoid this tax expense.

¶902 Multistate Tax Commission (MTC)

For this reason, states began programs of out-of-state auditing. However, performing compliance audits outside of an agency's home state is no easy chore unless the agency can afford to locate, hire and train local people to serve as out-of-state auditors. In the early 1970s, in response to this challenge, 19 states formed the first formal tax compact, the Multistate Tax Commission (MTC), originally based in Colorado. The MTC agreed to perform joint audits covering a wide array of taxes, and litigate or negotiate in behalf of its member states. A constitutionality challenge to the MTC was raised in *United States Steel Corporation v. Multistate Tax Commission*, 434 US 452 (1978). The Court ruled that the compact, having relatively limited authority, did not require congressional approval.

Today, the MTC is very prominent in the tax world, looking for seemingly inaccessible state tax revenues. One thrust of the MTC has been in the area of coordinated "nexus" projects. Beginning in 1986, the "Bellas Hess" project was initiated by 29 states to go after the direct marketing companies (mail-order catalogue businesses) who were hiding behind the protection afforded by the Court's decision in *National Bellas Hess, Inc. v. Illinois Department of Revenue*, 386 US 753 (1967) (protecting such companies, having no "nexus" in states in which they transacted business from afar, from registration and tax collection requirements). The project sought future voluntary compliance in return for tax concessions for prior years. Few companies accepted the project's offer.

As a result of the 1992 decision by the U. S. Supreme Court in *Quill Corporation v. North Dakota* (504 US 298 (1992)), the Court left Congress the option of legislating a national program of interstate sales taxation. At about the same time, the MTC attempted to gain the cooperation of the direct mail marketing industry in developing a tax reporting protocol. The MTC-industry effort failed, leaving a void which was addressed during the 104th Congress by U.S. Senator Dale Bumpers' bill, "Tax Fairness for Main Street Business" (S. 1825). This bill, which was never enacted, would have given the states authority to require sales and use tax compliance by out-of-state companies.

¶902

The MTC, the Federation of Tax Administrators (FTA), the Institute for Professionals in Taxation (IPT), and a variety of other organizations have published a number of reports under the moniker "the Steering Committee on of the Task Force on EDI Audit and Legal Issues for Tax Administration." (The FTA is discussed in the last bullet at ¶903.) The first report involved the development and publication of a standard for recordkeeping and record retention. The standard focused heavily on the issue of recordkeeping when printed documents are not available, e.g., electronic data interchange and evaluated receipts settlement. Several other related topics addressed by The Steering Committee include: auditing electronic data and handling procurement card transactions, sales and use tax compliance agreements, model direct payment permit regulation, and sampling for sales and use tax compliance. These projects also engaged taxpayer participation through a number of professional and trade organizations.

A separate initiative considered by the FTA and MTC addressed the implications for a computer manufacturer that hires local service firms to support its product in multiple states. The issue is whether this relationship between the manufacturer and service provider is an agency relationship creating nexus. These initiatives have not been adopted unanimously among FTA and MTC members.

Another initiative, and clearly the most significant, in which these organizations participate, which is discussed in greater depth at ¶2305, is the Streamlined Sales Tax Project (a/k/a. SSTP). This incomplete though maturing effort aims to simplify tax collection and reporting. The project remains less of a work in progress at the publication date of this book as the number of states that have gotten on the bandwagon meets a very critical threshold for implementation of the SSTP.

• *Sufficient nexus*

As discussed in the following chapter, states, prior to the decision in *Quill*, worked feverishly to redefine the term or concept of "sufficient nexus" to encompass the largest possible cross-section of the direct mail marketing community. Though the mail-order industry appeared to be the focus of this effort, fallout would be likely to have an impact on other industries and business environments as well. The "nexus project" referred to above, perhaps one of several, was aimed at not only the ranks of the direct mail marketing community, but industrial giants as well.

The issue for a large industrial combine is the relationship of the various divisions to the states in which only one division is engaged in business in a state. Only one division need have nexus in a given state to bring the registration and compliance requirements to all other divisions doing business in, or merely shipping property into, that state. Recent cases involving the mail-order industry, where a corporate parent is engaged in business through its retail outlet subsidiary and has separate operations in its mail-order subsidiary, will require that multi-unit corporations clearly understand the implications of such case law. The nexus in the example involving divisions is irrefutable, whereas the nexus of an

¶902

independent, out-of-state catalog mailer is in substantially less doubt under the *Quill* reasoning.

¶903 State Sales Tax Compacts

Several years after the formation of the MTC (1985), but before the MTC experienced any great tax victories, New York and New Jersey began addressing some of their more localized problems with a novel bi-state tax compact of information sharing. By the end of its first year, the New York Department of Revenue claimed to have benefited from the program with additional revenues in excess of $25 million. While the initial programs set up by this first regional compact offered voluntary compliance and participation, recent activities have been more aggressive.

• *Great Lakes Sales Tax Compact*

In the fall of 1986, the Great Lakes Sales Tax Compact was formed by six states—Illinois, Wisconsin, Michigan, Indiana, Minnesota and Ohio. This compact carried out its understood charter by mailing thousands of letters to potential multistate registrants who were believed to be transacting business in states other than their home states. Subsequently, audits of both customers and vendors in these states have produced hundreds of audit leads that are being investigated by the other compact states.

In 1987, Wisconsin withdrew its membership and in 1988, Iowa, Kansas, Nebraska, and South Dakota joined the Great Lakes Sales Tax Compact. During the past several years, this group has been less and less active as a compact, though it continues to meet on a regular basis. The lack of overt activity may not indicate a lack of interest. Rather, while the web of compacts and organizations may be dormant it is not necessarily dead.

• *Tri-State Compact*

The Tri-State Compact, consisting of Connecticut, Rhode Island and Massachusetts, began a letter campaign aimed at direct marketers in 1987, contending that any transactions in their three states that met some prescribed nexus guidelines would trigger tax liabilities or use tax collection responsibilities. Voluntary compliance was encouraged to obviate threatened assessments. The Tri-State Compact has been discontinued. However, in its place, the states of New York and Connecticut have formed an alliance that has provided information sharing on residents who cross state lines to avoid taxes.

• *Midwest and Northeast States Tax Compacts*

In 1988, the Midwest States Tax Compact was formed by the states of Illinois, Iowa, Kansas, Michigan, Minnesota, Nebraska and South Dakota. Also, in 1987-1988, the states of New York, New Jersey, Connecticut, Massachusetts, Pennsylvania and Rhode Island put together a traveling multi-state audit team that, preceded by a questionnaire mailing campaign, visited many unregistered sellers in Northern California in order to examine their books and assess taxes. The trial program was so successful it was moved to other parts of the country, notably Southern California, Texas and the Research Triangle region of North Carolina. Today, the Midwest States Tax Compact is increasingly inactive and the traveling audit squad from the Northeast is disbanded, however, not without significant success.

• Border States Caucus

In 1993, the states of Arizona, New Mexico, Texas, and California (and more recently, Oklahoma and Utah) formed a compact related to their economic border with Mexico and the implementation of the North America Free Trade Association (NAFTA). Of particular concern were activities in which property was being moved to and from Mexico. However, the compact has now grown into a major source of tax leads for the members. Much of the interaction between the members is now accomplished electronically.

• Other state sales tax compacts and the Federation of Tax Administrators

In the mid-1990s, the states of Arkansas, Mississippi, South Carolina, Tennessee, Virginia and West Virginia formed an information-sharing compact. The states of California, Iowa, New Jersey, New York, Texas, Florida, Illinois and Ohio initiated the voluntary mail-order pilot (a/k/a MOP) to clean up the mail-order industry registration problem specifically in their respective states. The program's success was reduced by losses in the courts sustained by California, a bellwether state. The courts are generally requiring that states cease in their efforts to require registration of mail-order sellers. And finally, the Federation of Tax Administrators (FTA), an organization of jurisdictional tax collectors, worked actively and openly to establish multi-tax, multi-state information sharing. Hiding in the tall grass will be more difficult for the business tax planner.

The most significant step to provide for comprehensive information sharing between jurisdictions was accomplished with the adoption of the Uniform Exchange of Information Agreement (UEIA). The agreement, a joint project of the FTA and 35 states and the District of Columbia, took effect January 1, 1993, to help achieve three objectives:

(1) establish better channels of communication among all signatory states;

(2) reduce the need for multiple bilateral agreements; and

(3) provide a mechanism for expanding the cooperative effort among the states.

Forty-four states, New York City, and the District of Columbia were signatories to the UEIA in 2000. Arizona, Massachusetts, Nevada, New Mexico, Oregon, and Pennsylvania had not signed on at that date. It is unknown if this agreement is still in place and whether all states are on board.

As noted previously, it is one thing for the taxing authorities to track the activities of the commercial seller to the commercial customer purchasing property through the invoicing process, or the retailer to the retail customer purchasing property with payment and tax being settled at the cash register. It is also a manageable task for the taxing authority to contact and audit registered purchasers that have made out-of-state purchases upon which tax was or should have accrued and should have been paid to the state. However, it is a more difficult problem for a jurisdiction to collect taxes from individuals on purchases from sellers not registered or when the property in question is brought into the state from outside of the country. The underground economy has always been a challenge for taxing authorities. How does a tax agency find sellers who deal in cash, do not register as sellers, and report nothing to anyone?

Again, the effort to achieve a trail of business activity through the out-of-state seller is receiving strong interest. The compact states can and are swapping mailing lists, customer payment and purchase records, etc., to locate the transactions upon which tax is not being paid. The voluntary programs are creating a cadre of sellers who have agreed to make every reasonable effort to collect the use tax, which may otherwise be ignored. And in very recent years, and with strong adverse criticism resulting in reconsideration of such policies, their respective taxing policy agencies, the states of California, Illinois and New York, to name the initial three, have secured access to customs declaration documents submitted by foreign travel returnees. The intent is to identify names and addresses of those upon whom the use tax liability falls who have no realistic means of self-assessing purchaser's use tax. At this time, it is believed that nearly all states are receiving declaration data from the U.S. Customs Bureau. It is likely that an increasing number of states will require personal income tax taxpayers to report use tax liability on their state returns.

Techniques are being developed by states to find potential taxpayers who claim to have no nexus but may be ignoring specific business activities that could indicate nexus:

(1) By becoming a registrant at a trade show, state audit and compliance representatives will be able to receive a listing of exhibitors which identifies out-of-state vendors taking orders either by their own employees or in-state representatives.

(2) States are sharing information within their own agencies to find potential taxpayers who: (1) place their names on state bid lists requesting to be notified of sales opportunities within the state, (2) request foreign corporation status for related entities, (3) sign up with the appropriate state agency for a payroll tax account, (4) enter into court actions, and (5) offer warranty or service coverage on property shipped in from out-of-state to in-state customers or state agencies.

(3) During a customary sales and use tax audit by a tax compact member, the auditor lists all of the expense reimbursement vouchers showing that company employees took business trips into adjoining states where no nexus was claimed. The auditor also lists customers in adjoining states with whom the taxpayer has a service contract for equipment maintenance.

In the future, states and localities will continue to share information, join compacts that perform multiple audits, and participate in tax administration associations where ideas and programs are developed. Beyond the FTA, MTC and the various compacts, we can find one other obvious place where jurisdictional tax personnel share information. There are four regional associations that attempt to meet (annually) to discuss common issues and concerns. Often top and second tier managers attend these meetings from the states agencies with the leadership going to the FTA and MTC meetings. The organizations are:

- NESTOA—North Eastern States Tax Officals Association
- WSATA—Western States Association of Tax Administrators
- SEATA—South Eastern States Association of Tax Administrators
- MSATA—Midwestern States Association of Tax Administrators

During the last several years, the FTA has worked on giving states on-line computer communications capabilities. An electronic mail system is in place allowing all jurisdictional participants to share information, download data files, inquire from databases containing research project results, etc. Virtually all departments of revenue, taxation, finance, etc, have Internet web sites accessible to the public. The information is plentiful, useful and free. (Refer to ¶1804 for research information on the Internet.) Ultimately, the purpose of all of this activity is to increase the level of taxpayer compliance with state statutes, rules and regulations. The task of the taxpayer is to deal fairly with these agencies, plan carefully, and reserve wisely for audit contingencies that may not be fully visible. One can run, but it is becoming increasingly difficult to hide.

¶904 Amnesties

Amnesty has become a popular program for states to use to attract wayward dollars into state coffers. These programs grant taxpayers that have not paid or have actually evaded taxes or registration obligations the opportunity to quietly come forward and meet the tax collector with the chance to cut a deal. The deal could mean no penalties, perhaps reduced interest, possible leniency in treatment by tax courts, etc. The programs typically have a very narrow period during which the amnesty applies and scofflaw taxpayers may come forward. Miss the window and you are out of luck if you are subsequently found out. There have been no fewer than two-dozen states that have employed this technique over the last several years. In fact, the Tri-State Compact was set up for such an amnesty. One of the more recent amnesty programs offering the largest stick and the smallest carrot was Illinois. A taxpayer that failed to take advantage of this program could expect the imposition of some very serious penalties for failing to participate. It is likely that there are many more unregistered taxpayers in high places than one might guess. Some of the nation's largest and most prominent corporate citizens are not in compliance and could benefit from an amnesty opportunity or two.

Chapter X
Nexus and Commerce Clause Issues

¶1001 Introduction

We have explored sales and use taxation in the context of activities occurring entirely within the borders of a given state or locality. State governments, based on federal constitutional authority, are empowered to impose taxes as they see fit. One limitation to any such tax enacted is that the tax can only apply to transactions or incidents occurring within a given state's borders. This concept of "within a given state's borders" should take on a new meaning as we investigate the laws and case law that define the authority of states to impose taxes. The purpose of this chapter is not to elevate a reader's legal consciousness to the point of becoming a constitutional law scholar, but rather to introduce some key cases and the laws to which they refer.

¶1002 Nexus

"Nexus" refers to whether one's presence in or proximity to the taxing jurisdiction and the way one acts are enough to require registration and compliance with the statutory requirements of the taxing authority. However, nexus is also about power, whether a state may have jurisdiction over those wishing to pursue business or commercial activities within that state's boundaries. As stated in Chapter I, in every tax code are definitions whose purpose is to clearly describe actions of persons or business entities that require registration and compliance with the conditions of the code. Within a given jurisdiction, the standards of nexus will probably vary from one tax to another. For example, the conditions that result in one's having sufficient nexus for purposes of sales and use tax may be different than the nexus standards for franchise or income tax. The concern of this book is nexus as it relates to sales and use tax.

Nexus issues fall into at least two categories:

(1) the imposition of registration and tax collection/payment responsibilities on businesses acting within the state, and

(2) the imposition of registration and tax collection/payment requirements on out-of-state businesses desiring access to the state's marketplace.

While a state may impose its taxes on services performed in other states on property to be shipped into and used within its borders, it does require that sales within its borders be reported and taxed by in-state sellers.

When viewing the nexus issue for sellers located within the boundaries of the taxing state, failure of the seller to register, pay, or collect and remit the sales tax commonly occurs when the seller believes:

(1) the sales are not viewed as related to those of a division within the state, e.g., a conglomerate's autonomous division does not recognize that a sister division's sales and use tax reporting in a given state obligate all other sister divisions, or

(2) the property owned by the out-of-state seller in the state is not enough to require the seller to be registered, e.g., a seller has no personnel, facilities, vehicles, etc., in the state, but does have merchandise it owns in the state on consignment with various prospective purchasers, or

(3) the activities of the out-of-state seller in the state are insufficient to require the seller to be registered, e.g., employees attend annual trade shows where products are exhibited and orders taken, or

(4) the activities of a related entity are insufficient to require the seller to register, e.g., employees of a related subsidiary are active in the state.

• *Compliance issues*

In contrast with the above nexus issues are compliance issues that exist for companies having sufficient nexus but that are often confused with nexus questions. Compliance issues may address such concerns as:

(1) the property is nontaxable, e.g., an artist prepares camera-ready art work for use by a printer and assumes that the activity is a nontaxable service rather than the sale of tangible personal property; or

(2) the sale to the customer is not subject to tax, e.g., an office supply company does not include in taxable measure sales to the state government in a state which does not exempt sales to political subdivisions; or

(3) the type of property being sold or service being provided is protected from the tax by the U.S. Constitution, e.g., a magazine publisher's sales are protected from the tax code because the tax upon the magazine sales would infringe upon one's right to freedom of speech; or

(4) the property being sold was already taxed, e.g., the sale of outdated assets sold in an auction of scrap property is not a taxable sale as the tax was paid at the time the assets were purchased new and the seller has not met the condition of selling tangible personal property; or

(5) the number of sales each year is not significant, e.g., a service company sells some used equipment at two separate times; or

(6) the seller makes no retail sales, e.g., all sales by the seller are sales at wholesale and are not subject to the state's tax.

A statute will prescribe the nature of the activity and number of transactions which are sufficient to require that a seller hold a permit to transact business (usually three or more in a given calendar year). The statute will further indicate the types of transactions or customers taxed, and the conditions which, if met, cause the seller to be required to register with the state. The challenges to most of these types of compliance issues are almost always related to the Due Process Clause of the Fourteenth Amendment or one of the rights guaranteed under the First Amendment. These challenges, being brought by persons using the courts in an attempt to diminish the power of the government, are often unsuccessful.

And what precisely is the Due Process Clause? The last few lines of the first section of the Fourteenth Amendment to the Constitution of the United States, ratified on July 9, 1868, also called the Civil Rights Amendment, contains the "due process clause." While the original purpose of the amendment in its entirety was to guarantee slaves the rights of citizens of both the United States and the states in which they were resident, the wording of the amendment has been called upon to hold that businesses are guaranteed rights and protections as well.

> Section 1. All persons born or naturalized in the United States, and subject to the jurisdiction thereof, are citizens of the United States and of the states wherein they reside. No state shall make or enforce any law which shall abridge the privileges or immunities of citizens of the United States; nor shall any state deprive any person of life, liberty, or property, without due process of law; nor deny to any person within its jurisdiction the equal protection of the laws.

On the other hand, the nexus issue, the imposition of registration and tax collection requirements on out-of-state sellers or vendors, has been receiving substantial attention. As noted, the issue has focused primarily on mail-order or direct marketing companies that sell through catalogues sent into jurisdictions by the U.S. Postal Service, receive orders by telephone, FAX or mail, and ship property to the customer by common carrier (UPS, FedEx, U.S. Postal Service, etc.) and never have any other presence in the state. More recently, nexus issues have attracted the attention of businesses engaged in electronic commerce.

In these cases, the Commerce Clause of the Constitution tends to be the basis for the seller's argument that its own insufficient nexus prevents the state from requiring registration and collection (and payment) of the state's use tax from the purchaser. Certainly, the state sales tax would not apply if the sale did not occur within the state.

And what precisely is the Commerce Clause? Within the text of the Constitution itself is Article I, Section 8, which deals with powers granted to Congress. The third paragraph describes one of the powers reserved for Congress, the right to regulate commerce.

> Article I, Section 8.(3) To regulate commerce with foreign nations, and among the several states, and with the Indian tribes ...

Giving proper concern for the converse of this power, the founding fathers adopted Article I, Section 9, which limits the powers of Congress. Pertinent to the Commerce Clause issue are the congressional prohibitions enumerated in paragraphs 5 and 6

> Article I, Section 9.(5) No tax or duty shall be laid on articles exported from any state ...
>
> Article I, Section 9.(6) No preference shall be given by any regulation of commerce or revenue to the ports of one state over those of another: nor shall vessels bound to, or from, one state, be obligated to enter, clear, or pay duties in another.

And finally, Article 1, Section 10, limits the powers of states regarding commerce and taxation.

> Article I, Section 10.(2) No state shall, without the consent of the Congress, lay any imposts or duties on imports or exports, except what may be absolutely necessary for executing its inspection laws: and the net produce of all duties

¶1002

and imposts, laid by any state on imports or exports, shall be for use of the treasury of the United States; and all such laws shall be subject to the revision and control of the Congress.

Taking these provisions as a group, one could conclude that states can control commerce within their own borders, cannot tax beyond their borders, and must live by congressional regulation of interstate commerce, providing Congress does not favor one state over another.

The following are a number of nexus questions and the cases that have been significant in providing potential taxpayers with a basis for testing their nexus status under a given state's statute. These questions may only address one of several issues decided by a given case. Do not rely on the following analysis in lieu of seeking advice from an attorney competent in sales and use tax law.

• *Nexus cases*

Does a mail-order seller in state A need to collect state B's use tax on sales into state B from state A when the seller also has retail locations in state B?

Nelson v. Sears, Roebuck & Co., 312 US 359 (1941)

Nelson v. Montgomery Ward, 312 US 373 (1941)

The Court found for the state of Nebraska (state B) in both cases, requiring the retailers to collect the state's use tax on their mail-order sales originating in state A. Nexus sufficient.

Does the presence of the seller's employees in state B taking and transmitting orders to and for delivery from state A represent adequate nexus to require registration?

General Trading Company v. State Tax Commissioner, 322 US 325 (1944)

The Court found that the state was not prohibited from imposing its tax upon General Trading as the presence of employees in the state met the statute's definition of "engaged in business." Nexus sufficient; taxpayer was required to register, collect and remit taxes.

Does the occasional entrance, into state B, of the seller's truck, based in state A, merely to deliver property to customers in state B constitute adequate presence to cause state B's tax statute to apply to the company?

Miller Brothers v. Maryland, 347 US 340 (1954)

The Court found against the state and ruled that the occasional delivery activity did not constitute the condition necessary to require the company to register in state B. Nexus insufficient.

Does the presence of seller's nonemployee representatives in the state constitute nexus requiring registration?

Scripto v. Carson, 362 US 207 (1960)

The Court found that solicitors and agents ("drummers") acting as seller's representatives gave the seller sufficient presence to require registration and tax collection responsibilities. Nexus sufficient.

¶1002

Can a mail-order house with no "presence" in a state, except that it sends catalogues to prospective customers through the U.S. mail, receives prepaid orders by mail, and ships property to customers via common carrier, be required to register, collect and remit the state's use tax?

National Bellas Hess, Inc. v. Illinois Department of Revenue, 386 US 753 (1967)

The Court found in favor of National Bellas-Hess, holding that the state had not demonstrated sufficient nexus to require registration on the part of the mail-order seller. Nexus insufficient.

Is the out-of-state mail-order operation of a company with in-state (unrelated) sales offices required to register and collect the state's use tax on its sales to state residents?

National Geographic Society v. California Board of Equalization, 430 US 551 (1977)

The Court found that the presence of the company's other offices, though involved in unrelated business activities, was adequate to require the company to register and collect the state's use tax. Nexus sufficient.

Is the regular and continuous solicitation of business in a state, even in the absence of physical presence, sufficient nexus under an "economic presence" or "economic benefits" test?

Quill Corporation v. North Dakota, 504 US 298 (1992).

The Court held that the prior 1967 *National Bellas Hess* Court's decision was still valid and that the state of North Dakota's law, while not being unconstitutional under the Due Process Clause, was unconstitutional under the Commerce Clause. As in the past, the Court left open the option of Congress acting in this arena.

As one can see, the majority of the nexus cases deal with mail-order sales. In recent years, the proliferation of mail-order businesses and the unrelated reduction in federal revenue-sharing with the states have placed the nexus issue in the forefront of sales tax battles. States that created statutory language broadening the definition of "being engaged in business" in an effort to capture mail-order seller activity would have to rewrite those laws based on the *Quill* decision.

The mail-order industry that gathered its wagons around the *National Bellas Hess* case has been vindicated. While the bright-line for sufficient nexus has again been drawn, there is no guarantee that congressional action will not ease the pain experienced by the states. Alternatively, legislatures will use the time-tested techniques of enhancing revenue (broadened definition of taxable sale, new definition of taxable sevice, limitation of exemptions, reduction in the collection discount, etc.) in the absence of the mail-order use tax collections. The last gasp from the states may be voluntary or mandatory use tax self-assessment, based on one's adjusted gross income, on personal state income tax returns. There are many ways to collect tax.

¶1002

¶1003 Commerce Clause Issues

As we noted, sales and use tax Commerce Clause issues are concerned with preventing one state from having or taking an unfair advantage over another by using taxation as a way to make the commercial playing field uneven. The Commerce Clause also deals with a state's ability to cross borders in an atttempt to assess taxes. Though Commerce Clause cases are not always concerned with sales and use tax, they establish criteria or tests that are available to test sales and use tax interstate commerce issues. The typical Commerce Clause test asks if the state tax code has exceeded its taxing authority by imposing its tax on transactions or property in interstate commerce.

• *Interstate commerce and Commerce Clause cases*

Can a state tax transactions in interstate commerce or did the state tax exceed its reach?

Complete Auto Transit, Inc. v. Brady, 430 US 274 (1977)

This is clearly one of the major cases of the century regarding a state's taxing scheme. The Court affirmed in a single case four individual tests which must be met for a tax to be viewed as constitutional in light of the Commerce Clause. In other words, while only the Congress can regulate interstate commerce, states may tax aspects of such transactions if the following four conditions are met:

(1) The activity in question is sufficiently connected to the state to justify the tax—*nexus* (see the beginning of this chapter for a discussion of nexus).

(2) The tax *does not unfairly discriminate* against interstate commerce—the tax does not favor the in-state vendor with lower rates or greater tax-cost reduction opportunities over, or at the expense of, the out-of-state vendor.

(3) The tax is *fairly apportioned*—the activities (taxable incident or moment) or property is taxed in proportion to the presence of the property or activity of the taxpayer in the state.

   (a) Internal Consistency - assume every state has a similar tax and confirm that no state is placing more of a burden on interstate versus intrastate commerce. If the test fails, it can be assumed that a state is trying to extract a greater tax from the party in interstate commerce.

   (b) External Consistency - attempts to verify that only the in-state component of the interstate transactions is subjected to tax.

(4) The tax is *fairly related to the benefits conferred* by the taxing statute—the state provides benefits to the taxpayer commensurate with the amount of tax paid.

As we move farther away in time from the Court's decision in *Complete Auto Transit*, we find that this case continues to be pivotal as the legal basis for viewing sales and use tax challenges. Notably, little has indicated that the "four prongs" of *Complete Auto Transit* are any less valid as a test of Commerce Clause constitutionality.

Is a state's severance tax, which appears to unfairly burden out-of-state coal purchasers when compared to the services provided by the state, unconstitutional?

Commonwealth Edison Co. v. Montana, 101 S.Ct. 2946 (1981)

The Court held the state superior court was correct in its finding that the tax was not excessive and that, even if found to be so, the taxpayer was not entitled to relief. Further, the fact that the tax appeared to unfairly target or discriminate against out-of-state parties who were the primary purchasers of the state's coal and, therefore, the major payers of the severance tax did not make the tax unconstitutional. The tax was, on its face, neutral.[1]

How does one measure the discriminatory character of a taxing scheme?

Armco, Inc. v. Hardesty, 104 S.Ct. 2620 (1984)

The Court found that the West Virginia gross receipts tax was discriminatory because local manufacturers were exempt from the tax, unlike out-of-state wholesalers. These two classes of taxpayers, manufacturers and wholesalers, were not comparable. Therefore, *Armco* could end up paying a home state manufacturer's tax as well as the West Virginia wholesaler's tax where the West Virginia manufacturer would not pay tax in West Virginia. This principle of "internal consistency," affirmed by the Court in *Armco* and reaffirmed in *Tyler Pipe Industries, Inc. v. Washington Department of Revenue*, 107 S.Ct. 2810 (1987), and *American Trucking Association v. Scheiner*, 107 S.Ct. 2829 (1987), holds that a state's taxing scheme will be viewed as unconstitutional if a higher tax burden would be placed on interstate instead of intrastate commerce should all states impose the identical tax.

Does an excise tax on originating and terminating long distance service violate the Commerce Clause?

Jerome F. Goldberg et al. v. Roger D. Sweet, Director, Illinois Department of Revenue, 109 S.Ct. 582 (1989)

In addition to confirming the four-prong test of *Complete Auto Transit* and the internal consistency test of *Armco*, the Court offered an additional test: "external consistency"—which deals with the question of whether the state has taxed "only that portion of the revenues from the interstate activity that reasonably reflects the in-state component of the activity being taxed." In this case, the Court held that the Illinois Telecommunications Excise Tax was constitutional.

Can the sale of an interstate bus ticket be entirely taxable in the state of origin although a portion of the service will be provided in a second state?

Oklahoma Tax Commission v. Jefferson Lines, 514 US 175 (1995)

---

[1] This type of tax has been called a "tailored tax" because of the way it appears to discriminate. However, the Court found no reason to reject it in this situation.

This most recent major decision was a surprise to many tax professionals as the questions of apportionment appeared to be at issue. The Oklahoma Tax Commission asserted its statutory tax on sales of transportation services claiming the full price of an interstate ticket was subject to tax in Oklahoma. In this case, no one questioned three of the four prongs of *Complete Auto Transit*, however, the questions of internal and external consistency were thought to be the case's undoing. The Court held that the tax would not be a problem if each state had a similar tax (internal consistency) and the tax was imposed on the activity in the state, the sale of a ticket (external consistency). The fact that the service might be interstate in nature did not require apportionment when the event, the ticket sale, was local in nature.

The above cases, which examine Commerce Clause issues, are part of the overall continuum of cases that have addressed the states' rights to tax in whatever manner they deem appropriate. There is more to be said about the relationship between the U.S. Constitution and state taxing schemes. This book limits itself to a non-legalistic discussion of the Due Process and Commerce Clauses. A tax professional's understanding of and attention to such legal precedents are important. Any compliance audit and resulting assessment can produce an issue which may become the next major court opinion. All the legal challenges to the multitude of questionable tax statutes in existence have yet to be made. Being prepared to contribute to legal history is a tax professional's obligation to the tax field.

Chapter XI
Sales/Use Tax Department Management—An Overview

¶1101 Introduction

The size and complexity of a tax department should reflect the size or complexity of its company. A large business with sales in only its home state should have a smaller staff than a comparably sized or smaller business in many states. Retailers will have tax accounting needs different than wholesalers or manufacturers of similar sizes. A small conglomerate is a more complex tax management problem than a single-line business of twice its size. How one determines the proper staffing and organization of a tax department is not a precise science. What one must grasp are the types of tasks every department must perform to be effective and beneficial to its company. Regardless of size, business type or business complexity, all tax departments must keep their eyes on the tax calendar. At ¶804, there is a state tax calendar.

¶1102 Compliance Functions

Compliance can be divided into four areas: registration and collection of tax, return preparation and filing, certificate file maintenance, and audit coordination and control. Every company, regardless of size, will need to address the first three issues at various times in the business life cycle. Small concerns may never be audited by a jurisdiction, though the requirement to be prepared for such an event should not be ignored.

• *Registration and collection of tax*

The requirement to register as a tax collector/payer in a given jurisdiction is a question of nexus. Once the issue of nexus has been settled and the company recognizes that registration is required, the issue becomes tax collection followed by the list of other tax tasks to be accomplished. Tax collection includes:

(1) determining what is taxable or exempt and what is included in the taxable measure; and

(2) establishing a collection mechanism and training personnel.

Mechanized point-of-sale retailers have a relatively simple tax collection task—program the cash register to automatically capture the tax at the time the transaction is rung up and have the sales clerk collect the tax with the sale. The less mechanized the cashiering, the greater the potential for error. Wholesalers and manufacturers have little problem with tax collection but a major concern with certificate file maintenance. A sale is taxable and requires tax collection unless a valid certificate of exemption(resale, direct pay, product or entity) is on file. Other types of sellers (or lessors) require collection systems with varying degrees of sophistication.

• *Return preparation and filing*

The preparation and filing of returns is clearly one of the most time sensitive aspects of the tax management process since the data accumulation activity ends very close to the commencement of the return preparation effort. Submission of returns on a timely basis must be achieved with a high degree of regularity. Multistate and multijurisdiction taxpayers should attempt to automate the return preparation activity. Ideally, tax data can be moved via computer link from sales records to tax return spreadsheets or programs. Such products are currently available from several vendors experienced in the design and marketing of tax-related software. Tax rate services may also be purchased both in hard copy and on magnetic media. A calendar of critical tax dates should be meticulously maintained in every company and posted for key personnel to see.

• *Certificate file maintenance*

Every sale is taxable until proven exempt. Therefore, as a form of insurance, one of the most important files in the tax department (or wherever it is maintained) is the certificate file. This file, at minimum, contains the original exemption certificate from every customer (providing one or more certificates) since the inception of the company. In addition, the file might also contain copies of resale or exempt purchase orders, export documents, bills of lading and contracts with special tax considerations. It is not important that such a file be maintained in the tax department, per se, only that it exist and be maintained. A specific individual(s) should be assigned the responsibility for this file. As with return preparation, automated tools are available to assist taxpayers in certificate management. The issue of automating the certificate management activity is discussed at ¶ 1503.

• *Audit coordination and control*

Audit coordination and control is one of those topics about which entire books could be written. In this book, we have dedicated a separate chapter (Chapter XIV) to this topic. However, in the context of the tax department management activities, there are four coordination and control functions which should be performed:

(1) scheduling and coordination—every audit should have been scheduled in advance of its actual commencement; the responsibility of overseeing the audit and auditor should be assigned to specific staff;

(2) record and data presentation—agreement should be reached with the auditor early in the audit process as to what documents and records must be made available (presented in a controlled manner) or located, how the data will be tested and projected, and what special needs may reasonably be filled;

(3) review of findings—items scheduled are questioned but not assessed until the taxpayer and auditor (and supervisor) either agree on the questioned items or agree to disagree that an assessment is justified; review procedures should be established early in the audit to minimize

pressure on either the taxpayer or auditor to rush to completion without giving proper time and attention to the audit findings;

(4) appeals and remedies—while the audit is in process, the responsible tax department representative should prepare and monitor a calendar of dates or deadlines which are to be met in order to preserve rights of protest and appeal.

At the conclusion of the audit, a file should be prepared containing all of the audit workpapers. Systematic and procedural changes should be addressed throughout the audit process when the audit findings demonstrate a deficiency.

¶1103 Company-Related Functions

Compliance functions are required to meet the needs of the taxing jurisdictions while company-related functions are those which meet the needs of the tax management process. These activities are internally directed, facilitating tax collection and payment in a manner that increases efficiency and results in full compliance while paying the minimum tax that is actually due. Communications with all areas of the company on an on-going basis is absolutely critical.

¶1104 Internal Auditing

#37 Traditionally, internal auditing is performed by an independent department whose charge is to make certain that the company's financial and accounting policies are being followed. The sales tax department activities are often at the periphery of this analysis as the dollars collected are the dollars remitted. However, within the tax department there should be a continuous internal audit. Issues requiring attention include (but are not limited to):

(1) the validity of data being passed from computer to computer and the instructions in tax programs;

(2) the precision by which personnel are following tax procedures in all departments having tax issues (e.g., accounts payable, purchasing, contracts, marketing and sales, etc.);

(3) the accuracy of the billing activity (tax rates);

(4) the proper tax coding of new accounts;

(5) the reporting of cash receipts and adjustments to the sales tax account; and

(6) the tracking of journal entries that may have tax consequences.

It should be understood that auditing the tax returns themselves is a regular activity which must not lapse into an occasional one. For compliance testing, one should work from a well-designed internal controls checklist. Do the numbers "tie-out?" Are all edit reports reconciled as they should be? Is the tax in the general ledger reconciled to the return? Is the amount due with the tax return actually sent with the return and timely?

¶1105 Intramural Training and Tax Procedures

The need to provide regular and systematic training of personnel having sales/use tax contact should not be ignored. Training should be performed in conjunction with dissemination of a company tax manual or other reference tools. Training should be available at all times and should be tailored to the needs and sophistication of the audiences. The company tax manual should be both instructional and a source of clear and concise tax reference. The use of charts and decision trees will enhance the user's desire to avail himself or herself of information, more so than a text presentation of the same information. Manuals should be updated whenever changes in business method, accounting policy or tax statutes cause their content to be outdated.

¶1106 Forms Management and Document Printing Control

There is little doubt in the mind of this author that this is probably one of the most consistently ignored areas of sales tax management. It is one of those functions that is best handled proactively. The issue is control over the publication of forms and documents that impact upon the sales tax area in every possible way. These printed pieces fall into two broad categories: printed material that is used solely in-house and printed material that communicates company tax policy outside the company.

The former group includes such forms as bid sheets, purchase requisitions, tele-marketing telephone crib sheets and order forms, and accounts payable vouchers or input forms. Concern for these forms should be oriented towards company tax policy. Of course, all forms should be dated for obsolescence control purposes. State tax policy is very likely to change more frequently than the forms themselves. While the content of most forms will not be tax-related, tax management must be responsible for reviewing the actual elements of the form related to tax issues.

Therefore, the proactive aspect of this management function requires that tax personnel be aware of the forms review process, frequency of forms issuance and target forms wherein tax issues must be addressed. Contacting key company personnel, to inform them of the tax department's interest in their forms, is critical to receiving the consideration required to keep tax issues in focus on company forms. The consideration given to sales tax on any form will help to ensure against audit assessment penalties.

Companies that demonstrate attention and concern through full documentation cannot be considered negligent unless no effort is made to attend to the tax issues addressed by the forms. Forms and printed material that are placed in the public view, and therefore represent company policy to the public, include the following types of materials: sales invoices; sales order acknowledgments; purchase orders; preprinted order forms; catalogues; price lists; certificates; etc. These materials should be very explicit in expressing company tax policy. Here are some examples.

(1) Does a company catalogue or price list indicate that tax will be added to all taxable sales and will be the contractual obligation of the customer?

(2) Does the sales order acknowledgment clearly indicate that, in the absence of properly completed resale or exemption certificates supplied by purchaser in a timely manner, taxes will be charged on all sales?

(3) Does the sales invoice provide for a breakdown of the taxes being collected, state and local, the rate being charged, the items being taxed and the subtotal taxable measure? Is it necessary to imprint a statement indicating that, where the seller has no nexus, the liability for the use tax will be on the purchaser?

(4) Are resale and exemption certificates properly worded?

(5) Do tear-out mail-order forms clearly explain how the customer is to compute and add tax in their local jurisdiction?

(6) Has the company reserved the right to recover tax reimbursement in the event that property or service thought to be exempt is ultimately determined to be taxable?

The list of issues is as long as a company's tax policy and sensitivity requires. Again, it is the responsibility of the tax department to impose its concerns on those that print documents for public consumption. What is placed in print and signed, even though it is "boiler-plate" material, can reasonably be considered contractually binding.

¶1107 Miscellaneous Tax Management Functions

Depending upon the size and complexity of a business and the size of the tax department (and the resources made available to it), there are several other functions that require attention. Following are these activities and examples of their significance.

• Tax planning

Too often senior company management contacts the tax department after major business decisions have been made rather than prior to that process. The tax cost of such myopia can be significant. Locating a production facility in the wrong state can increase the cost of purchasing assets by the value of the state and local tax rate as compared to placing the same plant in a state which grants an exemption for machinery and equipment used in the manufacturing process.

• Legislative surveillance

Elected representatives often meet the fiscal needs of their jurisdictions with taxes. If a company fails to keep a pulse on legislation under consideration, there is no room for complaining when a tax is imposed on transactions proving unfavorable to that company or its customers.

• Tax subscription and tax library maintenance

There are several tax subscription services (led by the authoritative CCH MULTISTATE SALES TAX GUIDE) that keep a tax department apprised of state-by-state developments. When such a resource is updated and read on a regular basis, along with other CCH publications, one is able to identify and correct misinformation in company procedures and instructional manuals. Nearly all large companies have some form of tax library. Increasingly large numbers of sales/use tax reference works, such as books, surveys, matrices, etc., should have a place in a tax library. Like tax procedure manuals, all materials should be kept current, be readily available, and be recognized for the level of authority that is represented by the content, source and bias. Increasingly, electronic versions of these resources are replacing the print versions, accompanied by excellent search tools.

• Record retention

Audit assessments are often diminished by those able to locate and document transactions questioned by auditors. Tax management must be intimately involved in all aspects of record retention related to company documents able to support an audit. While it is not necessary for the tax department to maintain its own complete duplicate set of paid invoices, customer invoices, assets logs, shipping logs, journal vouchers and tax returns, it is critical that the original entry data, or good micrographic reproductions thereof, be retained in such condition allowing ease of access. Within the tax department, records are normally filed by jurisdiction and period.

Tax record retention should follow this same pattern once the documents are to be archived. As is often the case, there is no universal method of record retention that will work for everyone. There need only be a system that works for one's own company. To assure the availability of records, it is strongly recommended that a representative of the tax department have a seat on any company-wide record retention committee. Departments not having a strong tax interest will tend to ignore issues that are important to the tax compliance function.

Finally, one should remember that records are not merely paper, micrographic reproductions or even optically scanned digitally recorded data, but also data stored on magnetic media. The importance of having full knowledge of the disposition of archived information surfaces during and following merger and acquisition discussions. What will be the disposition of records (all types) following the sale of a division or subsidiary if the records are integrated with other corporate data that was not sold? Did the attorneys address the disposition of records as well as the responsibility and liability for audits on a post-divestiture basis? The same issue arises for you in reverse if your company acquires part, but not all, of another company.

• Customer relations

The tax department has many customers or parties receiving its services. It is, first, a provider of collection services to the states and local jurisdictions. It supports the tax activities of the accounts payable, fixed asset, corporate planning, general ledger, and accounts receivable departments. It must interact with sales and marketing to be sure that bids, proposals, contracts, and general literature and advertising prepared by those departments are consistent with tax law and company tax policy. And when true customers have tax disputes, they should be handled timely and consistently to avoid damaging relationships.

- ● *Industry interaction and networking*

National professional associations for tax personnel are an invaluable source of guidance. The Institute for Professionals in Taxation (headquartered in Atlanta) is such an organization, comprised exclusively of industry representatives from many of the nation's major taxpayers. Meeting with these individuals, especially within one's own industry, is a certain way to share and compare tax management and audit issues.

- ● *Professional advancement*

The "Certified Member of the Institute" designation (CMI) available through the Institute for Professionals in Taxation is recognized widely as credible evidence that a tax professional has achieved a level of distinction in the sales tax field as measured by his/her peers. Such certification may be deemed worthy of merit by senior company management.

- ● *Legal research*

Audits inevitably produce legal issues requiring research. Access to company counsel (inside or outside) may be less productive than performing tax research within the tax department. Least of all, substantial legal costs can be saved by advance preparation and coaching of counsel where significant audit liabilities merit extensive use of due process.

- ● *Departmental management*

Someone must be responsible for job descriptions, hiring and training, performance evaluations, motivation and allocation of resources. Within the tax department, these activities are commonly performed by the manager.

¶1108 Department Organization

A survey of more than one hundred tax managers has resulted in the identification of four organizational structures for sales tax departments.

- (1) Centralized—For single or multi-line business, all return preparation, audit coordination, planning, general management and administration are handled in a single central office.

- (2) De-centralized—Typically, in a multi-line, multi-unit, or multidivisional business, all activities are performed at the business unit or divisional level with minimal support from a corporate tax department.

- (3) Functional—This is a combination of both of the above with consolidation at corporate headquarters (i.e., each business unit prepares tax return detail and transmits that data to corporate for inclusion in the returns completed and submitted by the corporate staff); individuals at both the corporate and business unit levels are assigned to functional areas of concern (e.g., research, audit coordination and control, legislative surveillance, etc.).

(4) Geographical—This is similar to the functional structure, except that the basic division of labor is by region, either physically, mechanically, or both.

There is only one requirement when selecting an organizational form: that it meet the needs of the company.

¶1109 Process Mapping the Workload

Much of life happens. Things are not always carefully, scientifically, practically, logically, or methodically planned or arranged. Over time, changes are the result of both planned and unplanned stimuli. In the sales tax environment we have numerous examples of processes followed because one person told another person to follow a series of steps to achieve a desired result. Is or was it the best plan? The result may be desired but the process may make little sense. Or, the result is not necessary but everyone is clearly comfortable with the process. Hence, the adage, "If it ain't broke, don't fix it."

For those more demanding tax professionals among this book's readership, this adage should find its way out the door. It is about time that we take stock of the process and make substantive changes. This is where process mapping is an ideal tool. A good map will identify non-productive sequencing of events, excessive time spent accomplishing the right or wrong function, and areas for natural improvement. As with any process that asks questions about the status quo, it will make some people in the organization very anxious. Accordingly, gaining employee participation in the process is critical to achieving change. People who invest become committed. Committed people take pride. Pride awakens passion. Passion gives life meaning. Jobs are more enjoyable. Doesn't this all sound wonderful? Perhaps your organization should take some time to ask these questions: What are we doing? Why are we doing it? How can we do it better?

True process mapping produces a literal map. The map shows events, decisions, actions, causes with effects, time duration, alternatives, documents, inputs and outputs, and terminal points. Your department may discover that, because of charting its processes, the effort to fix incorrectly accrued taxes is disproportionate to the time it takes to make the erroneous entries. That, by correcting the accrual process, e.g., changing the decision point or improving the availability of information about taxability, the time expended in repairing such mistakes is materially reduced. Process mapping is ideally implemented as an agent of change. Visualize the possible. Act to make it reality. Mapping skills can be self-taught or bought. There is simply no excuse to run a sloppy or thoughtless operation.

Chapter XII

Registration

¶1201 Introduction

The company senior vice president for administration and planning just completed a presentation to management and has indicated that the company will commit its resources toward expanding its operations. A manufacturing plant and distribution warehouse have been acquired in state A (new to the company) and sales offices will be established in states B, C, and D (new sales territories for the company). Preparation for market entrance is to be completed by the next calendar quarter with plant and warehouse occupancy planned for this quarter next year. Must the company register in all of these states? For sales and use tax purposes, what are the issues related to qualification and registration of the company which must be addressed?

¶1202 Obligation to Register

Every state has established activity thresholds which, if reached, require that a person or business is obligated to register and meet the responsibilities of registration in that state. Activities requiring franchise or income tax registration may not be sufficient to indicate business licensure for those taxes, whereas, under more aggressive use tax "economic" nexus provisions, sales and use tax registration may be required. To prevent a business from registering for only one of several taxes, most states have established information sharing between the various taxing departments—register for one and hear from them all.

Physical presence of property and/or personnel is the most common condition sufficient to trigger the requirement to register. Where property is the sole form, or one of several forms, of presence, e.g., a leasing company, property tax will be an additional tax obligation. And finally, city business license or occupation taxes are indicated for those engaged in business in some cities. California offers the broadest range and incidence of such taxes.

A more complex set of issues exists when a business has no physical presence but is active in the state in some lesser manner. Prime examples of businesses in this category are direct mail-order marketeers, wholesale distributors, and itinerant representatives (travelling salespersons). Their activities may be as minimal as sending catalogues into a state and filling orders by mail, providing toll-free telephone access to an order desk in another state, and making brief visits during trade shows. In recent years, many states have attempted to extend their licensing authority to include these activities, which appear to involve little contact with the state.

These are the nexus issues currently in the courts discussed in Chapter X. However, for the purpose of this chapter, our attention will focus on issues of registration where there is no question that a business is adequately represented in a state by its property, personnel or activities to create sufficient nexus.

¶1202

Clearly, a state has the right to control the activities of businesses within its borders. This right is guaranteed by the U.S. Constitution and is confirmed in state constitutions. Control of who engages in business within a state protects that state's citizens from unscrupulous, dishonest and malicious persons who would offer illegal, contraband, or dangerous products or services. This public protection is provided through a state's system of boards of control, boards of oversight and governmental commissions.

The advantages or rights accorded legitimate organizations include safety, health and sanitation services, access to the courts of the state, and use of various governmental welfare benefit services. On the surface, these considerations may pale in comparison to the obligations of businesses properly registered with the required jurisdictions and agencies, but, ultimately, some benefit will be derived representing the value of compliance.

¶1203 Registration Forms

A garden variety of names for the registration form have evolved over the years. The simple "registration certificate" is no more than a name and number verifying that the business is registered. Some states call the registration certificate a "license," a term that one may infer means its holder has met some minimum criteria to do business. A retailer's license should be distinguished from a license issued to one engaged in a special field of business governed by rules and regulations in an industry, e.g., construction, automobile repair, pharmacy operators, etc. Two of the more common terms are "certificate of authority" and "seller's permit." Both names suggest that the business has been granted permission to do something. And finally, a state or locality might have a "registered merchants certificate" or something similar which seems least presumptuous and most direct. What one must always keep in mind is that the physical document, such as a license, certificate, or permit, issued to a business granting a right to sell or carry on business, is vastly different from the document used to claim an exemption under the law.

¶1204 Completion of the Application

Most applications provided by states are used for several purposes:

(1) to record the location of the business, its owners, managers, and agents,

(2) to gather statistics to be used by the jurisdictional bureaucracy,

(3) to identify the business to other agencies, regulatory bodies, commissions and boards, and

(4) to place the business in its proper role as a tax collector and taxpayer in order to capture revenue.

Most applications ask for logical information:

(1) business name,

(2) address of main office where records are maintained and other in-state location(s),

(3) telephone number,

(4) business commencement date,

(5) type of ownership,

(6) names and addresses of officers (and directors),

(7) in-state agent for service of process,

(8) federal employer identification number or social security number,

(9) type of product or service, general nature of business, and

(10) estimated receipts for a given period of time.

Many jurisdictions require that new sellers furnish a surety bond. The estimated receipts often determine the amount of the bond. The bond is held as security that the new seller will remit taxes due and payable and, failing to do so, will forfeit the bond or deposit. Information concerning type of ownership often leads down the path of identifying other related entities engaged in business in the state that may or may not be registered. For large multidivisional organizations, this issue is particularly sensitive as all divisions of a single parent may become registered by the mere registration of a single division.

The type of business can determine the type of tax obligation(s) in a state that has various types of levies. A registrant may believe that registration for a seller's certificate of authority is the only tax registration required. Businesses making no retail sales may receive a wholesalers license and believe they are not obligated to report sales since no tax payment or collection is required. Most businesses having sales tax registration nexus will have an income or franchise tax obligation. Resident employees trigger payroll taxes. Property alone triggers property taxes. Essentially, the type of a business and the activities in which it engages will determine the taxes it must pay.

¶1205 Types of Registrants

On the other hand, not all businesses will want, or be able, to register for the same types of tax or permit. General sales activity at retail from fixed sales locations will require a customary sales and use tax style permit. The out-of-state seller, making sales on a regular basis into a state in which the vendor has a minimal presence, may be required to register to collect use tax in behalf of the in-state purchasers. A non-retailer, e.g., service enterprise, governmental unit (in a state that offers no exemption for same) or wholesaler, may be required to hold a use tax permit obligating it to accrue and remit the state and local use tax on all non-taxed taxable transactions. In states granting blanket exemption from sales and use tax to nonprofit institutions, hospitals, governmental units, religious organizations and/or educational programs, there is generally a registration which provides the registrant a tax-exempt permit.

Finally, some states have adopted statutory provisions granting special businesses, primarily manufacturers and natural resource processors, the authority to pay sales and use tax directly to the jurisdiction under a direct payment authority or permit (discussed in Chapter VI). Rarely is one's registration classification a matter of choice, and the obligation to register is nearly always clear.

There may be some costs (fees and bonds), there may be renewal requirements, and there will always be reporting, even when no tax is due.

Now, refer back to the original problem posed at ¶1201. The tax manager considers the planned construction of the factory and warehouse, recognizing that the factory will purchase raw materials which will be both self-consumed and further processed for resale. State A, in addition to requiring a basic sales and use tax license, offers a direct payment authority program which seems to be ideal for that facility. The warehouse will serve as a distribution center having no direct income and State A will designate the warehouse as a second in-state location under the same sales and use tax license as that held by the factory.

In States B, C and D, the company will have employees and rental offices and company-owned office equipment (personal property). The states all require those with owned property to register as a business. Each state will issue a seller's permit, requiring the company to collect the requisite taxes from all retail taxable customers purchasing taxable property or services. All four states, being eager to increase the grasp of their taxing authority, make it easy to register and require that registration be renewed annually. Fortunately, the tax manager has developed some excellent data processing capabilities which will allow for the proper self-assessment of use tax under the direct payment permit, collection of sales tax on taxable retail sales, and determination of use tax on all samples taken from inventory (and not sold) by the sales force. The new returns will be prepared using a mainframe download program to a spreadsheet which prints the returns on a laser printer. The states will automatically issue annual renewal notices with the first return each calendar year, charging renewal fees of $25, $100, $125, and $500. And life in the tax department will go on.

¶1205

Chapter XIII
Audit Support Documentation

¶1301 Introduction

In Chapter VI, we discussed two types of exemptions: those that are internally derived and those that are externally derived. Because a sale is deemed to be taxable in the absence of evidence to the contrary, the burden is upon the seller to demonstrate through proper documentation that a sale is not taxable, that tax need not be paid or collected and remitted measured by the gross receipts thereon. From an audit liability perspective, establishment, maintenance and retention of records are collectively the single most important facet of the sales (and use) tax department management function. Without proper documentation, which is clearly traceable for auditing purposes, transactions which are otherwise exempt become fully taxable, subject to interest for late payment and, probably, subject to penalty. As noted earlier, with sales tax, too often it is a matter of form over substance. How things look, that is, the manner in which transactions are documented, is often more important than the transactions themselves. To paraphrase the trite but true expression: it has to look like, walk like, and quack like a duck to be a duck.

There are four areas of activity which require thorough documentation: sales, purchases, journal activity representing intra-company accounting adjustments, and tax return preparation and related tax accounts. Auditors from jurisdictions will address each and every one of these issues, in summary, by statistical test and inference, or in detailed review, prior to accepting the taxpayer's reporting as being in compliance with that jurisdiction's tax statutes and rules. In the broadest sense, the books and records of the taxpayer must be made available to the jurisdiction auditor for purposes of verification. Each statute (and the related rules) provides more specific description of the records to be made available, the period of time for which they must be kept, and the manner by which the auditor may prove the veracity of the tax reported and paid, evaluated in conjunction with the company's actual records.

¶1302 Sales

The documents of original entry for sales constitute cash register receipts, cash sales receipts, commercial invoices, and credit sales invoices. All of these documents normally indicate the amount of taxable measure and the extended amount of tax at a given rate. Additionally, sales (tax) records should include customer purchase orders, bid and quotation information, copies of customer correspondence, bills of lading, freight invoices or shipping instructions, and copies of completed exemption certificates. Logically, all documents related to a given transaction should be filed together. Practically, this manner of filing is often unworkable. The compromise should represent a filing system that provides the necessary "hooks" or references to tie related transaction documents together. The customer purchase order and the seller sales order number are two commonly used document reference numbers.

• *Retail sales*

In the retail environment, cash register receipts and cash sales invoices (manual receipts) are the documents of original entry. In large volume retail facilities, retention of daily cash register tapes is nearly impossible. If 100 percent retention of daily register tapes is impractical, agreement should be reached with jurisdictions to provide either sample data retention or an alternative audit approach based on inventory purchases and mark-up analysis testing. Scanner data retained on magnetic media can provide similar supporting documentation, possibly eliminating the need for original cash register tapes themselves.

In states where purchaser-initiated exemptions (the product is taxable save the purchaser having a valid basis for making the purchase non-taxable) can be claimed at the check-out counter in the retail outlet, a policy requiring exemption certificate completion, prior to a cashier completing the exempt sale check-out, must be implemented. Exemption certificate retention and correlation to the sales documentation must be perfected.

In a retail setting, where the customer may finance the purchase through the use of revolving credit, a single finance agreement, lay-away, or other financial instrument, a careful handling of these types of arrangements must be described in a simple yet thorough procedure. Such a procedure takes into account the interest or carrying charges due, fees payable, etc., and the method of handling them on a state-by-state basis.

• *Business-to-business sales*

Business-to-business sales on commercial or credit invoices often involve purchase orders, sales orders, bills of lading and other related forms. The use of exemption certificates of all types is quite common in this environment. As with consumer retail, resale and wholesale transactions should not be allowed to reach the ship-and-bill stage until the sales (tax) file is complete. The proper solution, in either case, is to bill tax in the absence of the exemption certificate. However, the company attitude towards sales tax will determine one's success in achieving procedure compliance. After charging a tax audit assessment to the sales and marketing department one time, that department will not only lend a hand to your compliance effort, but may even become a champion for the sales tax department.

• *Size of transactions*

Finally, many auditors will ask to perform separate types of tests on sales, based on the size of the sales transactions. Daily cash receipts or small value sales by a wholesaler are often sampled in some random manner with the ratio of error being projected to the total sales population for the audit period. Large ticket sales are normally audited in detail, resulting in an audit assessment on a dollar-for-dollar basis. This natural and intuitive transaction stratification is not always best suited to all taxpayers. Determine in advance what will serve your company best and offer that plan to the auditor. Regardless of the audit plan, instances of improper documentation in a sample audit can have significantly greater financial ramifications than a similar problem affecting a few articulated transactions looked at in detail. In either case, it is better to have the file complete or the audit trail traceable than to suffer a burdensome assessment. Also, fewer jurisdictions are allowing taxpayers the chance to complete files once an audit has commenced.

¶1303 Purchases

As with sales, purchases are often audited in two separate groupings. Capital or fixed asset and large expense purchases (typically with high dollar values) are surveyed in 100 percent detail, while smaller value purchases are often audited in a block or random statistical sampling fashion. As with the small sales sample test audit, the ratio of error representing the taxpayer's failure to pay use (or sales, in some cases) tax is applied to the taxpayer's total purchase volume to determine the tax liability. The documentation which must be present to keep purchase audit assessments to a minimum are: purchase invoices; bills of lading (or freight invoices); purchase orders; and accrual records, evidencing the tax in question was either paid to the vendor directly or accrued by the taxpayer and paid to the jurisdiction.

¶1304 Journal Activity of Intra-company Accounting Adjustments

When property is purchased for resale (without tax) but is self-consumed by the purchaser, a balance sheet adjustment should be made to properly recognize the transfer of the property from one balance sheet account to another. Such a journal entry triggers a taxable moment which should also result in the accrual of use tax offset by charging the tax to the appropriate department or account. Examples of these types of transfers are:

(1) resale inventory is going to be used as samples by sales personnel; the inventory account is relieved and the samples account is charged with the inventory;

(2) resale inventory is used to make a piece of machinery for use within the taxpayer's plant; the inventory account is relieved and the capital asset or construction in progress account is charged; or

(3) resale inventory is used by the R&D department in the development of a new product; the inventory account is relieved and the R&D project account is charged.

The most noted weakness with journal entries (or journal vouchers) is their brevity. The person who made the entry may have known its purpose, but three years later that reason is all but impossible to fathom. Proper documentation of journal entries should provide enough clarity so that a stranger reviewing the transaction would understand completely how the values were derived, to what period they apply, why they were made, etc. Journal transactions which often have sales and use tax implications are those impacting the following accounts: sales, inventory, sales and use tax (the accrual or expense account), gifts and samples, gain (or loss) on the disposition of property, R&D, accounts receivable, and intra- or intercompany receivables.

Special industry accounting schemes may impact other accounts, but the above list is typical.

¶1305 Tax Return Preparation and the Sales/Use Tax Accounts

When a customer provides an exemption certificate after an invoice has been billed, booked, tax accrued, and paid, and the customer deducts the tax billed prior to paying the invoice, how does your system record the activity? How are tax invoices submitted to your customer after the original billing was rendered or booked, not only for purposes of reporting the tax but also to provide the tax department a trail to show whether what may have appeared as an exempt sale was really taxable? How does your company differentiate taxes for different states or localities in your tax account? These questions represent three examples of the importance of documentation in sales (and use) tax accounts. The tax practitioner should view the entire matter of documentation with the fear of coming down with amnesia tomorrow. If your job were secure, provided that you know today what you did before you forgot, you would work harder in documenting all tax-related transactions.

¶1306 Certificates and Customer Purchase Orders

In this and the preceding chapter, great emphasis has been placed on the form of documentation called the "certificate," that document which, when presented to the seller by the purchaser at the time of the purchase, results in the transaction being nontaxable. It is the document that keeps the seller from being assessed tax on a sale that was not previously taxed. The certificate, whether it be one for resale, direct pay or general (or specific) exemption, at a minimum, may be required to contain:

(1) the name and address of the purchaser;

(2) the name of the seller to whom it is given;

(3) a reason for the exemption;

(4) an authorized signature;

(5) the purchaser's license or registration number;

(6) the date; and

(7) the good faith of the purchaser.

This last ingredient means that the seller must view the certificate, in light of the transaction for which it was given, as being reasonably provided. For example, a resale certificate given by a restaurant for automobile tires probably was not given in good faith. The seller should have challenged the purchaser to explain how the restaurant will resell the tires. The seller must believe that the certificate is accurate and fits the business for which it is given. The certificate is not, however, a copy of the purchaser's business license, sales tax permit, sales tax registration or federal tax certificate. Sellers that accept such a document and presume that it will support the nonpayment of sales tax on a transaction will experience an assessment for such gullibility.

• *Certificate forms*

The form of the certificate may be very specific. New Mexico issues groups of prenumbered forms which are only available directly from the state. By example, California, Connecticut, Nebraska, New Jersey, New York, Ohio, Pennsylvania, Texas and West Virginia require that the form be worded in a very precise manner. Key to such wording is the fact that, should the purchaser use the property in a fashion other than that for which the certificate was given, the purchaser agrees to pay the tax for that nonexempt use. Currently, 26 states require their own form (wording) or the Multistate Tax Commission form.

Some customers and vendors may have their own forms preprinted in quantity which may be acceptable. However, if the content of the form does not appear to fit the statutory description, it should be rejected. Also, some states require that the form predate the transaction (the date on the form must be earlier than the date of sale). It is not a bad practice for the seller to require this regardless of the state in question.

It is also common for large wholesalers and manufacturers to send forms to their customers on a regular basis. The form may be a "one size fits all" (fitting many states and jurisdictions) and could be acceptable in some states. But no form fits all states. The form also may be issued to allow (when taken in good faith) the seller to place many customers on a nontaxable status for reasons of billing convenience. And certificate files should be updated on a regular basis, at least once every four years. In Nevada, new certificates are required every two years. Under special circumstances, when a state issues new registration numbers to its sellers, new certificates may be required from all customers.

It is important for the taxpayer to harvest all the certificates required to support customer exemption claims. An out-of-date certificate is worthless.

• *Types of certificates*

Two certificate concepts are widely recognized:

(1) *Blanket certificates* cover all sales for the product(s) indicated on the certificate. The seller accepting a blanket certificate that states, "see purchase order," should only accept the certificate if: (a) the customer always provides a purchase order that has tax instructions, or (b) the seller is willing and capable of billing sales or use tax in the absence of receiving the completed purchase order.

(2) *Unit certificates* cover only a particular job or order. Certificates of this type are widely used in the construction industry, where, by the very nature of the work, each contract tends to be separate and distinct, having a beginning and an ending with a discrete purchasing requirement.

There are numerous types of certificates, depending upon the state. Louisiana has approximately twenty types of forms alone. Often, it is beneficial for the seller to create a certificate to be completed by customers not otherwise required to do so, or without a standard document to provide the seller. If one looks at Chapter VI—Exemptions, one sees the many types of exempt transactions and customers requiring certificates.

One should be aware of the interesting issues often relating to certificates and what purchasers may offer as valid certificates.

(1) A letter from a customer stating that the purchase is going to be resold will not meet the definition of a valid certificate in almost every state. The approved certificate form is appropriate.

(2) A singular, all-purpose certificate with a list of states on the back in which the customer is claiming an exemption is likely to be rejected as unacceptable.

(3) A certificate from other than the actual purchaser will not be acceptable. For example, the Tomato Products Division cannot normally vouch an exemption for the Pesto Division if the purchased property is being shipped to the Pesto Division. Certainly, one subsidiary cannot vouch an exemption for another under any circumstance.

(4) A certificate that is not dated prior to the event to which it is related is unlikely to be accepted by the jurisdiction.

(5) An improperly completed or an incomplete certificate, a wrong form, incorrect wording in a form or certificate, or, in some cases, absence of the state seal on such documents, all offer the auditor a chance to assess.

In the absence of the certificate, some states will accept a customer purchase order as a document authenticating the nontaxable nature of a customer's purchase. Such a purchase order should contain all of the elements above. However, it is advisable that the seller confirm which states will accept a purchase order in lieu of a certificate and which will not before assuming the issue of valid documentation has been resolved. If properly completed, and acceptable in the view of the state, both documents relieve the seller of a tax collection or payment responsibility. The Institute for Professionals in Taxation in Atlanta, GA., prepared a survey, collecting and publishing the results into a pamphlet discussing the states' rules concerning registration (permit) numbers and exemption certificates. It is a useful document to have in one's tax library.

Chapter XIV
Handling Audits (and Auditors)

¶1401 Introduction

Audits can be very trying experiences even for the most skillful and experienced tax professionals because they are performed by people—auditors. That is not to say that auditors are a unique or peculiar breed of human beings, possessing strange and dramatic powers. More often than not, audits are lost by tax professionals who have failed to follow some very simple rules which facilitate completion of audits and dispatch auditors with minimal emotional, financial or productivity damage. Many years of acquired knowledge gleaned from some of the nation's foremost tax professionals combined with ample personal experience managing audits, auditors and tax functions for clients during this author's 30-year apprenticeship produced this list of "rules." If understood and followed, these rules should produce manageable audits, reasonable auditors and enhanced job security.

¶1402 Audit Rules

• *Rule No. 1—The audit starts before the auditor calls*

Audit survival results from planning and strategic thinking. Understand the auditor's concerns and anticipate the traps to be avoided and the questions which will be asked. Is a random statistical sample possible or should a block sample focus on a specific period when taxes were being paid correctly? What would be an acceptable sample population size? How should it be drawn? Are there any issues or items which would require stratification? What waivers should be signed for what period of time? If resale certificate files are not up-to-date, can they be updated before the audit?

A taxpayer should know where the "skeletons" are located. A pre-audit of those documents that will eventually be reviewed by the auditor should be performed on a regular and periodic basis. To survive an audit with the least damage, the taxpayer must be as smart as, or smarter than, the auditor, possess a silver tongue and gift of persuasion, or be lucky.

Auditors have time constraints and appreciate help in achieving a rapid completion of their audit assignment. The auditor will typically accept reasonable answers and workable approaches to getting the job done. If the taxpayer representative does not provide such assistance, the auditor must formulate an approach unassisted. Providing such educated direction can be helpful and productive. Advance planning and analysis make a taxpayer educated.

While an auditor may not be willing to agree with or accept the proposed audit plan one has "structured" in advance, such a proposal should be made. Similarly, the tax manager need not accept the proposed audit plan offered by the auditor; however, an alternative should be at hand representing a reasonable substitute approach. Arguing that a particular sampling technique is not allowable is often unsuccessful. Suggesting an alternative is a better strategy. Allowing the audit to be completed prior to asserting one's concern for the accuracy of an audit design is guaranteed to be rejected as a challenge if the design was originally agreed to by the auditor and the taxpayer. Once the auditor and taxpayer representative agreement on an audit plan, it should be committed to paper and signed by both parties if possible.

• Rule No. 2—Auditors are people too

Auditors are people with jobs who want to look good to their bosses, keep their jobs until retirement or until they take jobs elsewhere and, when treated with some degree of kindness, creativity, hospitality, respect and empathy, will often respond in kind. Auditors may be working for their jurisdictions because the work is challenging and always varied. The work may be a means of gaining valuable job experience or achieving economic freedom from parents, or a way of putting in time toward retirement. Most auditors are not heavily supervised and enjoy some degree of work "freedom." As long as a taxpayer representative remembers that an auditor is a person and not an enemy or adversary, per se, audits may be less stressful and anxiety-provoking. Mutual respect goes much further than shared hostility and abusive treatment. As with much of life, attitude plays a very big role in having a successful encounter with an auditor. Before the auditor arrives, consider personal attitudes, biases, hot buttons, etc.

• Rule No. 3—Keep the audit under control

Now that the auditor understands that help is on the way, be cautious not to do the auditor's work. In a "security" environment, the auditor should have a badge that indicates restricted access. The company telephone directory should not be made available nor should company personnel answer an auditor's questions directly. All requests for information and records should be channeled through the individual assigned to shepherd the audit. That staff member should be designated "audit coordinator," the liaison between the taxpayer and the jurisdiction.

All company employees should be notified that an auditor is going to be performing an audit at a given facility. An occasional story should be printed in the company newsletter explaining the scope of such an audit and the fact that casual conversation about company business with or around the auditor is not advisable. It should be made especially clear that the audit coordinator or liaison—not the auditor—is the individual to whom information should be given.

An auditor may request a tour of your facility to view its operation. The tour could be as formal as a gathering of managers to discuss all of the elements of production or as informal as a casual walk on the production floor. As with any interaction between an auditor and the taxpayer, contact should be controlled and planned. The phrase "loose lips sink ships" certainly applies to this situation. The taxpayer liaison should prepare all participants in such sessions with the advice to answer questions directly without volunteering information not requested. The ideal preparation for a plant tour is a dress rehearsal.

¶1402

If the audit is to be handled out of the tax area with less direct control over the daily comings and goings of the auditor, the affected organizations should be duly notified. A simple notification work sheet could be prepared describing:

> the jurisdiction, nature and scope of audit, period under review, scheduled dates for the audit, the name(s) of the auditor(s), and a brief explanation of what material should be given to the auditor without prior approval from a tax department representative.

A specific audit room, apart from other auditors (different jurisdiction auditors should not be provided access to each other on company premises), should be provided. These facilities should be spartan and simple. Great comfort encourages protracted engagements. A schedule of requested documents should be prepared by the auditor for review by the company tax representative. Only those documents requested should be pulled and presented to the auditor for review. The list of documents requested by the auditor should also be held as a reference for the audit for which it was presented as well as for use by company personnel in developing future internal audit parameters. Fishing expeditions are not an aspect of customary audit procedure. The auditor is expected to ask the questions. The taxpayer is only expected to answer the questions asked. Volunteering unrequested information is an invitation to possible trouble (of course, unless the disclosures relate to available credits not taken or given in the audit).

Finally, if the auditor is invited to attend the company Christmas party, department birthday or going-away parties, or to play with the softball team, the relationship has become too friendly. The audit has probably lasted too long and the auditor may be out of control.

• Rule No. 4—Be consistent in answering questions

Assume when an audit begins that both the auditor and the taxpayer are on a level playing field. Each action by either party produces a reaction by the other party. As long as the give and take of the audit continues on a mature and adult plane, both the auditor and taxpayer can expect to get an audit that is representative of the auditor's level of competence. As soon as either party in this relationship acts in a manner which causes loss of confidence, mistrust or questioned integrity, the relationship is damaged.

It is for this reason that the police inspector's statement, "The facts, only the facts," is particularly apropos. As a creative and imaginative individual, one may discover, and perhaps enjoy, "post-visualization" of what may have occurred at some time in the past. However, a bad story only tends to smell worse with age. If the answer to a question lacks certainty, choose the option of seeking out the answer and reporting back to the auditor rather than imagining what may have happened. The first time the auditor discovers an explanation is really a story will be the last time any explanation will be fully credible.

If a statement is made that is subsequently discovered to have been made in error, be willing to eat humble pie for the benefit of possible future reliability. And of course, if a post-visualization explanation is the most reasonable method of dispatching a question, be consistent with the explanation every time the question is asked. Few things can jeopardize the relationship between the auditor and taxpayer as much as a lack of confidence that an answer or the source of an answer is believable.

• Rule No. 5—Remember the audit diet

It is easier to keep it off than to get it off. As the auditor proceeds through the various steps of the audit, schedules are prepared representing the questioned items. If the answer to an auditor's inquiry is not satisfactory, the questioned items are placed on the audit schedule to be assessed unless the taxpayer is able to explain why the items were erroneously scheduled. Many states require that a written explanation be provided by the auditor for removing an assessable issue from an audit worksheet. In fact, auditors are often required to use ink, not pencil, on schedules, and will often fight to preserve the integrity of a completed schedule to avoid the hassle of justifying changes or corrections. For this reason, it is better to explain why an item should not be scheduled rather than convince the auditor to remove an item from a completed schedule. This point should reinforce the taxpayer's resolve in controlling the audit.

• Rule No. 6—Follow the prescribed remedies

A taxpayer's right to due process will be lost if the prescribed administrative remedies are not followed. (See ¶704 for a chart on Taxpayer Remedies by state.) The remedies begin with the injunction "to register and pay taxes timely." In the context of the audit, the taxpayer has obligations and remedies which should be followed.

(1) Advance the audit with reasonable dispatch. There is little advantage to stalling an audit once it has been scheduled and commenced. To the contrary, it is more often in the taxpayer's best interest to bring the audit to a prompt conclusion. Time is the auditor's ally. Time to think is time to assess. And the interest meter is running on an assessment while the clock ticks. It is rare that a taxing jurisdiction's interest rate on unpaid taxes is lower than a taxpayer's own cost of money.

(2) Request a complete set of the auditor's schedules including the "audit notes." As a licensed taxpayer, your records held by the jurisdiction should be made available upon written request. Each audit schedule should be provided by the auditor along with a clear and precise statement explaining how the schedules were developed. Auditors are generally required to provide a written narrative explaining how the taxpayer's records were reviewed. These notes are a useful tool for the taxpayer in developing strategic thinking on challenging the audit and looking for issues to appeal. Further, this written narrative may be used in correcting the systematic deficiencies which caused an assessment.

(3) Take advantage of all hearing levels. Where a taxpayer disagrees with the findings of an audit, a *timely* request for a hearing should be filed in writing. Each hearing or appeal level should be visited—in sequence— during the course of settling an audit in dispute. The discretion to

accept a taxpayer's explanation for a proposed assessment is given to each succeeding member of the administrative structure in a specific order.

Taken out of order, the rights of appeal can be lost. "Petition for redetermination," "statement of grounds," "request to be heard," "claim for adjustment or refund," etc., are phrases used by various jurisdictions to name procedures by which one requests a hearing or movement to another level in the appeals process. Beyond being heard by an administrative law judge, a member of legal counsel's staff, or a senior tax representative, one is entitled to a hearing by the taxing board or commission. And finally, with no other choice, proceed to courts.

• Rule No. 7—Negotiate

There are auditors who say they will never negotiate a proposed assessment. There are taxpayers who will not believe that an auditor can possibly possess a level of intelligence higher than two points above plant life. To every rule there is an exception. Auditors will negotiate and are not nearly as dumb as they may act. Many auditors adhere to the Lt. Columbo (the television investigator) method of inquiry. Ask as many questions as possible in a disarmingly simplistic manner, seasoned with a pinch of seeming forgetfulness, and answers will appear from where they are least expected. This technique can prove remarkably successful. If a taxpayer never offers to trade credits for liabilities in a casual manner, the auditor will not know that there is room for some give and take.

One should assume that auditors are expected to produce "x" dollars in tax collections as a result of "y" audit hours. Well thought-out "help" provided by the taxpayer, especially in a very long and complex audit appearing to produce a low tax dollar yield, may be an excellent first step in the negotiation process. However, remember, the tone set at the beginning of an audit will carry throughout every audit phase. Cordial, but firm, cooperation should produce a good negotiating climate. The goal is to end the audit with the smallest liability or largest credit.

This author and many other tax professionals believe there is nothing wrong with agreeing on parts of an assessment and making one's tax payment (usually with interest) as soon as possible. It is advisable to stop the interest meter from running, considering the exorbitant rate of interest charged by most jurisdictions. Paying accepted liabilities should have no impact on disputed issues that one intends to take through the appeal process.

Fewer tax professionals agree on paying the tax (and interest) on disputed assessments. If this is done, care must be given to confirm that the jurisdiction will refund overassessed tax (with interest at the same rate) should an appeal be successful.

Making payments "on account" should be done with extreme care. Such payments should be identified in writing as relating to specific issues. A taxpayer making such a payment may have it applied to tax due that is beyond the statute of limitations. The tax codes and ordinances may be written with the intent to protect jurisdictional interests at the expense of the unwary taxpayer. This forces the taxpayer to fight by using knowledge. Courts rarely support ignorance.

Finally, in many states, there are collections personnel whose sole responsibility it is to collect taxes (interest and penalties) which have been assessed and billed. It is possible to negotiate a payment schedule for large assessments, the lump-sum payment of which could irreparably damage the financial well-being of the taxpayer.

• Rule No. 8—Get help

There is great satisfaction in being able to manage and challenge an audit, successfully. However, it takes added courage to acknowledge that a totally objective outside set of eyes will likely view your company and its operation (from a sales/use tax standpoint) differently than a company employee, and, in so doing, will see opportunities and problems which may not be noticeable to an insider. A sales tax consultant familiar with the industry of which your company is a part may have some special insight borne out of viewing your competitors' tax procedures. As taxes are not normally a competitive issue, this expertise, which may be purchased, is well worth the cost. There is pride and wisdom in recognizing one's own limitations identifying when it pays to bring in qualified expert help. To have an assessment reduced at a cost of some percentage of the reduction (a typical fee structure for such consulting work) is better than paying the full assessment, even after factoring in the consultant's fees.

• Rule No. 9—Taxpayers must request credits

Compliance audits are supposed to look with objective eyes at the taxpayer's books and records. In theory, auditors are expected by their agencies to schedule taxpayer error, giving as much attention to credits as liabilities. The issue is "what is the correct amount of tax that should have been reported." However, in reality, auditors focus their greatest effort on identifying and scheduling understatement, rather than overstatement, of tax. Oceanfront property in Nebraska is available to be purchased by those that believe to the contrary.

In other words, taxpayers that believe they have overpaid taxes should prepare and present, to the auditor, schedules covering those overpayments for inclusion in the audit. If the auditor is willing to do the scheduling, taxpayers should cooperate.

On the other hand, it is not always an audit that identifies the overpayments. Internal auditing by internal auditors trained in sales and use tax issues, tax department random audits, annual certified audit examinations by CPAs trained in sales and use tax issues and reviews by contract tax specialists are all ways to locate tax opportunities. At times, it is best to "hide" such credits until such time as they can be used to offset liabilities scheduled in an audit. The decision to "hide" credits for use in offsetting audit liabilities should be weighed carefully against the cost of money and the jurisdiction's policy on granting credit interest. Often credit interest is not allowed for taxpayer sloppiness. Therefore, hiding credits is an issue of cash flow. Whatever one's choice on whether to hide or file for credits, one should not forget to file a protective claim for refund to keep a statute open for refunds.

¶1403 Managed Audits

As indicated at ¶302, managed audits are becoming an increasingly popular tool that taxing authorities use for large taxpayers for a couple of reasons. First, the states want to reduce their need to perform large audits repetitively. These audits can last for an entire open statutory period, involve several thousand hours of auditor time, and have minimal net tax impact. The option is to have sophisticated taxpayers perform audits for the state in exchange for possible benefits (reduced interest, penalty abatements, etc.). In so doing, the state enters into an agreement with a taxpayer, describing the manner in which the audit will be executed. The taxpayer performs most or all of the activities previously performed by the state agents. The state agent then reviews the audit findings and the taxpayer or state settles up.

Second, when performed on a direct pay permit taxpayer, this type of audit is often paired with the establishment of reporting tax on the basis of a computed percentage of taxable purchases, rather than reporting tax on a transaction-by-transaction basis. In this manner, the taxpayer and state agree to a reporting rate and also review the rate used (if one were previously established) for the period covered by the audit. This is known as a "rate true up." Once the rate has been recomputed, the taxpayer is granted permission to use the rate for a continuing period.

On the surface, the process of developing and implementing a rate for reporting, often using statistical sampling, provides the taxpayer a level of efficiency and accuracy that might not have existed when tax was reported on a transaction-by-transaction basis. However, developing such a rate or series of rates is not a matter to be taken lightly. A sampling project, performed casually, may provide efficiency in reporting with a higher effective tax rate. We have all learned that politicians and governmental bureaucrats can use statistics to prove whatever point they wish to make. Statistics can be both science and art, not to be placed in the hands of rank amateurs unless you want rank results.

¶1404 Conclusion

In the final analysis, the tax professional must carefully juggle many audits, protests and hearings, watch the tolling of statutes and expiration of waivers. He or she must come to grips with the issue of whether action or inaction is predicated on fear—fear of the known or unknown, fear of criticism, or fear of job loss resulting from poor judgment or the failure to adequately plan or strategize. Management by fear is not widely regarded in scholarly literature or real-life business as a recommended technique for running all or part of a business. This author does not recommend this technique, either.

Chapter XV

Automation Opportunities for Sales/ Use Tax

¶1501 Introduction

A very good friend, and the general manager of my previously owned consulting company, once said that he would give me his first-born son and a large sum of money if I could demonstrate how a business decision was not ultimately a question of money or time, and, therefore, ultimately money. While I had little use for his son (as I have my own), the money would have been beneficial and I accepted the intellectual challenge of the question and have not yet offered him an alternative answer.

In the sales/use tax environment, the decision to engage bits and bytes, "mips" (million instructions per second) and "megs" (megabytes) and all other forms of high technology is no less a matter of time or money. If one wants to save time in preparing returns in order to have more time to handle audits or prepare manuals, the price of data processing (automation) equipment and software should be weighed against the cost of additional personnel. However, in the short term, the time to become efficient in data processing may appear to adversely impact the anticipated savings from automation. The big picture purpose of applying automation to tax department functions should be threefold: increase accuracy, reduce the time required to accomplish tasks, and provide a greater opportunity to provide value in performing services not previously or optimally performed.

In assessing the need for implementing automation solutions in the sales tax environment, one has to consider both the cost and also the complexity of the solution. Often, a software development issue may originate outside of the tax department, with its conclusion directly impacting tax issues. For example, reporting sales tax in a retail business is ultimately an issue of cash register data accumulation. If data is not accumulated through an electronic check-out system, it is likely that the data processing solution is first an issue of data accumulation related to sales and, perhaps, inventory control. Only after the data have been captured does it become an issue of processing the data through taxability matrices created for the product lines sold and rates in various jurisdictions. Unfortunately, the decision to bring automation to the check-out function is normally driven by inventory planning and control or sales/marketing, not by the sales tax department.

As with so many issues in sales tax, automation is a matter of looking at several functional areas and determining how each can be moved into the twenty-first century. Some tax departments may never have breached the twentieth century but no matter. The time and opportunity are upon us. The needs of retailing are slightly different from those of wholesale distribution, which are different from manufacturing, which are different from "consumption" businesses (such as governmental entities, hospitals, contractors, etc.). Accordingly, in this chapter we will look at various automation opportunities that can reduce the time dedicated to crunching numbers and gathering data manually. If time is money, then reducing time in accomplishing tasks should decrease personnel costs and yield increases in profitability. However, if keeping or adding head count is important to a tax department manager, then, in the long run, automation should be avoided.

¶1502 Automating Sales/Use Tax Collection—Retail

In the retail environment (with the exception of Louisiana), inventory is purchased on a resale basis (free of tax). It is held for resale, demonstration or display without tax becoming due until a sale is made at retail to an end user. Four questions must be asked when determining the taxability of the sale:

(1) Is the measure of the transaction excluded from tax based on an exemption of some type (e.g., a prescription medicine for treatment of a human being, food for human consumption, repair labor, etc.)?

(2) Is the customer purchasing the property exempt from tax with regard to its purchases (e.g., a governmental entity, an instrumentality of the federal government, a not-for-profit hospital, etc.)?

(3) Is the transaction exempt from tax by its nature (e.g., a sale in interstate commerce)?

(4) Has the customer asked for, and is he or she entitled to, an exemption from tax (e.g., resale, direct pay, etc.)?

Of course, there is little universality in the way states and localities view these questions, nor is the list of questions all-inclusive. The questions are only a sample of issues for purposes of discussion.

First, the issue of taxability itself can be programmed. More than one vendor offers "canned" programs that tax sales through a system of customized product taxability tables. It is only necessary for the user to define the parameters of taxation, integrate the software into the existing data processing system and let the computer accumulate data. With the latest software solutions come "bolt-on" modules that first recognize taxability using tax decision modules, secondly attribute a taxing jurisdiction by examining the ship-to address, and thirdly provide a rate down to the local taxing level. The same vendors offering the bolt-on modules offer very complete services for updating tax rates on a regular basis. With periodic maintenance related to rate changes, the system operates with little difficulty.

As with most instances of incorporating new software into an existing environment, the largest task is the initial conversion from either an existing system or from a manual operation into an automated environment. Unfortunately, most software and hardware firms do not assist their prospective clients in understanding these hidden costs, thus generating client dissatisfaction because of unforeseen cost overruns. However, it is valuable to remember that, if the entire company is making a conversion, the tax department may get the items on its wish list provided under the company-wide software conversion budget. A word of caution and advice is in order. One must be vocal about one's wish list. If management does not understand the importance of the tax department's needs, then someone else will supply the wrong solution.

Given the proper product taxability, the data collection system must capture the tax collected cumulatively. The likely disposition of the tax collection data will be a general ledger account possibly titled "accrued sales tax," representing that which is being held for eventual payment to the states (and localities) with the periodic tax returns. Ideally, tax should be accumulated into sub-accounts coded to reflect the state, the locality and the respective rates for each. The end result should be a direct data dump into a return preparation spreadsheet. More sophisticated systems are required for sellers having complex taxability issues in multiple states. These systems are now fully integrated with scanned images of tax return forms and cumulative recordkeeping.

In our dot-com world, we have concerns over reporting tax on sales over the Internet. Brick-and-mortar companies have elected to operate in the electronic commerce environment and, in so doing, are required to collect tax based on rules that are both poorly defined and hard to decipher. The idealized solution for the electronic commerce taxpayer is to have the transaction taxed at the time it is entered. That is, every sale is completed and the "shopping basket" filled only after the seller's software queries for the purchase ship-to address, determines the jurisdiction, identifies the rate, computes the tax on the proper taxable measure, and adds the tax to the transaction. This is all done while the Internet purchaser is awaiting the sales total, before supplying a credit or debit card number to clinch the deal. A well-designed system will then provide summary reports for sales purposes, tax reports for tax purposes, inventory reports for inventory purposes, etc. The amount and quality of the data is the capitalist's tool to grow sales and tune the business.

¶1503 Automating Sales Tax Data Collection—Wholesale Distribution

There is a single glaring difference between the data processing needs of the direct retailer and the wholesale distributor. For the latter, the emphasis must be placed on certificate tracking, though the wholesaler's advance tax (in some states) will still be an issue similar to the sales tax issue for retailers. For the retailer, a limited number of sales transactions may be for resale or statutorily exempt, and certificates must support omitting tax on a customer's invoice or register receipt. On the other hand, the wholesale distributor who fails to effectively manage certificates may be liable for tax on all transactions (representing the bulk of sales) for which certificates are absent or in error.

Certificate tracking data processing is ideally integrated into the order-taking process. This type of program should be on-line, allowing the order taker to confirm the presence or absence of the appropriate certificate at the time an order is taken. A good system will offer:

1. immediate production of the correct certificates for mailing to, and completion by, the customer;

2. validation of the certificate's wording;

3. cross reference to multiple ship-to locations for the same customer; and

4. a method for scanning and cataloguing customer certificates.

Perhaps less obvious to most, but a natural time saver, the system should also provide for storage and retrieval of completed certificates along with a re-mail notification module for updating the certificate file. A certificate data processing program is essentially a dressed-up database product. As with other tax software, there are few such products currently available from tax product vendors.

¶1504 Automating Use Tax Payment—Accounts Payable Systems

Some of the least developed data processing products are found in the accounts payable/use tax environment. The fully automated application would involve recognizing the source location of property purchased, the destination of property received, the taxability of the purchase, the accrual of the correct tax (based on the rate in the receipt state, plus applicable destination or origin local tax) and, for those companies so requiring, the tax paid to the vendor. Much of this analysis can be greatly simplified by forcing the chart of accounts to recognize taxability as an issue. For example, in most states materials used for shipping products to customers could be charged to a nontaxable account, whereas materials used for shipping products within the company could be charged to a taxable account. By designating the former account as nontaxable and the latter account as taxable, one can accomplish such an objective. This does, of course, require accurate use of the chart of accounts.

As with many tax issues, the driving force for automating the accounts payable system is not normally the tax department. The decision to automate accounts payable is associated with the need for information related to cash management, general ledger interfacing, and liability accruals. It is only this last issue that brings the tax department into the discussion. Because the driving force for these changes is often accounting personnel, accounting industry software tends to ignore sales and use tax issues in favor of focusing on the accountant's concerns. As with sales tax reporting and collecting software, tax software vendors have created bolt-on solutions in the accounts payable environment as well. By creating a tax decision module that looks for a characterization of a purchase's taxability, the system is able to make accruals on an automated basis. There are, however, significant issues to be addressed:

1. How does one group purchases for taxability?

2. What happens with transactions covered by corporate procurement cards?

3. How will the tax decision module be populated with the required information?

4. What happens with special situations, such as construction contracts?

5. How will the system address electronic purchases with (EDI) and without (ERS) electronic invoices?

In the non-automated environment, i.e., the company in which there is no automated matching in the system for orders placed and property and invoices received, the task involves properly charging the department making the purchase with use tax and capturing that accrued use tax in the "accrued use tax" account. Many companies follow an excellent and simple manual procedure:

(1) Increase the amount of the taxable measure by the amount of the tax and charge the full amount to the required account [1];

(2) Post the added use tax to the tax accrual account for eventual payment to the jurisdiction(s) [2];

(3) Pay the net amount to the vendor through the accounts payable system, thereby crediting cash [3].

Example (to demonstrate accounting entries):

Taxable purchase value:	$1,000
Applicable tax rate:	5%
Account being charged:	8544 (general operating supplies)
Use tax accrual account:	2155

	dr	cr	
8544	1,050		[1]
2155		(50)	[2]
Cash		1,000	[3]

Some companies elect to expense the tax to a tax expense account rather than (as in the above example) to the purchase expense account. Either approach accomplishes the accrual in a manner that allows for simple general ledger tracking. With capital purchases, the contra-entry for the tax accrual is booked to the capital account rather than a sales tax expense account.

As with sales tax, separation of the major account into sub-accounts by state, locality and rate will greatly simplify reporting. For example, if tax had been charged by the vendor at the correct state rate, ignoring the local tax, the local tax could be charged (as above) to a sub-account such as 2155.5, meaning local tax at 0.5% rate only.

• *Tracking tax activity*

Additionally, some taxpayers want to track the total sales or use tax on purchases and have accounts payable personnel separately enter the amount of any tax paid to the vendor. This activity might be particularly important in a construction company or other firm that co-mingles resale and non-resale property. There are some benefits to such a procedure:

(1) The tax cost incurred by the company can be considered when planning for additional expansion. It may be to the company's advantage to favor expansion in a state offering some tax exemptions. Without

¶1504

knowledge of the taxes paid, the consideration of the tax expense relative to other issues would be made in a vacuum.

(2) Tracking tax activity can substantially simplify future compliance audits. The auditor is able to look at reporting by a single distribution account rather than viewing all invoices (or even a sample of invoices).

#45

(3) Tracking tax activity can also enhance the internal auditing process, both for the tax department and for general internal auditing. It becomes terribly obvious, and the basis for additional intramural training, when over-accruals are being made by a single clerk processing documents for given letters of the alphabet or specific types of transactions.

(4) When tax payment and accrual data has been captured in an easy-to-access system, answering inquiries from vendors under audit (wishing to know if a customer company has self-declared either sales or use tax on a nontaxed purchase) is greatly facilitated. There is little question that increased compliance audit activity by taxing agencies will result in an ever-increasing volume of such inquiry letters. Those companies capturing all types of such data will reduce their file research time substantially. This is especially true in companies filing documents by voucher or check number, rather than vendor name or number sequence, or for companies that must send documents off-site for archival storage.

• *Contingent sales tax liability accounts*

Finally, there are some companies that have set up a "contingent sales tax liability account" where seller's privilege sales tax liability was not billed by an in-state seller on a taxable purchase and it is anticipated that the seller may, at a later date, request the tax reimbursement. By using a separate account and tracking the activity through the automated accounts payable distribution reporting process, researching vendor inquiries is, again, greatly facilitated.

Ostensibly, the company purchasing property on which tax is not billed is demonstrating a very high level of financial accuracy by recognizing the potential tax expense (and the contingent balance sheet liability) in the period that the transaction occurs rather than waiting for the vendor's invoice for the unbilled tax. On a regular cycle approximating the outlawing of succeeding statutes of limitations, the contingent sales tax liability is reversed, benefiting the profit and loss statement. There is little doubt that automating the accounts payable use (or sales) tax activity is a valuable, albeit major, step in increasing data processing capabilities. It is also one of the more difficult steps unless there is strong cooperation between purchasing, accounts payable and the tax departments. One should not forget a cardinal rule of managing people:

People cooperate more and demonstrate greater care in performing their jobs when they have participated in making decisions that affect their work.

¶1504

¶1505 Automating the Tax Department

• *Return preparation*

Perhaps the greatest strides in automation in sales/use tax have come in return preparation. While numerous large companies, with their extensive information services departments, have developed custom mainframe software applications to meet their specific needs, even the smallest taxpayers are now automating with simple personal computer tools such as spreadsheet, database manager, and mainframe down-load programs. The most elaborate systems produce (by laser printers) facsimiles of state and local tax forms with all lines completed. The tax manager merely needs to sign the document prior to affixing the tax payment and sending the return on its way. Less sophisticated programs are mere automated number crunchers—still a far cry from paper and pencil technology. However, with these simple solutions, the programs are used to perform computations with manual entry of the resultant data onto the state-provided form itself.

While all such forms of automation, from the elaborate to the simple, are probably (or should be) contributing to tax department efficiency, they tend to have a single major flaw. Too often these programs are designed to gather data; however, little effort is exerted to test the validity of the assumptions underlying the data being collected. For example, does the purchasing department clearly understand what may and may not be bought for resale? Do the accounts payable clerks understand how to determine whether a purchase is subject to sales or use tax, or whether a local tax does or does not apply to a given transaction? Is the general ledger clerk following accrual instructions for booking use tax on self-consumed property purchased for resale without recognizing that the property in question is being purchased tax-paid?

Currently, there are no fewer than five major vendors offering tax return preparation programs. Various secondary suppliers selling to specific industries have programs which, after some refinements and customization, are able to achieve various levels of success in moving closer to an automated tax return. In nearly all cases, these programs are run in conjunction with tax rate software (discussed at ¶1502, above).

• *Compliance auditing*

A second type of automation in the tax department is being encouraged by jurisdictions using customized programs for compliance auditing. In an effort to pre-audit in advance of a scheduled compliance audit, tax managers are developing or using commercial auditing programs that largely simulate the activities of the jurisdiction audit. These programs will randomly select invoices for review from a universe of all transactions in a hypothetical audit period. These programs have not received wide use and are viewed with some skepticism by most tax professionals. A second reason these programs have not become widely used is financial. Tax departments tend to pick the short funding straw.

However, some tax departments are aggressively pursuing states that will accept statistical sampling audits performed by the taxpayer. These "managed audits" are tremendous time savers for tax departments using sampling software to select audit populations. Unfortunately, in the hands of tax managers lacking good statistical sampling skills, these programs are ill advised. See comments at ¶1403 under "Managed Audits."

• *Automated direct pay permit accrual*

A third type of automation used in the tax department is a corollary to the automated audit and accounts payable accrual programs: the automated direct pay permit accrual program, also known as rate studies or formula use tax reporting. The objective of such a program is to self-assess use tax based on a combination of ratios and selected accounts to which property is charged. While it is more timely to tie the accrual to the purchase invoice payment process, it may be more accurate to effect the accrual on a monthly or periodic basis when the general ledger and trial balance are run by the data processing department. The methodology for establishing the direct pay permit accrual is set by the state.

The program, if tied to purchase invoice payment, applies a ratio (developed and tested through some internal or external audit process) to amounts charged to particular accounts when the invoice voucher is processed for payment. The use tax is automatically added to the designated expense account while the tax is posted to the use tax accrual account. When tied to purchase invoice payment, all or part of the invoice can be charged with an accrual and the resulting report becomes the source document for future compliance audits. The impact of such a program is very similar to the results of the automated accounts payable system program for regular accruals.

The direct pay permit automated program tied to general ledger activity also applies a ratio to designated transactions identified by type, class or account within the general ledger. This would include accruals on transfers into accounts reflecting self-consumption of purchased property, constructed property, etc. The effect of this program is similar to that desired for booking use tax accruals on any general ledger account. However, this approach is only practical for those statistical universes for which the state would accept percentage reporting, not typically for very large or capital purchase transactions.

Finally, as more states use technology to analyze transaction populations in order to design acceptable statistical sample tests, tax managers will, of necessity, become more knowledgeable about the uses and benefits of the same tools. Many customized programs will be developed nationally, and some specialty software vendors will attempt to find and fill a market niche. However, indications are that most automation in sales tax will be limited to large concerns with substantial resources and staffs or small concerns using personal, customized computer-based software products. Forays into the sales tax market by consumer-oriented software developers have met with little market acceptance and have been largely discontinued.

¶1505

If recreating the wheel is not in the best interest of American business profitability, and if sales tax is really a noncompetitive issue, tax managers should make a greater effort to collaborate on software solutions. Within given industries are common problems. Sharing or selling the resource power should not be overlooked as a viable option for tax department management. Perhaps the tax department can become a profit center.

¶1506 Modern Technology Solutions

In the last several years, a number of software companies, old and new, have been moving their tax reporting from the 20th to the 21st century. In the 20th century in an enterprise-wide accounting package, complex matrices were established to address taxability issues for collecting and reporting sales and use tax. In a typical environment, each time a transaction surfaced in a given environment, the software would make an exit to a bolt-on package containing taxability information. If the transaction was determined to be taxable, this characteristic was returned to the enterprise software to be used in computing the correct tax due on the transactions based on various issues associated with whether the transaction involved a sale or a purchase. The tax information would then be recorded in the enterprise software for eventual reporting.

In the 21st century, not only is this activity linked to an intranet (accessible from anywhere in the world and requiring only one instance of the tax application), but it tends to be driven by rules established by the tax department and act on data rather than based on hard-coded matrices. These new age software products also address other transaction taxes, including but not limited to value-added taxes for any country in the world, but also contain certificate management tracking as well. To say we have the one multi-vitamin pill to solve all problems in sales/use taxation would be to oversimplify the situation. However, the web-based software solutions are powerful and desire serious consideration by medium and large taxpayers in search of automation. The best news is that a well-implemented solution will save time, increase accuracy in reporting and offer remarkable flexibility as a business grows and/or changes.

¶1507 Some Final Thoughts About Automation

Technology is a wonderful tool. It can make life appear easier, less "manual." Is manual always an incorrect choice? Let's consider a technology idea and a couple of non-technology alternatives. The idea is the tax manual (to be covered in greater depth in Chapter XVII).

We are in the information age. Company personnel need information at their fingertips to make good decisions. Whether those needing information are salespeople writing proposals, material managers disposing of old assets for resale or to end users, accounting personnel making journal entries, etc., a common concern of the tax department is the tax implications of these various activities. The automation solution might be an on-line intranet or local area network application allowing these individuals to find answers to common questions in a computerized database. A second alternative solution for providing information is an 8 x 10 (or whatever size is required) matrix of information, printed on paper and laminated with clear plastic. Be sure to provide a grease pencil for note taking. A third alternative solution is the traditional tax manual or binder. Which solution will be most widely and regularly used? Will less computer literate individuals who need information be resistant to a technology solution?

If we had the ability to measure worker access to the technology solution, (and we do in web-based solutions), we might discover an initial flurry of "hits" on our electronic tax consulting systems. After a while, utilization would appear to be sporadic or nil. Can one conclude that lack of use means lack of interest or that everyone has all of the answers they needed, wanted, but never openly sought? Is the same true of the manual that gathers dust on a workstation shelf or the laminated card that sits in someone's desk drawer? How does one measure the real benefit of an automation solution? Which costs more to create, a plastic laminated piece of paper with a simple matrix of rules to follow, a binder containing many pages of information, or a fully integrated, on-line, custom computer application? One doesn't need to be a rocket scientist to answer this question. Said another way, do not let technology give you useless and inappropriate solutions. Find the proper solution for the internal customer and the situation.

Chapter XVI
Tax Returns and Their Preparation

¶1601 Introduction

Assuming that a taxpayer accurately reports its sales, purchases and self-consumption of tax-free property on its tax return, over time the state will develop a fairly accurate transactional picture of that company. By grouping companies by industry type or classification of business, a state's commercial environment becomes a secondary image projected from the aggregate of the tax return data. The use of this data to formulate fiscal policy and legislative initiative is no secret to any observer of government. Simply, tax returns provide a regular and periodic method for a state (or other jurisdiction) to track the tax-related activities of taxpayers and, therefore, industries, localities, economic health of business, etc.

The information contained in a return is also invaluable to the state for establishing statistical images of what to expect in taxable sales reporting within a given industry. If few things in the world are new or different, then two businesses with similar product lines, markets, pricing structures, and selling methods should offer a basis for drawing conclusions, assumptions or expectations about such types of business. For example, one fast-food chain with a typical menu containing breakfast, lunch, dinner and snack fare and similar pricing structures can be expected to have about the same taxable sales in a given 24-hour period as any other comparable chain. Obviously, there will be differences based on location, clientele, community demographics, etc.

Auditors are often armed with these statistics when performing audits of similar establishments. This information is derived first and foremost from tax returns and, second, from actual audit confirmation. With this in mind, one is able to recognize the second way states benefit from return data. Compliance audits are the test to see that what is reported as taxable and the taxes remitted are a fair representation of a taxpayer's type and class of business. In other words, every tax return submission contributes to a large statistical database as well as reflecting a company's own business activities. The purposes of this chapter are to identify first, the types of information customarily reported on a return; second, the changing scene in the tax reporting and payment environment; and third, the various methods of handling the return preparation task.

¶1602 Returns

In Chapter XIII, we considered the documentation required to support an audit. Chapter XV presented opportunities to use data processing technology in gathering and presenting documentary data, information that becomes part of a company's historical file. Essentially, the information content of the tax return is depicted in detail in the support documentation and captured in bits and bytes in the taxpayer's computer. The return simply summarizes the data for gross reporting and record keeping purposes.

• *Form, function and timing*

Each state has adopted a return format that addresses the issues of taxation in the very broadest sense. Returns are sent to the taxpayer with ample time to allow the responsible manager to gather the data for a complete accounting period, close the books, and report and pay the tax collected and/or due. In deference to the uniqueness of businesses and their activity cycles, some tax agencies will tailor the return due date schedule to the company. Blank returns are issued and due dates adjusted to allow the taxpayer to include an entire accounting period on a return. The most common example relates to businesses with 4-4-5 (13 month) fiscal periods. The period ending dates and return due dates coincide with a calendar provided annually by the company.

Most lines on the return itself are for the taxpayer to establish the basis for any tax. Other lines further refine the data for purposes of local reporting requirements, actual computation of tax amounts, administrative fact gathering and transmittal. With the ever-tightening governmental financial crisis, jurisdictions are doing everything in their power to speed up the tax collection process. For example, certain jurisdictions have implemented prepayment or advanced payment requirements, mid-period reporting provisions, electronic funds transfer (EFT) payment procedures and electronic data interchange (EDI) protocols. More information on the last two issues appears later in this chapter.

Whether information returns are required to be prepared and submitted weekly, monthly, bi-monthly, quarterly, semi-annually, annually, or on a customized schedule, one can be assured the tax itself will be due at least as frequently. Never assume that the return due date is always concurrent with the tax due date. These two dates may be very different. Along with the task of remembering when taxes versus returns are due, there is the issue of the location to which they should be sent. Local taxes in home rule jurisdictions have reporting and payment requirements that are different than those of the state. Payment of tax to an improper jurisdiction does not mean a liability has been extinguished. Nor should one assume that the wrong jurisdiction will determine where the tax should have been sent and forward it. Auditing the general ledger tax account to confirm that all taxes were paid to someone in a given period will not suffice in determining if the proper party received both the return and the tax.

• *The how of reporting*

The second important variable on returns is the way the tax is reported. Paragraph 403 contained a discussion of accrual versus cash basis accounting. The issue is whether the activity being identified (sale, purchase, manufacture, etc.) is recognized at the time of its occurrence or at some later date. Whichever recording methodology is required (accrual or cash basis), it must be followed for purposes of tax reporting and payment.

The how of reporting also includes the issue of whether a jurisdiction specifies that return entries reflect the transaction plus the tax or just the measure of the tax. As with recording methodology, mixing types of entries (gross receipt or free of tax transaction) should not be done. Remember, states are very specific about whether sales tax can be absorbed. When allowed, if tax were included in the selling price, the customer must be so notified. The seller must indicate "price includes tax" if intending to "back the tax out of the sales price" by dividing by 1+ tax rate. The three common situations are displayed below.

Example: (to demonstrate reporting approach computations)

	Tax Added	Tax Incl.	Hawaii
Sales price of property	100.00	100.00	100.00
Add tax at 5%	5.00		5.00
Gross Receipts	105.00	100.00	105.00
Divide by 1+ tax rate		1.05	
Tax reported @ 5%	5.00	4.76	5.25
Measure of tax for the return	100.00	95.24	105.00

The above example makes it clear how the measure of tax for the return is very different when the tax is included in the sales price of property. Errors in properly reporting the taxable measure can result in a taxpayer being assessed tax on tax.

It is important to note that the state of Hawaii, for one, actually collects tax on tax by making the gross receipts subject to tax even though tax is already included in gross receipts. This usually results in the taxpayer collecting $5.00 from the customer at the time of sale and suffering a loss on the $0.25, for which the seller is not reimbursed.

• *The what of reporting*

Virtually all returns start with a line for entering sales, often followed by a second line for free of tax purchases subject to use tax. Do not forget that use tax is not only due and reported on out-of-state importation and use, but also for conversion of exempt property to a taxable use. When these two lines (sales and use tax) are added, the sum comes close to the income tax term of "taxable gross." To drive home this point, most jurisdictions require the taxpayer to provide copies of recent income tax returns corresponding to the periods of the sales and use tax audit. The auditor will verify that there is no disparity between what was reported as gross income and the amount of gross receipts. Any differences will have to be explained as (for example) uncollectible accounts, exempt sales, resales, etc.

Lines for these differences are the next most common on the returns: the deduction, exemption, and exclusion lines. These lines result in a reduction in the gross receipts subject to tax. Some common reductions to be reported on these lines include (but are not limited to):

(1) sales to the U.S. Government,

(2) sales in interstate commerce,

(3) sales of exempt property,

(4) sales to exempt customers,

(5) sales for resale,

¶1602

(6) discounts allowed on purchases, and

(7) uncollectible accounts written off.

A special line on some returns is used to reconcile maximum taxes collectible or due. A few jurisdictions have limitations on the total tax due on a given purchase or sale, piece of equipment, singular location, or other factor. However, do not assume that a line will be provided for this. This computation may be recorded only in the taxpayer's work papers but must be subject to auditability.

Generally, jurisdictions want a taxpayer to report all sales, taxable or not. This requirement helps increase the wealth of data used (and occasionally, abused) by tax administrators, legislators, lobbyists, etc., to prove a point or "gore the other guy's ox." The last line in this part of the return might be the net taxable measure line—the difference between total sales, or gross receipts plus amounts subject to use tax, and amounts excludable or deductible. Some jurisdictions provide the back of the return for listing and computing net taxable measure.

In states where local taxes are reported to and collected by the state, the return may provide for computing these taxes. The actual computation and allocation of the local tax amounts may be handled on the back of the state return or on an entirely separate form for concurrent submission. Other types of entries may be required where different types of tax are reported on one return, e.g., the Washington Business & Occupations tax is reported on the sales and use (excise) tax return.

The remainder of the data lines on the return will be used for:

(1) computing late payment interest and/or penalties,

(2) identifying prepayments posted to the tax collector earlier in a tax period, and

(3) adjusting for overpayments from earlier in the current tax period (but usually not on prior returns).

These lines require careful attention. The amounts recognized on these lines are deviations from what was collected or computed to be paid and held in the general ledger tax accrual account. It is the general ledger tax accrual account that is compared to the tax return data when the auditor performs a reconciliation of the general ledger account to the tax return, a standard part of most sales/use tax audits.

One additional computational line exists on some returns. This line is used to compute the vendor tax collection discount or fee—the amount a state allows the taxpayer for the cost of collecting the tax. The good news is that this fee is still available in some states. The bad news is that it is an easy target for elimination when a state's budget is looking lean on revenue.

The final two steps to complete the return are the signing and dating of the return by the authorized manager or representative and the posting of the return to the proper governmental agency. Until recently, these elements were very simple manual activities—sign on the dotted line, please. Some tax departments

¶1602

always use "return receipt" cards. Others use overnight mail or courier services. Both approaches provide for a delivery receipt though verification of the contents of the envelope or parcel is virtually impossible. However, with the advent of budget crises and advancing technologies, both the simplicity and vagaries of mail delivery have been replaced by electronic funds transfer (EFT) and electronic data interchange (EDI).

• *EFT taxes and EDI returns*

#49   For the uninitiated, EFT refers to movement of money via a bank wire. No physical instrument changes hands. Electronic impulses make entries in two accounts, moving funds directly from the taxpayer's checking account to the tax collector's checking account. The use of EFT virtually guarantees that the payment is made timely and that a clear record of the transaction is created by the bank to evidence the activity. States are solving some budget short-fall issues by accelerating the date EFT payments are due, changing the threshold at which a taxpayer is required to use EFT, or both. This looks like a one-time benefit to the states, but each month the money gets there faster obviating the need for greater borrowing at whatever cost.

EDI, on the other hand, is the movement of information via wire. To facilitate the processing of returns, states are requiring more and more taxpayers to file returns electronically. A return received via computer modem all but eliminates clerical input requirements at the state and virtually guarantees the accurate recording of return data. With a good connection, clear telephone line and properly established protocols, EDI is an efficient filing method. The main disadvantage of this modern age return submission is the absence of a hard copy document—a situation that will "take some getting used to."

A final note on the subject of returns relates to the growing trend to automate the process of return preparation. Return work papers are being reduced to computer spreadsheets fed by mainframe computer data extraction programs that are all but fully automated. Cost cutting by layoffs and restructuring jobs throughout corporate America is reaching into tax compliance operations. Those who were the employees of mainstream businesses are increasingly becoming consultants who contract to manage the tax compliance function for those businesses. If tax professionals are to continue in the employment of business, higher visibility and demonstrated value-added management will be required. Just getting the job done will not suffice. Technology in tax compliance has proved to be both a blessing and a curse.

Chapter XVII

The Art of Tax "Manualship" and Training

¶1701 Tax Manuals

Tax manuals are tools for taxpayers. The tax manual receiving the greatest distribution or having the most thorough presentation is not always most effective. The best manual is one that is fully accessible to the employee's needs and is used. In this context, accessibility is not an issue of physical location but one of user comfort. Does the employee feel comfortable seeking the answer to a question by using the manual or is the manual large, complex, difficult to understand and personally unapproachable? Is the material presented in a logical and easy-to-read manner?

Over the years, many tax professionals who have had the time have created manuals that were tombstones to their corporate existence and rarely opened by the employees needing to use them. Some companies even have departments that dispense written procedures like so many pills in a pharmacy. Each page in the manual is prepared in the same cryptic form, encapsulating the content and reading like instructions for building a model airplane or making a perfect souffle. Unfortunately, the relevant sections of such manuals, for those that truly need them, fail to consider the user's level of comprehension, time available to use the resource, or ability to craft the correct question to extract the needed answer from so much verbiage.

To create the truly effective manual, one needs to consider the user. Will the manual be referred to regularly or only for exceptional transactions? Does the user need to understand the reasoning for the answer or just the answer? Can the answer be presented in a manner that facilitates reference—a quick glance or the flip of a chart? Can the material be presented graphically, attractively, and with a feel, form and design to encourage its use? Can the information be placed in a location that virtually challenges the user to ignore it?

To answer these questions and appreciate the art of "manualship," which is really the job of information dissemination, let's consider places of information use and user needs. Focused user-oriented materials should not be presented to all users. That material which is peculiar to a given department should be presented to that department only. However, the tax department should have a complete version of all materials placed in the hands of field personnel. It is not only acceptable, but preferable, that few other departments should ever see the entire document. Following are considerations for customizing manual material to user needs.

• Purchasing and accounts payable

The purchasing buyer tends to be a fairly sophisticated individual, having some technical knowledge of the company's products, production methods, inventory and operational needs. In the purchasing department that prepares and issues purchase orders and (sometimes) certificates, the personnel must know when property used in a given manner meets the exemption conditions of the tax code. Purchasing people are accustomed to looking at catalogues and directories and calling suppliers to place orders. Purchasing information is commonly found on note cards, in traveling requisitions or in data processing systems. Buyers are always harried—the order was due to arrive yesterday and it is already tomorrow.

Processing invoices is a tedious activity often given to personnel on the bottom of the company pay scale. These clerks may not be brain surgeons but learn to be very effective in moving paper. From a sales and use tax viewpoint, they are concerned with whether the purchaser properly coded the order or if tax should be paid as invoiced or accrued and paid to the state. The accounts payable clerk's time is truly precious since job productivity is often measured in documents processed per day (or other period).

For personnel in both of these departments, easy reference flip charts, single-page matrices, and slide rules or data wheels are excellent formats used to relate tax information. When planning the form of presentation it is advisable to involve the user in defining the tools that will be most readily used. For example, if personnel are always looking at computer monitors, offer the possibility of data presented in a background file or pull-down menu on the computer. If charts of account or accounting cost centers describe property use, adjust these account numbers to reflect tax status.

• *Customer checkout and sales order entry/invoice processing*

Both of these departments are active in giving customers immediate feedback to sales and product issues—helping the customer complete the purchase order which becomes the written contract for delivery of property. In the retail world, either the sales clerk is required to decide the taxability of the sale at the time the transaction is being completed or the cash register automatically handles the tax status and tax charge on the receipt. Where the clerk must make a decision at the point of sale, tax information may be imparted on simple checkout counter-based flip charts, matrix guides or other simple hand-held transaction locator devices (slide rules, flip charts, data wheels, etc.).

In the commercial sales environment, sales order entry personnel are performing an order processing function either on a computer screen or in standard form. Taxability should be a function of several factors: customer-provided certification of resale, exemption, direct pay, etc., or the correct tax status for the item being sold or service being rendered. And in the absence of a valid certificate or certain tax exempt status of the product, the order is processed as taxable. For consideration of certificates, microcomputer database management systems can give rapid access to important and useful information with cheat cards and matrices available to lead the order taker through the proper set of tax questions.

¶1701

• *Tax department and general ledger personnel*

Previously, it was noted that one of Murphy's many laws provides that (paraphrased) documentation requested under audit is always missing, misfiled or stored in incorrectly labeled boxes, or was prepared by a capable employee who understood the issues, is no longer employed by the company and has dropped out of sight. Tax instructions for personnel in these departments, again, need not be more thorough than the individual's actual requirements, yet should be designed to reflect the true impact of the transaction or accounting entry. Often such employees can best relate to the presentation of sample data rather than merely an instruction of what to do. However, one of the most important considerations is the manner in which the individuals are trained to complete the entries required of their job.

Individuals who are given (receive) instructions without understanding the sources of the relevant data will find the work boring and produce output that reflects boredom. Regardless of the simplicity of the matter, help the individuals to be conscious about their activity in order to gain commitment to the work's accuracy and timeliness. When all of the instructions, charts, programs, etc., have been developed and placed in use, the tax professional must not only guarantee that user information will be updated as needed, that a master manual will capture the details of the various systems and tools in use throughout the company, that documentation will indicate when changes to procedures occur, but also that intra-mural training will be provided on a regular basis. Well-meaning employees carrying out incorrect procedures and giving erroneous tax information are a liability to the company. They are a responsibility of the tax professional.

At ¶1506, it was suggested that an intranet tax manual is an exciting alternative to paper in binders or laminated instructional material or matrices. The concept of an intranet manual is becoming easier to fathom and design as companies are becoming more electronically linked. There are many software database tools and search engines allowing one to create a rapid reference program. Such a program can be accessed on all employee personal computers through a wide area network (WAN) or local area network (LAN). As an alternative to an intranet solution, one can establish a secured-access Internet solution. The programs are the same; the access is different.

Creation of such a tool requires selection of a software application, development of a design and structure, inclusion of a search engine, accessibility and facility for updating, and embellishment of information with interest-creating attractiveness. The more intuitive the structure of the material and the fewer key strokes the user makes to both enter the program and glean information therefrom, the greater the likelihood that it will be used by the intended target "customers." Use of a program that provides for nested "pull-down" menus adds to ease of use. For example, an electronic manual designed for use by a manufacturer might include pull-down menus referencing different manufacturing activities, assorted overhead and support activities, various products, categories of materials, etc.

¶1701

Another approach to the design of an information solution is the voiceless telephone. When employees have questions they simply type them out and submit them to the tax department via the company electronic messaging system. Every time the tax department responds to such an inquiry, the answer is placed in a searchable database. Over time, nearly all of the important questions will have been asked and answered. This type of electronic manual is truly customized to the needs of the user; however, it should probably be seeded with some of the obvious questions and answers.

Regardless of the approach one uses in sharing information with fellow workers, remember two simple rules:

(1) Any user who participates in the act of creating the tool gains the enthusiasm and commitment resulting from the "buy-in" process and will tend to use that tool in the job.

(2) Whatever solution is created to tackle the issue of information presentation, sophistication does not imply facility of use or accessibility to human minds; therefore, one should guard against complex solutions for remedial problems.

¶1702 Training

Again, that which is elaborate may give one great ego satisfaction while producing few real benefits. Training programs can be as simple as brief instructional seminars, as exotic as videotape or audio cassette instructions or as advanced as employees attending tax schools, conferences and symposia. Discussion seminars are an ideal method of accomplishing two goals: imparting your concern for, or satisfaction with, getting the job done and encouraging company personnel to share their questions and (mis)understandings about what they are (not) doing. Discussing tax concepts and how they relate to the workings of the company is a worthwhile investment in time.

The purpose of any training program is change. Accordingly, tax training seminars should have as their purpose a change in behavior:

(1) *increased awareness* of tax issues;

(2) *proper treatment* of use tax on nontaxed out-of-state purchases;

(3) *use of information* charts prepared by tax department personnel; and

(4) *reduction in the overall rate of error* related to tax transactions and issues.

Such training should include the use of real life sample documents, systems, procedures and issues. Keeping seminar training at an abstract level is unlikely to cause work habits to change. And ultimately, follow-up with feedback is as important to training as the training itself. A tax professional cannot hide his/her company behind a veil of ignorance or incompetence. Also, tax compliance auditors ignore the fact that a taxpayer has received training. If a company employee does not follow the trainer's instructions or if trainers fail to verify that the task assigned is being completed, unpaid tax will still be assessed regardless of intent. The taxable sale is still taxable; the tax will be assessed.

¶1702

As a supplement to training seminars and refresher classes or to provide field location training where tax-related functions are decentralized, some tax departments are considering the preparation and circulation of video cassette recordings or audio cassettes of basic training materials. These types of aids, used in conjunction with qualitative auditing or follow-up, should not replace interactive training classes. A library of such materials can effectively guide an individual through the basics of taxation but should not be used for instruction on actual procedures. Of course, with any material of this type, regular updating to ensure accuracy is imperative and may be the single most persuasive reason to avoid the cost of this media form.

One of the best training environments for personnel dealing with tax issues is the tax school, tax symposium or industry tax conference. In recent years, selected industries have created consortia to develop, share and discuss issues in taxation that are common to its members. The air transportation, telecommunications, leasing, direct marketing, manufacturing and retail industries have been very active. These groups offer not only formal and informal training and symposia, but frequently meet to discuss issues of common interest such as proposed changes in statutory provisions affecting tax policy, audit and assessment issues and court cases.

In addition to industry-related instructional and training programs, there are programs offered by professional associations such as the state CPA societies, associations of tax professionals (e.g., Institute for Professionals in Taxation, Tax Executive Institute, Committee on State Taxation, etc.) and bar associations' continuing education programs. While tending to be offered away from one's office, for a fee, such programs are an excellent way to gain access to one's professional peers—clearly one of the best ways to learn valuable tax concepts and techniques. While higher education has yet to embrace the field of sales and use taxation as a discipline justifying separate classes or course of study, some individual programs are offered on an occasional basis.

Finally, a tax professional should not view the task of training as one that only applies to others. Because the tax laws are ever changing, the process of education must continue. With the implied job security inherent in this dynamic field comes the added requirement to remain on the leading edge regarding tools of the trade and the issues which are the boon and bane of one's professional existence.

Chapter XVIII
Tax Research

¶1801 Introduction

At some point in the experience of every budding tax professional is the moment of truth. Someone within your company (or a client) asks a question and the answer is not readily available in the recesses of your mind. It is not simply a matter of saying, "Follow these instructions." The question is a new issue, to your knowledge, never before broached. The answer is certainly available from some source, but which one? The following process is divided into five steps:

Step 1 — Find the issue
Step 2 — Frame the question
Step 3 — Select and employ the preferred research tool
Step 4 — Test the conclusion or answer
Step 5 — Reduce the answer to a simple instruction

¶1802 Step 1—Find the Issue

There is a series of activities in step one which precedes any other action in researching the questioned matter: *listen* carefully to the question; *ask* questions to gain additional insight and a clear frame of reference wherein the issue arises; *listen* to the answers provided by the questioner looking for any special words which lend clarity to the issue; *repeat* the question back to the questioner; and *confirm* that what you heard was what the questioner meant.

¶1803 Step 2—Frame the Question

Step two involves determining the true nature of the issue. For example, consider these questions:

(1) What kind of tax is at issue?

(2) Is the issue related to reportable sales or merely the self-consumption of property not previously taxed?

(3) Is the customer in question really the taxpayer (party in action) or has that status been shifted?

(4) Are there different categories under which one can caption the issue?

It may be necessary to segment the issue into two or more smaller pieces which may be considered in an "if-then" format, for example,

(1) If the tax to be collected is sales tax, then which party is the seller, what type of tax is at issue and upon whom does the liability fall?

(2) If the property is self-consumed, (a) was the property merely held for demonstration or display prior to being resold or (b) was there constructive use prior to sale?

(3) If the tax was paid to the seller in error, then will the seller or the purchaser have the ability to claim the refund?

The beginning practitioner may consciously follow these first steps in the research process while the more experienced practitioner is likely to use these steps unconsciously. However, the end result should be a clearly framed question.

¶1804 Step 3—Select and Employ the Preferred Research Tool

After the question has been carefully framed, is understood and has been broken into its various parts, one can select the tool(s) for developing the answer. The tax professional has only to determine which source of information is best suited for assistance in solving a particular problem or question.

To begin with, here are eight different types of information sources, all of which are valid under given circumstances. Mention of any specific source is not meant to be an endorsement of that source, only a statement that it exists and is available to the practitioner. It is important, however, to understand how a source is to be used prior to employing it. Misuse will waste one's time.

• Call the jurisdiction

While this source of information is generally readily available and inexpensive to use, it is not always as dependable as one might expect. Individuals hired by jurisdictions to provide answers to questions are not always well trained. They probably lack specific knowledge of your industry and, most important, will give your question a verbal answer which should not be relied upon. Ideally, one should prepare a written request for advice from the taxing authority's officer for legal affairs or legal counsel. In some states, a written response from this individual may be relied upon (a fact which should be confirmed in the advice or opinion letter) for purposes of a future audit.

• Use taxpayers' networks

Everyone is part of many different sub-groups or networks. As a tax professional, one belongs to the networks consisting of (by example) all tax professionals, tax professionals from a specific industry, tax professionals doing business in a given state or multiple states, sales tax professionals, etc.

Many of these groups are organized, have meetings, offer instruction and training, publish written materials and have membership rosters for use by members. As with many other topics, there is little that is truly "new." Most questions have been asked and answered by others. It is a matter of determining who asked the question, comparing the situations to see if they are parallel, and confirming if one may rely on the conclusion reached by or for another.

The following are organizations which exist either to benefit those in the field of sales and use tax or to sell, solicit or share information:

(1) *Institute for Professionals in Taxation (IPT):* This is an association comprised of sales and property tax professionals from industry, not taxing authorities; it offers seminars, symposia, schools, a newsletter and a tax issues bank (for use by members).

(2) *Council on State Taxation (COST):* This is an organization related to the National Chambers of Commerce which offers a forum for taxpayers; it also offers some conferences and seminars.

(3) *American Bar Association (ABA) and American Institute of Certified Public Accountants (AICPA):* Both organizations are comprised of admitted members of their respective professions; they offer "continuing education" and some printed literature.

(4) *National Tax Association (NTA):* This is an association of educators, theorists, practitioners and representatives of taxing authorities, which develops issues and presents papers (in all taxes); it offers printed material and conferences.

(5) *Federation of Tax Administrators (FTA):* This is the main organization of jurisdictional tax representatives (and other interested parties) whose primary focus is on tax law administration and tax collection; it offers a good opportunity to listen to "the other side" either through attendance at programs or through reading its newsletter; it also offers excellent opportunities to meet key members of state staffs.

(6) *Various regional tax conferences:* These are local organizations interested in treating taxation issues in given geographical regions; they offer conferences and topical meetings.

(7) *Privately sponsored educational programs:* These include trade associations, professional organizations, institutions of higher learning, industry associations, publishers, taxing authorities and various others; they offer a broad range of meetings, conferences, symposia, written material, etc., typically for a fee.

• *Ask a qualified professional consultant*

Times will arise when outside assistance is not only advisable but necessary. Internal limitations, e.g., financial, personnel, time, and experience, may preclude successful completion of indicated projects. In today's tax environment there are an ever-increasing number of persons and organizations that are claiming to be "qualified tax professionals." Unfortunately, there are no standards by which the taxpayer seeking assistance can gauge the quality, ethics, proficiency or competence of these parties. And, as with any business opportunity, the chance to "make a buck" brings out opportunists willing and able to claim acts which are both remarkable and incredible.

The tax professional should not be reluctant to engage the services of truly ethical consultants, as these qualified practitioners can be extremely useful in a variety of circumstances. However, determining the competence of such parties is a separate issue altogether. Consider some of the following criteria on a "consultant's" selection checklist:

(1) Is the expert new to the field? Familiar with the industry? Certified or trained in sales and use tax specifically?

(2) Are references available and have they been contacted?

¶1804

(3) Are the services available responsive to company (client) needs?

(4) If there is a potential problem with the service of the consultant, what is the likelihood the consultant will be around in a year or through the closing of a statute to satisfy any questions raised by jurisdictions?

(5) In contingency fee contracts, are the fees conditioned on success in recovering overpaid taxes only, or overpayment recoveries plus future savings (the latter approach being exceedingly dangerous)?

(6) In fee for service contracts, is the job to be accomplished by the consultant clearly defined?

(7) Is there any question about the point at which fees (plus expenses) will be payable and upon what the fees are based?

Expert consultants, in addition to designated specialists, may be found in the public accounting and legal communities. Most of the "major" accounting firms now have a national practice specializing in sales and use tax. The depth of experience is not often prevalent at the local level. Similarly, most of the larger law firms in the major metropolitan areas provide legal advice in taxation. Some of these firms also have one or more partners who are knowledgeable and experienced in sales/use tax specifically. Unfortunately, in either profession's schooling, few, if any, courses include sales and use taxation. Accordingly, it may be ill advised to refer sales tax questions to general corporate counsel or a company's certified public accountant without determining the extent of the experience of those individuals.

• Find and review speciality monographs

All of the organizations listed at ¶1804, above, have published articles, monographs, survey results and papers on numerous sales and use tax subjects. Some of this material is free or discounted to members of the organizations. The content may not always be authoritative or quotable; however, every source has potential when preparing a position paper and is worth considering.

• Read the jurisdiction's code, regulations, rulings, annotations, commission or board minutes and information brochures

A situation described in the state's own literature is a much easier issue to argue with a compliance auditor than is a nonpublished example. Fortunately, most states publish not only their own laws and regulations (also called rules or advice), but also make other materials available at little or no cost. Most states publish rules or regulations that provide examples of how their law should be interpreted by taxpayers in a number of popular trades or professions, covering a majority of typical conditions and transactions. Never rely on one state's interpretation of another state's law.

• Use legal information and research products

Legal information about sales and use taxes is available through a number of private publishers and in a variety of formats, including print, CD, on-line, and Internet. Publishers that offer tax legislation, regulations, forms, judicial cases,

¶1804

administrative and letter rulings, explanations and analysis on a multistate basis for "one-stop information shopping" are often the most efficient services. For example, **CCH** INCORPORATED's State Tax Reporters provide comprehensive, ongoing coverage of state tax issues, including sales and use taxes for all states. Their products are typically available as subscription services with continual updating, and they are published in print, CD, online or Internet mediums. In addition, CCH offers condensed, specialized versions of its information in products such as the MULTISTATE SALES TAX GUIDE (state-by-state summaries of sales tax laws with topical charts) and the *Sales Tax Alert* newsletter.

A clear trend in legal and tax research is the growing demand for electronic media—CD, on-line, and Internet—to house all the relevant information. Tax research on electronic media can be intimidating to researchers who are more familiar with traditional print products; however, the convenience and expediency offered by electronic formats simply cannot be matched by paper publications. Moreover, most publishers have made their electronic products much more intuitive and easier to use during recent years. To illustrate the capabilities of electronic research, consider the following example. Assume you wanted to research every state on the topic of whether your use of the Internet for solicitation of book orders created a taxable nexus for the state's imposition of sales tax. Using CCH's Internet product, the Tax Research Network, you would simply:

— Log in: Using your user identification and password (encryption is available for enhanced security)

— Select the State tab on the first screen

— Click on "Select All" for all State Tax Reporters

— Select the Power Search button

— Select the desired tax type (Sales and Use)

— Enter a search phrase, such as: nexus and Internet. (This search would capture documents that used both terms: nexus and Internet. Singular and plural forms of the terms would automatically be included and lower/upper case distinctions are ignored. In addition, CCH's legal thesaurus would enhance your search so that, for example, all legal equivalents of the term "nexus" would be included in the search, e.g., "doing business," "minimum contacts," "link" and "connection.")

— Execute the search by clicking on the Search button.

The resulting document list would include a search of CCH's fifty-one (D.C. included) state tax reporters for relevant explanations, annotations, cases, laws, regulations, and other official information (e.g., administrative rulings, comptroller decisions, MTC bulletins, etc.). Viewing any particular document is as simple as a mouse click on that document. A user-friendly tool bar on each screen allows you to easily alter your search, initiate new searches, navigate and locate prior searches, printout document lists or source documents, search by citation, and other helpful options.

¶1804

Due to the growing accessibility and usefulness of the Internet, researchers should also explore state government homepages, where relevant department of revenue information is sometimes available for no charge. In addition, several Internet sites contain directories of tax information providers, with links to beneficial sites. For instance, the Tax and Accounting Sites Directory (http://www.taxsites.com) supplies links to state government tax cites, tax software and forms, accounting articles, academic resources, private publishers, tax service directories, on-line tax preparation, and accounting and tax associations. In particular, association and government organization homepages are often good starting points for identifying current tax trends and key government or association personnel. (See Federation of Tax Administrators (www.taxadmin.org), Multistate Tax Commission (www.mtc.gov), Institute for Professionals in Taxation (www.ipt.org) or the American Institute of Certified Public Accountants (www.aicpa.org).

• *Read the relevant cases*

Ultimately, it is the courts that interpret the laws when taxpayers and taxing agencies are unable to settle disputes. In Chapter X, "Nexus and Commerce Clause Issues," one may gain a brief appreciation for the types of issues that have reached the federal courts addressing matters pertinent to the U.S. Constitution. There is a similar body of cases at the state court level that have interpreted state law; however, some states have minimal litigation.

One does not have to be an attorney to read and benefit from court cases. It is, again, a matter of understanding how a case is organized and how it should be read to gain insights from these writings.

(1) Each case has a plaintiff or petitioner, the party that seeks a remedy or judgment against the other (the defendant). If the first case in a series of appeals has the taxpayer suing the state for a refund (the most common occurrence), the taxpayer is the plaintiff and the state the defendant. If the taxpayer prevails at the first court level and the state appeals the verdict to the next court, the labels for the parties are changed. The state becomes the appellant and the taxpayer the appellee. These designations will flip-flop back and forth through the appeals process.

(2) At the beginning of every case there is a synopsis which, in brief, tells the findings of the court. Often, there are keynotes that identify the most important issues of law that were considered. The text of the case follows with an exposition of the facts followed by the arguments presented by the parties. The court discusses the merits of the arguments, frequently citing other cases as precedents, concluding with an opinion. Where the case is heard by several jurists, a majority opinion cites the points of law and reasoning that brought the court to reach its decision. A concurring opinion agrees with the majority on the result but not the reasoning in reaching the result. A dissenting opinion is rendered where one or more of the jurists disagree with the finding of the majority.

¶1804

(3) It is important to review the other cases cited in a given case as they are likely to help clarify or demonstrate a particular concept or point of law. As such, that case which has set a precedent, e.g., *Complete Auto Transit, Inc. v. Brady*, 430 US 274 (1977) and the four-prong interstate commerce test, is considered a landmark case serving as a basis for many other decisions.

(4) Learn to analyze a case simply and cleanly—read, extract and write. What are the issues and the remedies being sought by the plaintiff or appellant? What are the facts of the case? What are the main points of law at issue? How did the court find?

Once a trained tax practitioner, though lacking a law degree, uses a court case to extract an answer to a question, the fear of law may all but disappear. This is not to suggest that attorneys are not useful or necessary. In some states, only those admitted to the bar may handle a hearing, as issues not addressed at the earliest hearing levels cannot always be entered in subsequent appeals. Certainly, one should always (and may be required to) retain counsel for appeals. Remember, counsel is only as good as the information provided by the party retaining counsel.

¶1805 Step 4—Test the Conclusion or Answer

The issue is reduced to clear and concise question(s). Everyone agrees on the framing of the question(s). All appropriate research sources have been used with the general conclusion taking form. However, prior to implementing the conclusion, one should test to see if the conclusion, action or inaction, is reasonable, has a material financial impact which is cost justified, can be implemented in a timely and methodic fashion given the tools available or which can be developed, and is not contrary to company policy.

¶1806 Step 5—Reduce the Answer to a Simple Written Instruction

The final step in the process for which tax research was performed is likely to be an action or a policy producing an action. Whichever the outcome, a simple written procedure or instruction should be prepared and presented to those who need to know. The form of the notification should follow company standards. The notice or instruction should be clear, concise and, perhaps, above all, dated. The bane of a tax department is actions without consistency and undocumented procedures. In the final analysis, the compliance auditor will probably want to know why and when. If the answers to these questions are always very explicit, assessments will be realistic, if there is an assessment at all.

Chapter XIX
Record Retention

¶1901 Introduction

Company policies regarding record retention may not meet the needs of the tax department, in general, and the sales and use tax function in particular. In fact, one may find that, in reviewing record retention practices of a sampling of companies, there is likely to be a direct reverse correlation between the quality of this activity and the size of sales/use tax audit assessments. This conclusion should not surprise a seasoned tax professional. One's ability to dispose of a "questioned" item on an audit schedule is invariably tied to the issue of documentation. If the requisite paper work can be found, the question can usually be answered in the taxpayer's favor.

One of the most important benefits derived from rigorous record retention is the general discipline implicit in a thoughtfully planned and well-executed system. There are many methods of cataloguing archived records, all of which have arguable benefits. Documents and storage boxes may be numbered and logged in a manual or automated system. Companies with micrographic record-keeping have probably created several different indices to allow "rapid" location of a sought-after transaction. But, ultimately, knowing where to look for a needed document, and knowing that it is there, is what is important.

(1) Correspondence may be retained in date sequence within an alphabetical filing system.

(2) Accounts payable files are normally stored in vendor number, vendor-alpha, voucher or check number sequence, in groupings of a year at a time.

(3) Purchasing records are likely to be filed by purchase order number and, perhaps, by vendor as well.

(4) Sales records and invoices are often filed by sales order number and cross-filed by customer and, therein, by invoice number or date. In larger companies, filing may be by billing unit, marketing group, or any of a number of other ways designed to frustrate the sales tax professional.

(5) Shipping and receiving records may be logged by date.

(6) Sales tax exemption certificates for customers and permits issued by the company itself, if filed at all, may be filed in one of several functional systems.

(7) Closed audits, tax returns, data processing documents, research projects, internal memoranda, and other pertinent documents are probably kept in the tax manager's desk until he/she resigns or is terminated, or the files outgrow the space provided for filing (in which case a transfer box is filled and sent to storage).

The best record retention system is one that is designed to accommodate search and recovery activities. When one understands what may need to be recovered, the logic of how it is stored should be self-evident. If one's company has a "manager of records retention" or "company archivist" or "records librarian," it is desirable to work closely with that individual. A trained archivist should be able to translate sales tax department needs into a functional system. Therefore, the first step in designing a functional record retention system is understanding when stored records may require access. Unfortunately, the sales tax professional may not have the final say in record storage policy.

¶1902 Accounts Payable and Fixed (Capital) Assets

There is one significant reason to access archived accounts payable ("a/p") records: to meet the needs of audits (internal or external, procedural or compliance). Since few audits are performed employing a 100 percent review of all documents in an open statutory or test period, planning for the inevitable statistical sample audit is an excellent idea. Some data should be maintained, accumulated on a current basis, and retained by a designated staff member:

(1) the quantity of checks issued per period (month, quarter, or year);

(2) the check numbers used during the period;

(3) the total value of the a/p checks issued;

(4) the complexion of a/p records (i.e., what types of transactions are paid by accounts payable—inventory, expendable supplies, capital assets, travel, taxes, and miscellaneous) and the dollar distribution to the various types of transactions.

Actual documents are probably placed in the archives by the accounting department. Regardless of the manner in which current records are filed and eventually boxed for storage, it is imperative that they be clearly labeled for easy identification. Copies of all asset purchase invoices should be kept in a separate file as most states perform 100 percent audits on these transactions. Notations concerning use tax accruals on all purchases should be made on, or kept with, the original file document. The ability to track such entries or notations, to either the general ledger or tax return back-up, is extremely important.

Purchase invoices should be retained for the term represented by the longest open statute of limitations which remains subject to audit. However, because a period has been audited does not mean the same documents may not be open to review at a future date. Of course, record retention requirements for other purposes may have more demanding standards than those prescribed by state and local sales tax laws. Therefore, the greatest retention period should be set by the most demanding standard.

¶1903 Purchasing

Sales/use tax audits will tend to rely on purchasing records only when a/p data is inadequate to substantiate a given allegation concerning the disposition of a purchase. Because most states have a minimum four-year statute of limitations on a written contract, purchasing records are often kept longer than most. The tax professional should understand how the records are maintained, the procedures used to gather the data comprising a typical order, and the rules followed by the purchasing department for issuance of an order.

If it is the responsibility of purchasing to determine the taxability of purchased material, access to and an understanding of the decision logic may be very important in dealing with an auditor. If the purchasing department issues current resale, direct pay and exemption certificates, the tax department staff must have a thorough knowledge of the files representing this correspondence. It is very easy for a vendor to mistake a unit resale certificate for a blanket resale certificate, thereby erroneously placing the customer's entire account on tax-free status. If such a decision is incorrect, the provider of the certificate wants to be able to readily locate the document copy that properly evidences the facts. The same condition applies to company responses to after-the-fact requests for certificates. The extreme importance of these documents suggests that a dual filing system may be appropriate—file once by vendor to whom the document was issued and once by date, chronologically.

¶1904 Sales Order and Invoice Files

A compliance audit of sales (tax and use tax) has as its sole purpose the verification that all taxable transactions resulted in the payment of the correct amount of tax to the jurisdiction. The customer's written statements concerning purchase taxability are strictly viewed in determining whether the seller has properly taxed a given transaction. Random statistical sampling techniques are replacing full detailed reviews and block samples as the audit procedure of choice. While large value sales invoices are often reviewed in detail, smaller, more frequent, transactions are nearly always sampled. Retail environments, where a sample may consist of several randomly selected days' cash register receipts, offer an extreme in sampling methods.

To guarantee that the proper records are retained in the "correct" order, consider either (a) how the auditor will get from the tax return to the raw data (customer invoices, register tapes, sales receipts, etc.) or (b) how the auditor will get from the raw data (reviewed under some sampling strategy) back to the original tax return entry. Designing the appropriate retention system for sales invoice records is simply a matter of developing and implementing a logical system for reconciling the preparation of the tax return itself. Whatever logic is dictated by the reconciliation process also dictates the preferred filing methodology.

For example, in a manual or automated system, every invoice should be discretely, if possible, serially numbered. If the return is prepared from sales journals, the invoices should be filed in the order of the sales journal evidencing a clear reference to the sales order file where the order information is retained (including the requisite certificates). It is immaterial which box contains needed documents provided there is a "road map" to get to the desired box.

With advances in technology, magnetic images of customer invoices will be retained in easily accessed databases. This will allow selection of any document by calling up one of a variety of record fields. Therefore, if an invoice is a record, one could select invoices to be reproduced based on customer number, ship-to location, date and tax status. Auditing is then reduced to verification testing without the need to physically view original documents.

¶1905 Shipping and Receiving

One of the forgotten areas of record retention concern, primarily for multi-state companies, is shipping and receiving. Delivery tickets, shipping instructions, bills of lading and way bills are all critical to proving shipment method, point of title passage, date and location of last possession, etc., of property sold or purchased in interstate (or inter-locality) commerce. Again, as with all other sales or purchase-related documentation, it is not necessary for extra copies to be kept in a variety of file locations. Just be certain the trail of access to a document is made obvious through a system of file location notation. If the sales invoice copy or data processing record is the centrally controlling document in the audit trail, all other records may have their own location, without duplication, providing the invoice *always* gives the needed reference to those documents.

¶1906 Certificate Files

Copies of certificates, issued to vendors, should be retained in the purchase order file (when unit certificate) or a general certificate file, probably alphabetically by vendor (when blanket certificate). These documents, including any special letters of clarification and responses to vendor audit inquiries, should be retained for the requisite number of years based on the state's rules concerning longevity of certificates. Some states require annual updating of certificates. In other states, the certificate is valid until rescinded.

Original unit certificates from customers should be filed with sales order files, with a copy of the certificate in a separate customer file. Blanket certificates may be filed in customer alphabetical or numerical order, by state, or by such method that best lends itself to rapid document retention by the tax professional. Again, with the advent of greater levels of automation, certificates can be filed in any random order provided each document is catalogued for easy location. Originals should always be maintained even if micrographic reproductions are made for daily accessibility.

¶1907 General Tax Department Records

There is no magic to archiving general department records except to say that retention periods should be adequately long and destruction instructions very clear. General correspondence with company personnel, state and local authorities, other tax professionals, and internal and external auditors should be maintained in a simple alphabetical system, by state, locality, company location, etc. Audit records should be maintained in separate files along with related appeals and copies of verification correspondence. Remember, certificates gathered under the pressure of an audit may also require filing in the certificate file.

Record retention is not difficult. Good record retention can be the difference between major assessments and minor inconveniences. In creating a system, think about the concerns of a compliance auditor. By so doing, one not only structures data for accessibility, but also recognizes the critical audit issues, a step towards liability reduction.

A final and very important record retention issue has become a cause of great concern for many tax managers. In Chapter XV, the issue of automation was discussed. Replacement of legacy software systems is both a problem and an opportunity. A major problem that must be recognized by every tax manager is the need to secure data for future audit review. In the past, this has not been as much of a problem because the system under which the data was archived would be available to give the data accessibility if and when it was needed. Y2K has come and gone and, we are still replacing entire systems and throwing out the software and hardware that support legacy system data. How will one respond to an auditor's request for a three-year data file if the data is inaccessible? What extraordinary costs will be required to deal with this problem? Does senior management understand this is not simply an insurance issue—will the data be available when it is needed? This is a statutory issue because most states require the data to be kept available (read accessible). Ultimately, will anyone who understood the old system be around to explain its contents (if it can be found and read) when the time comes to look at the old data?

As if that question does not give a tax manager heartburn, consider that, under client server distributed software solutions, data will be truly distributed. One may not simply say, "Give me a dump of the accounts payable file." That file may be in many separate pieces, depending on which departments own what pieces of the data puzzle. Taxpayers with SAP software are none too familiar with the problem of getting a programmer to write the variant that will collect data needed to compile a return or support an audit. As life gets simpler and more automated, we will be required to develop new foci. Record retention is no longer only a paper issue. With EDI (electronic data interchange) and ERS (evaluated receipts settlement), both paperless approaches to selling and purchasing, will come new issues of record retention.

Chapter XX

Answering Questions and Questioning Answers

¶2001 Introduction

In the operation of any business, there are many employees who will ask or be asked a variety of sales tax-related questions in the regular course of their activities. Often the questions asked, and the answers given, may appear entirely reasonable and acceptable. However, on closer examination, one will discover that further probing is necessary to protect the business from large avoidable assessments resulting from improper answers. The ways one asks and answers questions may be the difference between undesirable tax assessments and surprising and large tax savings. Accordingly, in this chapter several departments have been identified with sales/use tax activities followed by a discussion of some questions and answers that have a direct tax impact.

¶2002 Purchasing

• *Tax status and the purchase order*

Question: When placing an order, either verbally or in writing, is it necessary to indicate that the property being purchased is taxable?

Answer: While it is imperative to inform company accounts payable personnel that a purchase should be subject to tax, it is probably only necessary to indicate nontaxable purchases to the vendor.

Purchases of tangible personal property are presumed to be taxable while the taxability of services must be determined on a state-by-state basis. Exemptions should be noted on the purchase order accompanied by the appropriate certificate form. If the transaction is not taxable due to an exclusion, e.g., repair labor is excluded from taxable measure, the clause "nontaxable labor" should be in evidence on the purchase order.

The burden for either paying or collecting *sales* tax falls first on the seller. In seller privilege states, the sales tax liability falls solely on the seller and can only be passed to the purchaser contractually. In non-seller privilege states, the tax collection responsibility may be on the seller, but the payment responsibility will likely fall on the purchaser and, therefore, is not "solely on the seller."

However, if property is likely to be subject to use tax (out-of-state purchase), it is always advisable, for the benefit of the accounts payable department, to indicate the tax liability in the text of the purchase order itself. Some companies, using multi-part forms, will have the vendor's copy of the order printed with black-out scribble print in the tax extension area. This block-out technique places the responsibility for proper tax invoicing on the seller, leaving the purchaser's accounts payable department the verification task. The implied (and appropriate) relationship between accounts payable and purchasing departments places the responsibility for determining taxability with the order placing function—the buyer is more likely to understand the intended use of the product ordered—leaving the vendor invoice processing and verification activity with the paying function—accounts payable personnel normally match terms on a purchase order with the billing from the vendor. Also, accounting personnel will be more inclined towards challenging tax on an invoice if the account being charged is a "nontaxable" account.

• Tax status and confirmation of purchase orders

Question: Is it necessary or advisable to issue a confirming copy of the purchase order if the purchase is not taxable?

Answer: It is both necessary and advisable. States that accept purchase orders as evidence that sales are not taxable require a copy of the order in the seller's file as supporting documentation for selling property on an Free of-tax basis. However, there are a number of states that also require the purchaser to complete and submit a certificate along with the written order. In these situations, the order alone is inadequate documentation for the vendor.

• Wording the purchase order

Question: Do states require special wording on the purchase order for the seller to be reassured that the purchase is not taxable?

Answer: Use caution in both creating the purchase order form and completing it. Some states require special wording concerning resale, e.g., the phrase "for resale" must be present on the purchase order. The imprint of the seller's permit, resale certificate or direct pay permit number (in cases of direct pay) would be required on purchase orders where a separate certificate is not required. In the case of purchase orders issued for multiple states, a listing of the appropriate state numbers is required.

The words "exempt" and "nontaxable" or "not taxable" may be meaningless without an explanation. If tax is included in a price (in states not requiring separation), that fact must be spelled out on the purchase order, for the benefit of both the seller's and the purchaser's accounting departments, as well as proof during an audit.

• Certificates issued by purchasing

Question: Is it necessary for the purchaser to keep a copy of all certificates issued separate from the purchase order file?

Answer: As with any document issued to anyone, it is valuable to keep copies of certificates. There will be occasions when having a record of such a document issuance will be helpful. For example, some states require that new certificates be issued on a periodic basis. Having a certificate-issued file will facilitate review of re-issue deadlines. One's purpose in carefully monitoring certificate validity should be the removal of doubt in the mind of the vendor. Ultimately, paperwork that is kept current will result in fewer time-consuming inquiries for all concerned.

¶2002

• *Tax status and telephone purchase orders*

Question: When placing an order, the order taker asks the buyer, "Are you exempt?" What is the correct response to this question?

Answer: First, verbal representations by purchasers to sellers are not binding and are definitely not considered by state auditors who are auditing the seller for proper compliance. Therefore, whatever response a purchaser gives to the question is only as good as a written statement (a purchase order and/or certificate) confirming the verbal representation. The request for such a written confirmation is the seller's concern.

Second, the question may be an attempt by the seller to determine if the property is being purchased by or for an exempt entity (where the state statute provides for entity exemptions) or if the purchase is for resale or exempt for some statutory reason. An improperly asked or ambiguous question can place either the buyer or seller in a future liability situation as the answer will almost surely be used incorrectly.

• *Impact of shipping instructions on purchase order tax status*

Question: How will the routing of the property (ship-to instructions) impact the order and what should the buyer do to gain maximum advantage from such a situation?

Answer: There is little question that avoiding tax by having property shipped directly to a state offering an exemption is both good business and alert tax planning. If a company has its headquarters in a state without a machinery and equipment exemption and a plant in a state with such an exemption, it is foolish to land the equipment in the home state and trans-ship it to the plant in the second state. No state sales/use tax law taxes sales based on the purchaser's ordering location, though some local taxes are (and many business license, franchise, and other taxes may be) based on where the seller takes the order.

However, if property is shipped out of state, the seller should always (unless the transaction is not a sale) invoke the interstate commerce clause for the property origination state and must comply with the use tax law (if applicable) in the property destination state. One should be cautious not to confuse the concepts "shipped" and "destined." The former commonly refers to property transported by the seller, while the latter may involve a customer pick-up in the state of origin with the destination being another state. Of course, tax is likely to apply in the destination state.

• *Purchase orders with mixed tax status*

Question: What is the advisability of mixing, on a single order, taxable and nontaxable transactions?

Answer: It is often difficult or costly to make this separation as a purchaser. If placing a purchase order costs $75-$100, it is prudent to keep paper to a minimum and combine similarly taxed purchases on a single order, wherever possible. However, in some industries this policy would be difficult, if not

¶2002

impossible, to follow. It is crucial that tax status by line or item be an available option in the purchase order generating system. If orders can be separated between taxable and nontaxable purchases, both the seller's and purchaser's accounting personnel should have a simpler processing task. Notwithstanding, one should strive to meet the goal of not mixing taxable and nontaxable purchases on the same order.

• Sales of scrap property

Question: We have some scrap property to be salvaged. What are the tax issues, and how should such transactions be handled?

Answer: More often than not, disposition of scrap assets is left to purchasing or material management with little instruction other than to get top dollar for the property. Scrap property should be sold, or at least processed for sale, through the accounts receivable billing system just as customary commercial sales are handled. Invoicing should include sales tax to the extent of the state's definition of "sale."

If the property is (a) being purchased for resale, (b) a sale in interstate commerce, (c) sold to an exempt entity, or (d) not taxable for some other reason, the documentation in support of the pertinent claim must be attached to the sales package. Sales of scrap assets are always reviewed by compliance auditors, often in the analysis of the account dealing with profit and loss on the disposition of assets. Simply, any revenue hitting the "cash" or "receivables" accounts without some explanation why the transaction was neither taxable nor exempt will be regarded with suspicion by an auditor.

¶2003 Accounts Payable

• Purchase invoices with unbilled sales or use tax

Question: The vendor sends an invoice to the company requesting payment of previously unbilled sales tax. What is the correct action?

Answer: Regardless of the state, the *first* issue to resolve is whether the purchase is taxable. *Second,* if taxable, was tax accrued and paid directly to the state? *Third,* was the tax already paid to the vendor on a separate invoice? Often companies will provide follow-up tax billings and not necessarily tie the separate billing to the original transaction. Most auditors will not research such separate tax billings. *Fourth,* was the tax paid directly to the state under an assessment? Care should be used in qualifying what type of tax (sales or use) actually applied to the transaction. It is not necessary to substantiate that the actual purchase was assessed in a statistical sample audit, only that the period and type of activity would have been covered in the assessment. *Fifth,* if company policy is to add tax to all nontaxed invoices (a bad policy), separate research into the payment history will be required.

• Purchase invoices with improperly billed sales or use tax

Question: The vendor's invoice itemizes tax incorrectly. What is the appropriate response in accounts payable?

Answer: The recipient of the incorrectly prepared invoice should pay the invoice in full and prepare a debit memorandum to adjust for the overcharge. The debit memorandum form should be set up for easy completion (fill-ins) and should contain the information necessary to meet the permit requirements of the state in question.

If the company does not use a preprinted debit memorandum form, such a form should be developed, printed and used. It is both inadvisable and poor accounting procedure to simply deduct erroneously billed tax from the vendor's invoice, thereby making a short payment. The better procedure is to pay the invoice in full and concurrently process a debit memorandum to resolve the tax (or any other) error. If such an adjustment is made on a current basis, the state's only concern may be a timing issue regarding what tax was due, and when.

If, after an extended period of time, the purchaser notes that several paid invoices had been taxed in error, it is not fair to the vendor for the wronged purchaser to simply prepare a deduction to be taken against current open balances due the vendor. Nor is it correct to deduct the overcharges from the next return to be filed by the purchaser with the state. Many states require the party who collected the tax to file for the refund.

If the invoicing error is an undercharge of tax, the liability is best extinguished by accrual and payment of the correct additional tax due with the regular periodic tax return. Paying unbilled tax to a vendor may only guarantee that the vendor will have a bigger and better Christmas party, not that the liability will be properly extinguished.

• *Procurement cards*

Question: How should one handle procurement cards?

Answer: Procurement cards are company credit cards that typically assigned to designated managers who are authorized to make low-dollar-value purchases without a purchase order. The concept of the card is to reduce the cost of purchasing by eliminating low-dollar, high-volume purchasing activity. Cards may be associated with cost centers or types of acceptable purchases. The holder of the card is normally liable for the purchase that is reimbursed or actually paid by the company. The issue is use tax—how does one know if use tax should be accrued and paid on a procurement card transaction?

Most companies either:

(1) report tax on a percentage basis based on a study,

(2) accrue tax on all purchases assuming no tax was paid, or

(3) accrue no use tax assuming all purchases are tax paid.

Each approach has its shortcomings. All approaches require document retention (of all vendor invoices, not simply the credit card receipts), which is an ugly task at best. Although card issuers are attempting to provide greater information on their statements, their own systems leave much to be desired as the merchants must provide pass-through information and frequently do not. Perhaps some of the most successful programs restrict the purchasing activity of the card holders, establish structured procedures, and require that complete documentation be forwarded for imaging and/or archiving. Before "signing off" on the design and implementation of a procurement card program, the tax manager should be very thoughtful and thorough in research and planning. Few tax managers are fortunate enough to participate in program design let alone have time to determine the ideal structure of the program to minimize exposure.

In the direct pay permit taxpayer environment, the issue of the procurement card can be more easily handled if the taxpayer is on a rate reporting methodology. When establishing the rate, one should ideally evaluate some number of transactions associated with procurement cards and incorporate this information into the reporting percentage. Consider all of the possible combinations. Was the transaction taxable and tax paid at the correct rate? Was the transaction exempt and taxed in error? Was the transaction taxable and not taxed?

• On-line purchasing activities

Question: How should on-line purchasing activities be addressed, either at the purchasing or accounts payable level?

Answer: There are many types of purchasing that no longer involve purchase orders. We have moved from warehoused expense supplies to on-line malls. When the vendor of stationery supplies receives an electronic request to fulfill (complete delivery of) a shopping list of 20 items for various departments, it is likely that the vendor will bill the tax. However, it is also possible that no tax will be billed, and the transaction is potentially subject to a tax owed by the purchaser. In this situation, it is probably appropriate for tax management to engage the vendor in a discussion of how sales and use tax issues should and will be handled. Without "traditional" documents and processes, alternatives must be consciously developed and implemented. One cannot leave the proper settlement of a tax liability that is electronic in nature to chance.

¶2004 Accounts Receivable and Billing

• Short payment of tax on customer remittances

Question: What does one do when a customer short pays or entirely omits payment of sales tax billed on an invoice?

Answer: Unless the customer provides the proper documentation, e.g., resale certificate, direct pay permit, exemption certificate, resale or exempt purchase order, the unpaid tax should be regarded as a balance due and placed in the normal collection procedure. When adjustments to the sales tax account are made reflecting short or nonpayment of tax, it is critical that a written explanation be placed in the sales tax work papers for the period of the adjustment. Remember, unreconciled differences in the sales tax account are almost always the basis for an automatic assessment.

• Customer requests for tax refunds

Question: How does one handle a customer's claim for tax refunds involving multiple periods?

Answer: First, if the periods are closed due to the tolling of the statute of limitations, the claimed refund (for the periods beyond the statute) should not be allowed unless the seller is willing to suffer the cost of the refund without state reimbursement. The issue of foregoing reimbursement from the state under any customer claim is probably best decided by the sales and marketing department (and could be charged to sales expense).

Second, if: (a) the period has already been closed due to an audit, (b) the period is not beyond the allowable statute of limitations, and (c) the jurisdiction does not prohibit re-opening of an audited period, the seller should file a claim for refund with the state. A deduction from a current return which relates to a closed statutory period will probably result in an assessment during the next audit.

Third, if the period covered by the customer's claim is part of the open statute of limitations and has not been audited, the seller (a) may deduct the refund from the current liability in some states, (b) must file amended returns in other states in order to recover the refunded tax, or (c) must actually file a claim for refund in the balance of states (in some cases, on a specific form). Merely making a deduction from a current return without authorization can cause a liability in the current period offset by a credit in a closed period with the net impact being an assessment of interest for the timing difference.

Fourth, if the refunds requested are in a current period, the refund should be processed immediately resulting in an adjustment on the current return. However, when making such a refund on a current return, one must be sure to correct the measure upon which the tax is reported to the full extent of the adjustment, i.e., if the refund measure is $1,000 and the tax $50, be sure to reduce the current reportable measure by $1,000, not $50.

In any event, any claim or request for an adjustment should be handled promptly, either through an immediate reduction in the current tax liability or through processing of the proper request with the state. Timeliness preserves the refund for the customer (to the extent that the period is not outside of the statute) and assures the seller of reimbursement for the tax being refunded.

• *Errors in sales order processing*

Question: The sales order entry department discovers that a customer was improperly coded in the order processing system as nontaxable, i.e., the customer account was set up as a resale account in error. What action should be taken?

Answer: There are two approaches to this problem: cautious and deliberate. Using the former approach, notify the sales and marketing department of the scope of the problem. Confirm that billing the customer will not create a serious problem with the customer relationship. Ask that the sales-person calling on the customer account assist in identifying the proper customer contact with whom to broach the issue and carefully present the request for unbilled tax in a personal visit (if the amount is significant) or in writing.

¶2004

The deliberate approach involves simple and direct correspondence stating: tax should have been billed and was omitted in error; there is no apparent basis for not taxing the transaction(s) in question; in order to properly extinguish the liability for the tax we have attached this separate tax-only invoice; unless appropriate and complete exemption documentation is provided in lieu of the tax owed, a tax payment, in the amount noted on the enclosed invoices, is expected in fifteen (or however many) days.

This list of questions and answers can be expanded to cover every possible situation in all 6,500-plus state and local agencies. This author can only begin to stimulate the imagination with some of the numerous possibilities. Questions and answers are the material from which manuals are made. Each question results in a procedure for someone within the company who is required to handle the issue. The tax professional's exercise involves writing the questions and procedures based on the questions asked and the answers to be given. The wording in the preceding examples can be used to address a myriad of related problems having many of the same answers. A new term has evolved in the World Wide Web environment—FAQ or frequently asked question. If you enable a tax information system for your employees to access over the company Intranet, you should give them the FAQs and the answers and make sure you date and sign what you do. Take pride in your work and make currency (timeliness) both a high priority and visible.

Chapter XXI
Some Final Taxing Issues

¶2101 Introduction

There are several random issues that should be addressed, though not in great depth. They are issues that: (1) offer the tax professional slightly more challenge than the daily fare of sales and use tax, or (2) make little or no rational sense and, therefore, merit some mention and discussion. The issues include:

(1) third-party drop shipments,

(2) third-party refunds,

(3) purchasing and leasing companies

(4) interest on assessments, but not refunds, and

(5) statutes of limitations for refunds and assessments.

As with many other tax issues, the tax professional may not perceive relevance for his or her company, yet there is a strong likelihood that one or more of the issues will surface at some time in a tax professional's career.

¶2102 Third-Party Drop Shipments

The Bermuda Triangle of sales and use tax is third-party drop shipments. Such transactions involve at least three separate parties and two separate sales. Significant confusion is added to these transactions when all parties are in different states. The following chart portrays one typical third-party transaction.

Company I		Company II
	sales invoice →	
Located in State A		Located in State B
Registered in State A	← Payment	Registered in State B
Nexus in C		No Nexus in A or C
		sales
property	↑	invoice
↓	$$$	↓
	Company III	
→	Located in State C	←

In this and most other third-party drop shipment transactions, the issue relates to documentation. For example, will State C accept a resale (or other) certificate from Company II in State B related to the shipment by Company I in State A to Company III in State C? State C takes the position with Company I that a sale has occurred and seeks sales or use tax from Company I for its sale to Company III in State C. Because Company II has no nexus in State C, it is unable to present the necessary State C resale certificate to relieve Company I of its collection responsibility as a registered seller in State C.

There are numerous variations on the conditions indicated in the chart, as well as variations on the documentation question:

(1) If Company I is not registered in State C, should it be so registered?

(2) If the shipment of property is not to Company II's actual customer (Company III) but to a vendor providing services to Company III, what certificate is appropriate? For example, Company III's service vendor(s) may be further fabricating, forming, painting, anodizing, plating, assembling, packing, etc., the product shipped by Company I.

(3) If Company III is purchasing the property for resale, who provides what certificate to whom?

(4) Does the use of Company I's delivery equipment or contract carrier, instead of the use of a common carrier, alter the tax collection responsibility or documentation requirement?

(5) Do the FOB terms change the tax collection responsibility?

(6) If Company III is an exempt entity, what certificate is appropriate, and provided by whom?

(7) Is there a standard affidavit form that can be used by Company III or Company II to satisfy the documentation problem for Company I?

(8) How would installation of the property by Company I change the documentation requirements?

One can find many more variables to investigate. Unfortunately, most states do not answer the above questions in their statutes, regulations and rules leaving most tax professionals to their own devices. As with registration (permit) numbers and exemption certificates, the Institute for Professionals in Taxation has also completed a survey on third-party drop shipments. This booklet is available (at a small cost) and should be part of one's tax library. The Institute does update these booklets on a regular basis. Make certain that you have the latest version.

¶2103 Third-Party Refunds

When a company performs an internal review of its purchase transactions, it is likely to find instances where sales or use tax may have been collected, by its vendor, in error. Such overpayments could arise where items purchased were used in an exempt fashion, were resold prior to first use, or were exempt from tax by their very nature. In most cases, such claims for refund must be filed with the vendor who collected and paid the tax to the state. Unfortunately, the customer has little leverage with the vendor and less leverage with the state in encouraging a timely response to the claim. More interesting yet, the state may not be required to provide interest on the refund when the claim is filed by the vendor. Is there a solution to this inequity?

Unfortunately, the laws are not written to anticipate refunds with the same focused attention given to assessments and compliance. One may argue that a refund is simply a credit assessment; however, this is not likely to be persuasive. Certainly, whenever possible, refunds should be claimed from the state to keep the transaction on a first-hand basis. If this is not possible, a lawsuit against the state, brought by the company claiming the refund and joined by the vendor, is the only method of pressing this issue. It is unclear whether there is a U.S. constitutional question implicit in this situation, but evenhandedness appears to be lacking.

¶2104 Purchasing and Leasing Companies

#64

In recent years, several companies have implemented purchasing and leasing companies as part of an overall tax minimization strategy. How are purchasing and leasing companies useful, and what are the problems inherent in their use?

The captive purchasing company involves establishing an independent (wholly owned subsidiary) to purchase everything for resale to be sold to its related operating unit. This structure works effectively where the operating unit maintains a stock of taxable material at one or more centralized depots or warehouses and it is difficult at the time of purchase to know where the property will be ultimately used or consumed. The strategy places the retail sales activity in the hands of the wholly owned subsidiary and takes it away from the operating unit's suppliers. All purchases by the wholly owned subsidiary are made on a "for resale" basis. All sales by the wholly owned subsidiary to the operating unit are made based on knowing the precise location of the operating unit's facility and based on a purchase order from the operating unit. There is a significant compliance obligation for the wholly owned subsidiary to compute and collect (pay) sales tax measured by its gross receipts.

Issues arise relate to inbound separately stated freight charges and other reimbursed costs (service fees, data processing services, management fees, etc.) that may be considered part of gross receipts not excluded from taxable measure of the wholly owned subsidiary. This strategy has one distinct advantage of allowing the operating unit to pay sales tax at the precise rate associated with the destination of the property (possibly lower) instead of the central warehouse location (possibly higher). The second advantage is control of the taxing activity (increased precision). A third advantage is a one-time cash flow delay in payment of the sales tax. A fourth possible advantage may include the ability to establish "tax incentives" for local jurisdictions where the centralized depots or warehouses are located.

Sounds good? Why isn't everyone adopting this approach? First, purchasing companies are ideally suited to companies with repetitive mixed taxability purchases and no access to a direct pay permit. A company with a direct pay permit has the luxury of purchasing property without tax and applying the tax based on use. It is also useful when multiple locations use identical property that can be centrally warehoused and distributed conveniently. Secondly, purchasing companies cannot easily be used to purchase construction contracts for resale without being viewed as a contractor, which can create some unanticipated and undesirable liabilities. Thirdly, it cannot be assumed that reimbursement of the cost of the operation can be paid for independently of computing tax on those operating costs (noted above). In other words, gross receipts or taxable measure includes payment either in cash, in kind, or by the indirect payment of payroll and expenses through separate reimbursement. Fourthly, the costs of delivering property on one's own truck may be includible in taxable measure.

On the other hand, leasing companies are often set up to take advantage of state income tax opportunities. However, since leases are often regarded as continuing sales, there are clearly sales tax implications in their operation. Unlike resale rules, the laws across the states are inconsistent concerning leases. One cannot always purchase leased property for resale. There are various types of elections that must be made, tax collection and payment rules that must be followed, etc. The captive leasing company involves establishing an independent entity (wholly owned subsidiary) to which the operating unit contributes or sells all of its capital assets (furniture and fixtures). When this occurs, there is a one time benefit of either a cash infusion or provision of capital stock in the leasing subsidiary. The operating unit cleans up its balance sheet with regard to owned and depreciated assets and the new subsidiary now has new (used) owned assets to depreciate. The subsidiary then leases the property back to the operating unit for a fixed term at an agreed upon fair market value lease price. The leasing subsidiary incurs a sales (or use) tax liability associated with its activities as a lessor. Sales (or use) taxes are reimbursed by the operating unit. One can see that the sales tax compliance implications of such a transaction are significant to the new leasing subsidiary and that the sales tax obligations increase rather than decrease. This initial transaction is a bulk sale. The on-going transactions create gross receipts likely to be subject to tax and having major compliance ramifications.

In conclusion, purchasing companies are a nice idea, offering some tax simplicity but adding some administrative and hidden complexity and cost. If adopting either strategy, it is absolutely critical to address the issue of change management. Will there be employee transfers? Will there be service requirements? Will people need to think and act differently, reflecting the reality of the strategy, not merely the concept? Before restructuring, one should do a careful study of the soft and hard costs of establishing a purchasing or leasing company. There could be some unanticipated surprises.

¶2105 Interest on Assessments, but Not on Refunds

#65   A directly related issue, which appears to have much stronger implications in U.S. constitutional law, involves states that either arbitrarily, or by statute, provide for interest on assessments, but not on refunds. The added code feature that creates more confusion and difficulty is the concept that "negligence" need not be present for interest to apply to an assessment and, if present, prevents interest from applying to a refund. It is certain that changing this type of one-sided provision is unlikely in the absence of a lawsuit at the federal level. It is clear to this author that no jurisdiction should be allowed uncompensated use of a taxpayer's funds for any reason.

¶2106 Statute of Limitations for Assessments and Refunds

A final related point to the issue of refunds is the inequity present in some statutes that sets the statute of limitations for assessments at a period of time greater than that provided for refund claims. In other words, the state may audit for compliance and assess additional tax thereon for, as an example, four years, while a taxpayer may only claim refunds of taxes for three years. One could infer from state rules that the purpose of this distinction is to force all refunds into audits, i.e., that is, taxpayers bringing refund claims are bothersome but jurisdictions will adjudicate refunds otherwise disclosed as part of an audit under the statute of limitations associated with the audit. Again, while a state may have received a challenge to this inequity litigated through the initial levels of the appeals process, it is not known to have been tested for validity under the U.S. Constitution. As with the preceding issue, the author believes such statutory language would not survive a federal law challenge. Is this a due process issue?

One can surely find similar issues giving the tax professional cause to join the ranks of alternate professions; however, these facets of taxation also make the field both dynamic and exciting. There is certain job security in the confusion and challenge offered by 7,000-plus jurisdictions seeking a tax computed at rates from less than 0.25% to combined rates exceeding ten percent. The task of remaining sensitive to change is critical in order to avoid those unpleasant surprises called large assessments.

Chapter XXII
Tax Considerations by Industry Segment

¶2201 Introduction

Throughout this book, references have been made to applications of tax concepts in different environments. What types of businesses would be most likely to hold a direct pay permit, and how would it be used? What environments are most likely to have a use tax under-accrual problem and why? What records must be retained for review in an audit in a given industry? Regardless of the fact that a tax law in its entirety is a single statement of a state's tax rules, there are differences in the levels of concern that need be demonstrated by various businesses.

Accordingly, in order to provide the reader with some insights, this chapter describes many of the more important sales and use tax considerations by industry segment. Due to the continuous hybridization of business, the segments have been drawn with some poetic license. In light of the explosive growth in electronic commerce and its associated issues, Chapter XXIII takes a separate look into taxation of electronic commerce.

(1) Retailers, or more appropriately and hereinafter "resellers," include businesses whose sales are of property sold in the same form as that in which it was acquired, whether at retail or wholesale. See ¶2202.

(2) Manufacturing includes businesses that process property from one form into another prior to its sale to either another manufacturer, end user, or reseller. See ¶2203.

(3) Construction companies are those businesses that enter into contracts resulting in the creation, modification, alteration, enhancement or demolition of real property, or the fabrication and installation of that which becomes a part of real property. See ¶2204.

(4) Leasing involves granting the right to use property, information, or services for a fixed or indeterminate amount of time, for consideration and with the ownership of the property remaining with the grantor of the right. See ¶2205.

(5) Telecommunications is one of the rapidly growing industry segments, which includes carriers of information, regardless of the medium of transmission (sound, sight, electromagnetic, microwave or other), type of customer, origin or destination of transmission, or equipment or facilities used to accomplish the transmission. See ¶2206.

(6) Services are associated with performance of some activity in which there is minimal transfer of ownership or use of property, or no transfer of property at all. See ¶2207.

In all cases, there will be overlap between the industry segments: telecommunications companies perform services, resellers may lease as well as sell, manufacturers are sellers, often at retail, and those providing services can be as diverse as governmental units, hospitals, banks, insurance companies, airlines, etc.

Finally, for ease of review, the material in this chapter is presented in parallel structure for each industry segment. That is, each segment will have a review of (1) sales issues, (2) purchase issues, (3) special problem areas often buried in the general ledger or journal voucher world, and (4) constitutional considerations. Examples by state may be scattered throughout this chapter, since it is not this book's intent to cover specific codes or jurisdictions.

¶2202 Resellers

Resellers include those businesses that have single or multiple locations, make direct mail sales, or engage in wholesale distribution sales activities. Products sold, as represented in this segment, include everything that would be found in a full-line department store or general store (from auto parts to musical instruments, gardening supplies, clothes, tools, sporting goods, furniture and appliances, bulk foods, etc.). Outlets in this business segment would be called, by example, department, hardware, sporting goods, auto parts, grocery stores, restaurants, mail-order catalogue or direct mail sellers and automobile show-rooms. Many telecommunications companies are resellers; however, their activities involve no tangible personal property. Again, the distinguishing characteristic of a reseller activity is simply the resale of property in the same form as it was acquired.

• *Sales*

Whether the sales of a reseller are at a single location, at many individual locations throughout a single state or multiple states, by mail order, or under a third-party drop shipment arrangement, a single statement is uniformly applicable in all jurisdictions having a sales or gross receipts tax. If the reseller meets the nexus standards of the jurisdiction, tax must be either collected and paid or simply paid on taxable sales, depending upon the nature of the imposition of the tax. Further, an assumption should be made about sales. In the absence of information to the contrary (e.g., that the property being sold, the customer to whom the sale is being made, or the documented and intended use of the property by the customer will be free of tax, or that the commodity or property itself is by nature exempt), the sale will be subject to tax. While there is certain comfort and safety in operating from this assumption, it is a position that most sales and marketing managers find difficult to swallow. A proper policy of "bill the tax in the absence of *documentation* to the contrary" is both wise and prudent.

The various sales tax statutes also direct the taxpayer with regard to whether the tax must be passed on to the customer, separately stated, or whether it may be absorbed by the seller as a sales incentive. Accordingly, statutes give explicit instructions regarding how the tax must be identified on the invoice and what is included in, or excluded from, the measure of the tax. In the case of wholesale resellers or retailers selling nontaxable property or property to those able to avail themselves of exemptions, a critical issue is the manner in which the excepted transactions must be recorded. Let's take a look at several examples.

¶2202

A department store retailer must be able to track property by unit code (often referred to as the SKU). This unit code should be marked for taxability. Requiring sales clerks to make decisions concerning keying of proper tax status should be kept to an absolute minimum. Where a state offers exemptions to types of purchasers who provide proper identification or documentation, a simple but firm procedure must exist that may be learned and tracked. The clerk must know what is acceptable to be viewed and what is necessary to be placed in the "file" as documentation. If the retailer has multiple locations within a state or locality, certain identification of the appropriate tax rate is required.

If one remembers the rule that all sales are considered taxable in the absence of documentation to the contrary, a program of training and tracking is required. Laminated, spiral-bound "crib notes" or instruction cards affixed to cash registers are effective methods for keeping clerks informed. Be advised, however, that the decision to change the format or content of such material is often decided in a department that may have no functional understanding, let alone concern for, or interest in, sales tax issues. Attention to this level of detail is an absolute necessity in the retail environment. Following are examples—certainly not an exhaustive list—of the details to which attention must be paid:

(1) Is bulk food sold in the store in states having a bulk food exclusion?

(2) Are repair charges in a department store having an auto center properly identified? Is a distinction required between parts and labor?

(3) Is there a lunch counter, popcorn stand, ice cream counter, etc., making single sales of walk-away food? Does the state consider these sales taxable as prepared foods or non-taxable as sales of food where there is no facility for the consumption of that food?

(4) Where large appliances or other deliverables are sold, is the delivery made via company equipment, contract (captive) carriers, or common carriers, and is this issue of tax on the delivery service properly addressed? How does the system handle a sale at the store and a delivery into a jurisdiction in which the store is not located? What if there is another company outlet in the jurisdiction into which the property is delivered? Where does the sale really occur, and which tax applies?

(5) Are there ever charges for installation of the property at the customer's premises?

(6) How are extended warranties handled? Are such service agreements handled differently whether they are mandatory or optional?

(7) If purchases may be financed, charged on company revolving credit cards, placed on lay-away, or otherwise given special handling, what are the tax implications for these alternative sales and finance strategies?

(8) When property is returned by a customer, is the return handled through the same system as the sale to assure that the proper tax coding is used to credit tax back to the customer (if allowed)?

A wholesale reseller (one that customarily sells business-to-business) has a very different set of concerns. Because sales are often for resale, this type of reseller must be most concerned with having properly completed and timely received customer purchase orders and exemption/resale certificates on file, along with copies of pertinent invoices, shipping information, etc. Success in achieving full documentation often rests with the field sales staff or the order entry department personnel who accept orders and process them into delivery requests. Generally, where resales are involved, the nontaxable tax status of freight charges follows the nontaxable tax status of the resale order. Similarly, returns are credited without tax as long as the original sale was made tax-free.

However, in business-to-business retail sales, the tax applicable to the sale may not follow the tax application on a return where an arbitrary amount is charged for restocking. Similarly, all of the example issues addressed for the department store retailer apply to the business-to-business retailer. The singular difference is that the sale is not normally rung at a cash register. In the case of both department store and business-to-business retailers, a sale can turn from a sales to a use tax transaction when property is required to be shipped to another state. Determining whether one has nexus in the destination location is simple if one's company ships to a jurisdiction where the company meets the destination jurisdiction's nexus standards. Finally, the taxability of trade-ins becomes a serious issue where equipment sales are involved. Some jurisdictions allow the value of the trade-in to be deducted from gross receipts. Some allow this deduction only on property of like kind and, of course, there are those jurisdictions that do not consider trade-ins deductible from gross receipts, taxing the entire sale regardless of the trade-in value.

Direct mail sellers are now breathing easier in those states where they have insufficient nexus as defined in *National Bellas Hess* and *Quill*. Because these sellers typically have only one location nationally, their retail sales to all other states, except the one in which they are resident, are not subject to sales tax but are absolutely subject to use tax if the property being sold is taxable. However, because the customer is usually an individual who has no practical method of, nor is likely to, self-assess and remit use tax, the direct mail seller with insufficient nexus may elect to register with the state and collect the use tax from the customer/user voluntarily.

A requisite of collecting tax is the need to implement a fairly sophisticated billing/use tax system that looks at each purchaser's ship-to location and all state and local tax rates. Unfortunately, this procedure does not address the matter of dealing with those customers who did not remit correct tax on self-completed order forms submitted with payments for purchases. The economic and marketing cost of back-billing these customers may force the seller to bear the tax cost burden, a condition prohibited in some states. The issue continues to be discussed widely in the direct marketing industry and among the various states, particularly those participating in one of several MTC-Nexus Projects.

Finally, there are specialty outlets that have to be attuned to the tax issues of their specific business segment. Automobile, boat and aircraft dealers make retail sales of vehicles, watercraft and aircraft, which may have special tax, registration, and licensing requirements. Due to the dollar size of their sales and the various bureaucracies to which they are required to report, their problems are often very unique.

¶2202

Non-dealers are also occasionally involved in disposing of such property in a used condition and must meet some of the same standards of compliance when completing their transactions.

Grocery stores are retailers selling mostly unprepared food to end users. Most states have exempted from taxable gross receipt amounts attributable to the sale of such bulk foods; however, the definition of what is included in bulk foods or food products is often irrational and absurd. This condition is best exemplified by the "snack tax rules" imposed by the state of California. In July 1991, the state began taxing only specific food products that seemed to fall under the category of junk foods. Unfortunately, correct identification of these newly taxable foods is a challenge even for the most highly qualified nutritionist.

In a similar sense, reseller distributors of medical-related products are often confronted with the same type of problem. States often develop irrational bases for defining which medical products are or are not taxable. The "however not that" and "yes, but not those" conditions create a monster nightmare for these companies. A central invoicing function and billing software can be severely tested when the same product sold to the same customer under two different intended uses may or may not be taxable. When one factors in multiple states, multiple types of customers, and multiple uses, a tax manager could simply lose it. The vision of the half-crazed tax manager is found where a company sells in many states having exemptions and exclusions that do not follow a rational pattern.

In an attempt to accelerate tax cash flow, states are beginning to look at collecting tax even on resale sales. The tax collected becomes an advance payment by the ultimate seller against which a deduction is taken at the time its taxable sale is made. Louisiana introduced the concept, and other states are giving it serious consideration.

The statement that all sales at resale are not taxable is simply not correct.

• *Purchases*

Purchases by resellers are much easier to address as a topic as the exceptions are fewer in number. Inventory is not taxable at the time of purchase since the tax is paid, or an exemption certificate taken, at the time the sale is made. However some purchases may be subject to sales or use tax as explained below.

(1) *Property purchased for resale:* When a reseller gives its exemption (resale) certificate to its vendor, it is agreeing to be responsible for all taxes due whether the property is resold at retail or self-consumed. Self-consumed property is resale property converted by the reseller to its own use.

(2) *Taxable assets acquired for displaying or shelving inventory:* Although this is not a universal condition, this type of property is traditionally taxable. It is not resold and is consumed by the reseller.

(3) *Taxable expense materials:* This category of items might include everything from cash register tape, sales receipt books, sales clerk uniforms to sweeping compound. However, greater attention must be paid to packaging materials. States treat these products as either taxable (ex-

¶2202

pendable supplies) or non-taxable (resold with contents). Advertising newspaper inserts and catalogues delivered from the printer to the common carrier to the ultimate recipient are taxable in some states and nontaxable in other states. Litigation to resolve this issue proliferates.

• *Special sales and use tax accounting issues*

When a company uses property for demonstration or display while "holding it for resale," it may benefit from a use tax exclusion accorded property used in such a manner. Most states have defined such use as nontaxable. However, once the property is sold or given away, the incidence of taxation my be triggered. Sale of demonstration property is taxable even if the sales price is discounted. The donation, destruction or giving away of such property after it has been so used is likely to result in use tax coming due. The common accounting treatment of this type of transaction is to remove the property from inventory via journal voucher. The inventory account is relieved, and the demo, samples or donations account is charged with the expense. When such a transaction occurs, it is important to confirm that the appropriate taxable value is used to measure any liability coming due (see ¶503). For resellers that also enter into leases with customers, special rules must be reviewed to properly account for the taxability of the lease revenue.

It is important for multistate resellers to establish a system for properly accounting for tax by jurisdiction. It is significantly more difficult to determine the tax jurisdiction from which collections are received after they have been pooled. The better method is to create separate accounts.

• *Constitutional issues*

The single most important issue today for the reseller generally (and mail order resellers specifically) revolves around nexus, the sufficiency of a seller's activity to create an obligation under a state's code to register and comply with that state's laws. However, it is not only the direct mail marketer that must address this issue. Multistate sellers in business-to-business as well as consumer sales must look carefully at their products, the sales calls made by their personnel and representatives, and their related entities or casual sales activities to properly determine the extent of their nexus. Is there a risk to not registering? Perhaps there is. The issue is simply one of risk aversion, or how much risk one's company is willing to assume.

The second issue that has received much court action, usually initiated by retailers that use catalogues to pitch their wares to the mail-order market, relates to the taxability of those catalogues that are printed in one state and shipped across state lines to be placed in a prospective customer's mailbox in another state. What made the issue problematic was the challenge that was brought by a party having nexus in the destination state. This issue was addressed in *D.H. Holmes Co. v. McNamara*, 486 US 24 (1988). Suffice it to say, the taxpayer did not prevail.

The third issue, which has not yet received any court attention, concerns the purchase of goods from a retailer by someone other than the ultimate consumer, when the ultimate out-of-state consumer receives the property as a gift. This situation is different than the pure vanilla nexus issue when the order is placed and implied control is granted to the purchaser at the time consideration is presented to the seller. Is it not possible that the transaction is really a sales tax transaction, due to the implied control of the property by the purchaser? Although the property is used in the recipient's state, there is no consideration presented and, therefore, there may be no purchase. However, the recipient's state may claim that the property moved into the state at the instruction of the purchaser and therefore, if all other nexus considerations are met, the purchaser is subject to use tax in the destination state. The "jury" is still out on these types of transactions. As we look in greater depth at the manner in which transactions take place, we will continue to find situations that challenge our case law and tax sensibilities.

¶2203 Manufacturing

Of all of the industry segments discussed in this chapter, the manufacturing segment is most complex. It leases, sells and resells. It fabricates from raw materials and creates products from elemental resources. For these reasons, it is not enough for one concerned with the tax consequences of this segment to read only this portion of Chapter XXII. Read all of the chapters, as they are all likely to touch your realm. Manufacturing's most significant tax issues are distinguishable from those of the reseller due to the complexity of its purchases, the uses of those purchases, and the vagaries of the tax laws concerning those purchases.

• *Sales*

Manufacturers are sellers of the products they fabricate or assemble from raw materials. Whether the products are computers, automobiles, jumbo jets, or hat pins, the sales issues are largely identical to those of the reseller who sells for resale. The manufacturer, with the exception of those that make capital products, will almost always be selling for resale. The capital equipment manufacturer will possibly sell for resale but will more than likely sell at retail. These sales, rather than being subject to a resale certificate, may be subject to a special business/ public benefit exemption, e.g., sales of equipment qualifying for industrial expansion or pollution control exemption status. They could also be subject to one of many specialty business exemptions, e.g., sales to common carriers or hospital, governmental units or non-profit educational institutions. Of course, what is important to remember is to timely acquire a properly completed certificate, taken in good faith, pertinent to the exemption being claimed.

Manufacturers are often involved in third-party drop shipment transactions. Their customer is not the party to whom the property is shipped. If the relationship is truly complex, the customer and recipient of the property will be located in two different states, with the manufacturer in the third state. Extreme care must be taken to properly analyze these types of transactions in order to gather and retain the correct certificate from the appropriate party. When the sale moves from the manufacturer to the customer, with no one in between, the transaction is either a classic retail or resale, exempt or direct pay permit sale.

The traditional manufacturer sells on credit, i.e., extends credit terms to a customer who pays in a given amount of time. There may be prompt payment discounts, trade discounts, rebates, trade-ins, and perhaps some leasing activity. The leases can be written by the manufacturer who thereafter holds the paper;

the paper can be sold; or the sale can be to a third party financing organization that writes its own lease paper. In all of these situations, the manufacturer must attend to the requirements of the jurisdiction. The most significant responsibility to be assumed by the sales tax professional in a manufacturing environment is that of learning how one's company conducts its business.

Manufacturers can be grouped in three broad categories.

(1) *Resource converters:* These companies take a raw resource (e.g., iron ore, bauxite, crude oil, soya bean, corn, etc.) and convert the raw resource into either a finished product (e.g., aluminum foil, gasoline or diesel fuel, heating oil, etc.) or a raw material to be used by someone else (e.g., steel castings, aluminum sheeting, soya oil, corn sweetener, etc.).

(2) *Material processors:* These manufacturers take a converted resource and process it into another product, which they may sell for resale or retail. A paint manufacturer will take petroleum distillates and pigments and turn them into paint. A food processor will take corn sweetener, flour, cocoa butter, sugar, and nuts, and produce a candy bar. A chemical plant will take a variety of raw ingredients and fragrances and produce perfume.

(3) *Assembler/fabricator manufacturers:* This segment is widely known as the rust-belt companies; however, they also include a variety of other companies, such as computer, medical durable equipment, furniture, aircraft, and appliance manufacturers, etc. The output from these companies represents the durable goods of a society.

The resource converters will make exempt sales in many cases. Even when selling a raw resource converted to a finished good, these sellers are often selling through a separate retailing or distribution entity.

Perhaps the single issue of greatest concern to the manufacturer would be the vertical transfer of converted resources within a single company. In such situations, a seller may be making a taxable inter-company sale as distinguished from a largely non-taxable intra-company transfer. Often, when property crosses entities, the activity is a sale, as contrasted with mere self-consumption. This issue is covered in greater detail in Chapter V at ¶503 and 504.

• Purchases

Sales tax issues for manufacturers are not a simple matter to manage, and purchases are even more complex. With sales, the customer dictates by action or omission the taxable status of its purchase. When presented with a customer's resale certificate or direct pay permit, the seller is probably safe in not billing tax, provided the certificate or permit is properly completed, timely received, and taken in good faith. However, the manufacturer, taking the role of the customer, either contracts to pay or acquiesces to reimburse sales tax, or must provide the seller a proper document to relieve the seller of the liability to collect and/or remit sales tax. There are many issues that come into play for the purchaser in making the tax/no-tax decision. The results of these decisions often produce troublesome use tax audits. A discussion of the purchases made by a manufacturer would not be complete without including a discussion of the following issues: (1) machinery and equipment, (2) pollution control and energy conserva-

¶2203

tion, (3) raw materials, (4) manufacturing aids, (5) utilities, and (6) expendable supplies and services.

Machinery and equipment (M&E) includes some tangible personal property usually classed as capital assets or fixed assets, but does not include furniture and fixtures, real estate, buildings, etc. The useful life of a piece of M&E is often measured in years. Parts often replaced are frequently viewed as consumable supplies if they have a life of, for example, less than one year. States have taken one of two broad positions regarding machinery and equipment. M&E is either exempt from tax when used directly or perhaps exclusively in the manufacture of the product, or completely taxable regardless of how it is used. A chart portraying the manner in which the states tax M&E appears at ¶ 602.

The significance of understanding the taxing rules must be recognized if one is going to avail oneself of tax exemptions at time of purchase or to take a credit after the purchase. States that provide for the latter may do so under a provision that calls for a refund of the tax based on the percentage increase in the productivity of the machinery purchased, on increased employment, or on location in enterprise zones, etc. Furthermore, one must look at the definition of manufacturing to be certain that the use of the property is consistent with the law. For example, states defining manufacture as the activities during which raw materials are combined would not exempt some conveyances (cranes, loaders, conveyor belts, etc.) used to move property, not to combine it. Other states consider manufacturing machinery that comes in contact with the raw materials from the time the materials are at the plant until the finished product is shipped. Suffice it to say, M&E is very state- and definition-specific.

The other significant issue with M&E concerns where the property is being used within the manufacturing facility. A machine used in research and development may benefit from an exemption, but the same equipment used in production might be taxable. Much more likely, the converse could be true. A piece of test equipment that assures quality has no impact on the fabrication of the property but directly impacts upon the acceptability of the product in the customer's eyes. For example, a tester in a lab used to test chemical balances during a manufacturing process to confirm the ingredient purity may be treated differently than a test oven in a production area that allows the manufacturer to certify that a given product will withstand specific heat ranges.

Many states have granted *pollution control equipment* exemptions in an effort to reduce the quantity of industrial waste effluent or byproduct. The provision of such exemptions gives the citizenry a sense of comfort that living in the vicinity of a factory does not represent a health risk. When this exemption is paired with an *energy conservation* exemption, the combination is a powerful encouragement to the business that is ecology-minded and energy-aware. The number of states offering exemptions for energy conservation equipment is dwindling in light of the relative (compared to the oil embargo years) availability of energy and state government budgetary insolvency.

Raw materials are one of the most common sales and use tax exemptions granted by states to manufacturers. The definition of a raw material varies from state to state. The simplest definition is "that property becoming an ingredient or component part of the property being manufactured." For example, these raw materials might include everything from the wing assemblies on a jumbo jet to the fine gold wire used to connect the leads on a microprocessor to the microlithographed image on the silicon chip. Qualified more restrictively, the definition might read "that property becoming an ingredient or component part of the property being manufactured that becomes indistinguishable as a part thereof." An example in this situation would be the vegetable oil in the salad dressing. Viewed liberally, the definition of raw materials might be expanded with the phrase "or materials that, by coming in contact or combination, bring about a chemical or physical change." These raw materials would include such products as chemicals and catalysts, items often classed simply as manufacturing aids (discussed below). In all cases, raw materials are normally expected to remain a component part of the finished product. Some states even specify the extent to which the material must remain present.

Manufacturing aids or *consumables* are a class of products that is often defined as "being consumed or used in the manufacture of resale property that brings about a physical or chemical change," or "is consumed in the production process but not incorporated into the finished product," and "has a useful life of six months or less." Again, there are numerous variations on this theme. How does one class cleaning materials, clean room uniforms, or refrigerants? There may even be different rates applied to these consumable materials when distinguished from raw materials or expendable supplies, as is the case in Louisiana and Hawaii.

Utilities and fuel have been regarded as exempt from tax in some states as raw materials or consumable supplies used in the manufacturing process. For example, in Texas, exempting utilities used in the manufacturing process requires separate electric meters or engineering certification for manufacturing plants for one to avoid being taxed on used in manufacturing. Otherwise, all utilities, including those for administrative office uses, are taxable. In a state with this type of exemption, when there is a single meter, the taxpayer must have an engineered study performed to determine the apportionment of the utility charge to benefit from the exemption. Utilities and fuel could include electric power, natural gas, water, coal, etc.

The final category of purchases made by manufacturers are those involving either *expendable supplies or services*. The supplies include office, data processing, janitorial, shipping supplies, etc. Perhaps the most confusing matter involves the determination of whether packaging or shipping supplies are taxable. Commonly, nonreturnable packaging materials sold with the product are not taxable as a supply purchase. The tax is due, if at all, on the sale of the container plus its contents. Nearly all other types of expendable supply purchases are taxable.

On the other hand, purchases of services could involve anything from refuse collection to contract engineering to legal services. The services can be of a strictly overhead nature (supporting the administration of the manufacturer), contracted manufacturing or engineering skills not available internally (provided by a temporary agency or consultant), repair to M&E, etc. In most states, those services applied to resale material directly may be purchased for resale, e.g., anodizing or plating products for resale, testing products for certification that they meet weight, heat, cold or other minimum or maximum standard. Services of an overhead nature would be taxed based on state code. Importantly, one can no longer presume that services are always going to be exempt from tax.

As a final note, whatever the tax status of the purchase, or however the property or service will be used, the purchasing manufacturer must be certain that the proper purchase order and/or certificate is filed with the seller to gain the advantage of the desired tax benefit. Training of purchasing personnel must be performed on a continuing basis to recognize both turnover in employees and changes in buying assignments.

Similarly, if the accounts payable department does not understand the importance of accruing use tax on taxable transactions where the purchaser is liable, the surprising news may come in the form of a job-threatening audit.

• *Special sales and use tax accounting issues*

The most severe test of the sales and use tax accounting methodology of the manufacturer centers around the matter of taxing self-consumption of resale property. Accounting entries that tend to be red flags to jurisdictional auditors are those that relieve an inventory, work-in-process or finished goods account, and charge an expense account. A simple self-audit of the journal vouchers impacting these resale material accounts should be performed for confirmation that tax is being correctly accrued and paid, if it is due. However, investigation beyond the pure account numbers themselves should be part of such a review. Some of these entries may not have a tax consequence.

Secondly, if free-of tax property is acquired by one's company under some specific premise and the plan is not followed through, a use tax accrual is likely to be required. For example, a company makes an asset purchase intended to be resold to its off-shore subsidiary. Prior to the sale of the asset to the subsidiary, the company decides to place the asset in use domestically. In this situation, a use tax accrual is required when the entry (credit) relieving the intercompany receivables account is recorded offset with a charge (debit) to a domestic asset account. Take care to make the accrual only if the domestic location does not offer an exemption for which the purchase otherwise qualifies.

Also related to assets is the disposition of depreciated assets. Taxpayers often ignore their liability to collect and/or remit tax on such sales. This transaction is often recorded as a charge to a profit/(loss) on the sale of assets account offset by the relieving of the net book value asset account. Other related issues are discussed in Chapter V and in this chapter at ¶ 2207 in the section dealing with special tax accounting issues. There are likely to be issues related to other types of taxes. However, this discussion addresses sales and use tax concerns only.

• *Constitutional issues*

As with the reseller, the nexus issue is important for the manufacturer. The vertical integration of a manufacturer may mean that the products are fabricated in one state, assembled in a second state, held in distribution centers in several other states, and sold at retail in all states. In such a scenario, it is incumbent upon the sales and use tax manager to carefully review operations to determine where the registration and filing requirements exist. For the manufacturing conglomerate comprised of several individual divisions operating autonomously, the same nexus problem may exist. Division A filing in its home state casts the cloak of nexus over all other divisions doing business in that state, and vice versa.

To conclude, manufacturers have significant opportunities to be creative in tax planning, thus avoiding problems in the future. However, the other edge of the sword represents the complexity of the manufacturer's operation and the potential hidden tax pitfalls. The variety of contractual relationships between the manufacturer and its customers or vendors is not found in most industry segments. This variety can be a tremendous source of satisfaction or frustration. Audits of manufacturers are often very complicated. After all of the schedules are spread out on the table, one can be sure that an adjustment in one schedule is likely to cause a second schedule to "move" or require adjustment. Such an audit tests the mettle of the best auditor and sales tax professional.

¶2204 Construction

Before entering the realm of construction contracts, it is helpful to come to some agreement about terms. To do so, let us develop a small list of key definitions. A construction contractor is a party that enters into an agreement with a customer in order to perform some type of work related to real property. Most commonly, the work contracted for is the construction, improvement, modification, or demolition of that real property. The prime contractor is the lead contractor having the relationship with the customer or client. The sub-contractor(s) perform aspects of the contract for the prime contractor and normally has no contractual relationship with the customer or client. Most contracts are granted to the contractor as a result of a competitive bid, which serves as the contractor's commitment to perform the job for a given sum of money (or other valuable consideration) at a certain place in a stated amount of time.

Contractors may sell individual elements of tangible personal property, such as ovens, boilers, HVAC (heat-ventilation and air conditioning) systems, etc., or may make sales of these items in conjunction with their installation. A construction contract may include the use of materials (e.g., wallboard, joists, conduit, plaster, etc.) that become an integral part of the real property structure or machinery and equipment that may be removed without damaging the structure.

Aside from these basic definitions describing the parties and their relationship to one another, there are terms under which these services are provided. The most common type of construction contract is a *lump-sum* contract in which the contractor agrees to perform the contract for a lump-sum amount, inclusive of materials, services, overhead and profit, not billed separately but rather combined. The price could be increased during the course of the contract, however, but only a single combined billing is rendered. Increases are normally handled via change orders.

At the opposite end of the billing spectrum is the *time and material* contract. In this case, the contractor bills based on actual rates for laborers, supervisors, skilled artisans, etc., and separately charges for actual materials. In a time and material (T&M) contract, the contractor will likely bill separately for overhead and profit margin.

¶2204

Two other types of contracts commonly found in dealings with governmental entities are *cost-plus* and *fixed price* contracts. The cost-plus contract is often open-ended, since the total costs will not be known and there is little competition for the contract. The customer pays the contractor's actual costs plus incremental overhead and profit margin percentages added thereon. Cost-plus contracts are often subject to large cost over-runs, which must be paid for by the customer.

By contrast, the fixed price contract is an agreement wherein the contractor is bound by its bid to produce the desired result for a set price, which is fixed before the job begins. The contract, if there are over-runs based on poor estimating by the contractor and not unforeseen circumstances, can produce large losses for the contractor, who must bear the burden of over-runs. Fixed price contracts may not be modified by change orders similar to the lump-sum contract.

• *Sales*

Sales by construction contractors normally begin with a bid process. A request for quotations (RFQ) or request for proposals (RFP) is issued by the party interested in the service desired. The result of the RFQ or RFP is a written proposal, which includes a description of the project, time schedules, suggested billing method, pricing structure, etc. Some contract proposal requests are issued with the requirement that the bidders provide their bids using a specific type of contract form, e.g., lump-sum, fixed price, etc. It should be noted that the form of the contract will likely determine the method of taxation, whereas the method of billing may be ignored. For example, a given contractor, for internal accounting purposes, may show a detailed breakdown of all costs, while the contract may be a lump-sum contract.

Generally, with the exception of retail sales, where sales taxes are determined by the terms of the state tax code, sales by contractors are not subject to sales or use tax. The exception states are Arizona, Mississippi, New Mexico, Washington, and West Virginia, where the construction contractor is considered a retailer of new construction. In other states, new construction is not taxable at retail; however, repairs, remodeling, maintenance or demolition might be taxable. Most states consider the materials incorporated into a construction project and the tools, expendable supplies and machinery and equipment used by the contractor to be consumed by the contractor and, therefore, subject to sales or use tax when purchased by the contractor.

Perhaps the most significant issue for the contractor is that the exemption from tax accorded to the customer may flow through to the contractor but generally does not. This is absolutely a state by state issue and should be addressed carefully by contractors. It may be beneficial for the exempt customer to purchase the materials that would otherwise be incorporated into the real property and consumed by the contractor. The customer would supply the materials to the contractor following their exempt purchase. By so doing, the exempt customer may benefit from its entitled exemption on the material. Tax, if due at all, would only be due on the balance of the construction service.

Contractors must use extreme care in accepting exemption certificates. Real estate construction cannot normally be "resold" in the traditional sense, which is why a resale certificate taken by a contractor is likely to be a flawed action.

Similarly, care should be shown when contracting with the U.S. Government. The common exemption accorded sales to the Government normally does not apply in the case of real estate contracts.

• *Purchases*

Consistent with the concept that the contractor tends to be the consumer of that which is incorporated into construction projects, there is little that a contractor purchases that should be tax free. This means that the tax should either be paid to the seller (material supplier) or accrued and paid to the state as use tax. However, there are several issues that require attention by the contractor.

(1) *Commingling of resale and consumable materials:* Some contractors make retail sales as well as performing contracts in which they are the consumer of that which they install or incorporate into the property constructed. The contractor having both types of activities should determine if his (her) state will allow the otherwise consumable materials to be purchased for resale, thereafter accruing and paying the use tax on that which is consumed versus taxing that which is sold at retail. The converse of this situation involves the contractor who buys all property tax-paid or places all property on a tax-paid basis and must then take a credit for the tax-paid cost of otherwise taxable materials when making retail sales on which the tax must be declared (collected and/or paid). In either situation, it is critical that the contractor be consistent in following the taxing methodology selected.

(2) *Materials to be used on projects out-of-state:* When contractors enter into contracts that result in taking materials across state lines, the tax-wise contractor determines whether its home state requires that the tax be paid even if the property will be consumed elsewhere. As a planning consideration, a contractor needs to address this situation early in the bid process. Bidding a project solely on the belief that tax may not be due in the destination state could be a costly error. Many states collect tax on all purchased property held for use, regardless of its final destination.

(3) *Purchases contracted for prior to a rate change:* Filling state coffers with revenue adequate to support the common good will continue to be a major problem for legislatures. The simplest solution, a tax-rate increase, causes an interesting problem to the contractor in particular, and to any purchaser that enters into a contract, with a long lead time to delivery or job completion. Many states and localities have taken this into consideration when passing rate-increase legislation. Contractors and purchasers are often given the benefit of the rate in effect at the time the contract was signed by the parties, rather than being subjected to a new rate.

For the contractor, materials that have been bid at a given price with tax at a set rate are the basis by which a contract may be measured for profitability. When a rate increase is forced on a contractor, the increase in tax from 4 percent to 5 percent, for example, represents a relative increase of 25 percent. When applied to the cost of all materials, such an increase can be a significant amount

¶2204

of money in a tightly contested, high-priced bid. The ability of the contractor to hold the rate in effect at the time the contract was signed is referred to as having rights under a "grandfather clause." It is important to note that strict rules often apply to such clauses. For example, the contract might have to be at a fixed price, without a right to terminate except under penalty, etc. When invoking a grandfather clause, all of the conditions must be met by the contract.

- ### *Special sales and use tax accounting issues*

There are few special tax accounting issues for contractors other than those previously discussed. Familiarity with the code and rules/regulations in the states in which one is engaged in business is of paramount importance. Most states provide instructional presentations for their construction contractor taxpayers. A minor misunderstanding on a multimillion dollar contract could result in a jurisdiction's assessment capable of placing a contractor in receivership.

- ### *Constitutional issues*

One of the most significant constitutional issues to be addressed by the contractor has been mentioned. It is the issue of a contractor's rights and obligations when availing itself of the constitutional prohibition of states to impose sales or use tax directly on the U.S. government. The second major constitutional issue has to do with where the contractor is performing its service and whether that performance places the the contractor's activity within an otherwise foreign jurisdiction for reporting purposes. It is likely that if a contractor is required to be registered with a state's contractor board, it is probably also required to be registered with the state for sales and use tax purposes. The right to use the state courts for perfection of contractor's liens certainly implies an obligation to comply with the state's tax registration requirements. Maintaining an inventory of materials and supplies, equipment and machinery, vehicles and, most important, construction workers meets every state's sales tax nexus standard. The fact that billings are sent to the customer from a different state, or that the home office of the customer is in a different state, is immaterial. Again, considering the value of most contracts, it is foolhardy for the contractor to challenge the state tax on some imagined constitutional issue. Few such challenges will result in a victory for the contractor.

As a final note, the tax professional in a non-contractor industry needs to be fully informed of the issues related to construction contractors. Relying on the contractor's own knowledge to understand sales/use tax issues is no less dangerous than presuming that one's own purchasing department can properly evaluate the sales/use tax implications of a major construction order. These are great planning opportunities that can result in the tax professional being viewed as a hero with vision.

¶2205 Leasing

On the surface, one might consider leasing as a relatively monolithic industry, having a singular type of transaction that would be easily understood. Nothing could be further from the truth. The industry is composed of several segments, based on the relationships between the lessor and the lessee, the property being leased, and the manner of acquiring the property to be leased.

(1) Manufacturers often establish leasing operations to enhance their sales opportunities to customers who are unwilling to make the outright purchase of their products. These lessors are often referred to as OEM, or original equipment manufacturers. Their leases are often written through wholly owned subsidiaries or financing units.

(2) Financial institutions have engaged in the business of providing leasing services to their customers. Leases by banks and insurance companies are frequently structured as lease lines where the lessor provides an "accommodation" line of credit that is "taken down" by the customer until the line is fully used. The line is then converted to a financed lease or other instrument for a set term.

(3) An entire industry has been established that serves as a funding vehicle for businesses interested in leasing property. These third-party leasing companies provide the funds to their customers who want to acquire property but are unwilling to part with current cash. The third-party lessors often make advance arrangements with manufacturers unable to write their own leases. This is a competitive tool for the company wanting to compete with larger or well-financed OEM lessors.

(4) There is a very large group of companies that rent tools and equipment, typically on an hourly or daily basis, where the transaction is simply construed as a short-term right to use. Most tax codes address these types of transactions separately. So, too, are those involving the rental of equipment with operators and the rental of real property, e.g., office space, retail stores, apartments, etc.

(5) In an industry represented by special rules of its own in most states, the vehicle leasing industry writes paper for the short-, medium-and long-term lease-financing of cars, trucks, and trailers. Waterborne vessels and aircraft are often included in this grouping.

Generally, with all leases, the lessor retains ownership of, and title to, the property being leased, with the right to use being granted to the lessee during the term of the lease. There are two significant categories of transactions entered into by lessors that, while being defined with poetic license by some jurisdictions, have characteristics that can be clearly stated. These types of transactions are the "true lease" and the "conditional sale." For sales/use tax purposes, it is critical that the distinction be understood. Three issues are compared to help explain the difference between these transactions: the right to purchase, the purchase price, and the disposition of the property at the conclusion of the term.

(1) *True lease:* With a true lease, it is said that there is no option available to the lessee concerning the right to purchase. Because the leased equipment traditionally reverts to the lessor, the lessee desiring to purchase the equipment must pay the fair market value, or other preestablished price (e.g., 10 percent of the original cost) for the property at the end of the lease term.

(2) *Conditional sale:* A conditional sale, which may also be known as a finance or security lease, involves a definite purchase option (really not an option, but a provision) that is clearly spelled out in the lease

document. The price to exercise the purchase is a nominal amount (often $1). Because the purchase is mandatory, the lessee keeps the equipment at the end of the lease term.

• *Sales*

What are normally considered sales, for the purposes of this chapter, are those transactions involving the taxpayer and its customer. For leases, we will view the true lease, conditional sale or other transaction as the sale. Generally, conditional sales are taxed at their inception. The lessor purchases the property tax-paid and effectively finances the tax and interest (which must be separately stated). Such leases may not be taxed beyond the tax payment measured by the initial purchase price when the lessor is a third party. When the lessor is also the manufacturer (OEM leasing), and the lease paper is not held by a separate entity, the option to pay the tax at the inception of the lease may not exist.

In the instance of a true lease, sales tax treatment varies widely from state to state. The lessor may be required to pay the sales or use tax at the inception of the lease, measured by the purchase price of the equipment, or may elect to purchase the equipment without tax (effectively, for resale), measuring the (normally, use) tax by the monthly or periodic lease charges. The choice may be restrictive based on the term of the lease (short-term or long-term) or based on the condition that the property must be leased in the same form as acquired (the equipment must be purchased by the lessor in the form in which it will be leased, rather than as parts that are assembled). This provision, also evident for conditional sales, keeps the manufacturer from measuring the purchase price of the equipment to be leased prior to including the elements of labor, overhead and profit. For example, the cost of the components of a micro-computer might be $350, but the selling price of the same computer, after adding in the labor to assemble the components into a computer, overhead to operate the computer company, and profit for the shareholders, is probably $600 to $1,200.

There are two other broad considerations regarding true leases. First, a few states create a separate "rental tax" to cover these leases, rendering the equipment purchased as consumed by the lessor and not resold. Therefore, the tax may be paid on the purchase of the equipment and also be required to be collected on the lease receipts. Rental taxes are an effective method of revenue enhancement without the need for sales tax. Secondly, many of the charges related to true leases are also subject to tax. This is accomplished by considering these related charges part of the total taxable measure reportable under the lease. These taxable amounts might include the following:

(1) property tax paid by the lessor on property under lease (and yes, this is a perfect example of legitimate double taxation);

(2) charges to terminate or cancel a lease;

(3) amounts paid to purchase the property from the lessor at the conclusion of the lease term;

(4) costs to maintain, transport, temporarily store, or insure the property; and

(5) charges related to casualty value of damaged property.

Ultimately, the problem with leases for the lessor centers around the lessor's failure to follow the rules and finalize agreements with lessees that support the proper collection and/or payment of tax. Other problems are created by the lessor allowing the lessee to dictate the terms of the lease without having adequate knowledge of the sales and use tax code for the state in which the property will be resident. As leases may be subject to use tax, not sales tax, the lessor's failure to collect and/or pay may result in the lessee being assessed for the tax. From a public relations standpoint, it is more palatable for the lessee to pay tax periodically rather than all at once under assessment, with interest.

The special consideration given to vehicle leases arises from the different set of licensing and fee laws that govern vehicles. Further adding to the complexities of the issue are the rules covering equipment used in the "for hire" transportation of persons and property in-state and/or across borders. To increase the level of tax capture in these transactions, states have devised all methods of apportionment applicable to leased transportation equipment. The automobile rental industry, which rents vehicles on a short-term basis, is expected to assist in the enhancement of tax revenues by collection of all forms of user fees in support of tourism, airport construction and maintenance, etc., beyond the sales/use taxes. However, care should be given in addressing the taxation of special charges, e.g., drop-off charges, gasoline charges, rental of cellular phones and their charges, etc.

The short-term equipment rental companies are customarily required to collect and/or pay taxes measured by the total charge passed on to the customer. The exception to this might include situations where the equipment is rented with the operator, e.g., heavy equipment, sound or video studios, etc. These rentals may be perceived in the state's eyes as representing the purchase of services, incidental to the provision of property.

And finally, many states are focusing attention on collection of tax for the rental of real property. This may be limited to a simple hotel bed tax or may include tax on actual rentals of individual residences, stores, and offices. As companies search for methods to creatively use existing resources to generate supplemental revenue, greater attention may be given to such ancillary businesses that are departures from the company's purpose for existing. These situation will challenge the tax professional once again.

• Purchases

The issue of tax on purchases by lessors is integrally tied to the rules related to the lease transaction itself, as discussed above. When the issue can be problematic for the lessor, and more important, for the lessee, is when the lessee first purchases the property and then consummates a sale-leaseback. Many states have been careful to address such arrangements in their statutory language or rules/regulations. Problems occur when the future lessee purchases the property for resale and makes substantial use of that property prior to selling it to the lessor for leaseback. This fact pattern, viewed by an alert auditor, is often the basis for first collecting use tax on the cost of the original purchase for resale and then as sales tax on the sale of used equipment by the lessee to the lessor.

¶2205

Companies that use lease lines are advised to focus considerable attention on such transactions.

• *Special sales and use tax accounting issues*

It is easy for legal counsel to devise creative lease arrangements that offer the lessee the best financial terms possible. However, when these agreements run afoul of the tax code, the code will control the transaction. For example, giving away income tax benefits (such as depreciation) may be contrary to the rules protecting the lessee from having to pay tax on an otherwise ideal, and nontaxable, sale-leaseback transaction. Additionally, some privilege states will call the tax due on leases a use tax but will administer it as a sales tax, going to the in-state lessor for the tax. Terms related to lease assignments need to be studied carefully to avoid transferring unnecessary or inappropriate tax liabilities to an assignee. Assignments are not clearly addressed by most tax codes.

• *Constitutional issues*

A single vexing constitutional issue is often overlooked by the leasing company. By entering into lease agreements in states in which they have no obvious nexus, lessors acquire immediate nexus due to the presence of their equipment in the state. Although it may take time until the state finds the unregistered lessor and asserts its right to have the lessor register, the discovery is likely to occur. The lessor will probably execute a UCC filing and pay property tax to a county. Both actions also serve to raise the lessor's visibility in the state's eyes. For the lessor with even a small portfolio out-of-state, careful consideration should be given to attending to the matter of nexus. A national association of equipment lessors could be an excellent place to network with others sharing a similar tax interest.

¶2206 Telecommunications

When the country's entire telephone system was comprised of "Ma Bell," her regional carriers, and a handful of independent telephone companies, tax issues were relatively simple. There was little reselling of telephone services, billing was largely centralized, equipment was mostly leased (it seems, forever) and the word "cellular" was thought to be an issue in the field of microbiology. In fact, prior to 1982, no states imposed transaction taxes on interstate telecommunications.

Today, we live in a radically different world of telecommunications. Non-telephone companies have their own telephone systems, using communication satellite technology, from which they resell services to others. The alphabet soup of today's telecommunications industry is defined by LECs, CLECs and IXEs. These renegades, along with numerous independent up-start (they all began as start-ups) telephone companies, are buying telephone service in large quantities from their competitors and repackaging those services to generate incremental revenue. Teleconferencing and video conferencing are becoming almost as commonplace as companies that own their own telephone systems. Cellular phones are everywhere. Pagers can find you with a shake, beep, or message on any inch of the globe and relay a message from any other inch on the globe. The idea of the comic character, Dick Tracy, having a telephone in his wristwatch is nearly passe. With the proliferation of personal digital assistants (first sold as Palm Pilots), we are now capable of interacting fully with voice and data wherever our networks are in place. Even though Iridium, the satellite telecommunications company, is struggling, we cannot imagine where the next telephonic invention will surface. Telephones can now be rented from automobile rental agencies along with the rental cars. Conference calls can be made from airliners at an elevation of 35,000 feet, crossing several states and multiple localities in an hour-long flight.

Simply put, telecommunications is no longer limited to what people do with a telephone handset. A data file can be sent via computer modem over a cellular network while a car is "roaming" across multiple cellular networks. Data can be transmitted via fiber-optic glass cable to a satellite dish, which bounces the electromagnetic impulses off a satellite positioned in orbit over another country. Once received, it is printed out in the form of a photograph, which is scanned into a printing negative used in the production of tomorrow morning's newspaper. Telecommunications now includes the live streaming of radio and video and the use of a computer as a telephone via the Internet.

State-of-the-art telecommunications involves interactive "tel-data." An individual can watch a television program on a monitor connected to a computer with a telephone line linked to the stock market. Orders can be placed to buy and sell stock, transfer funds to cover purchases, review account balances, view a corporate balance sheet and financial statement, etc., or merely order tickets for a transcontinental plane flight or the opera (or country music concert) being staged in the local amphitheater. The array of services described in these paragraphs represents the interaction of numerous service providers in multiple states, crossing telephone lines, satellite interconnects, microwave repeater stations, and lease equipment owned by as many different companies.

As one can see, telecommunications involves a diverse grouping of providers in an environment that is in rapid and dynamic growth. Companies in this industry are fiercely competitive and incur large capital costs to establish their businesses. They create complex billings to explain who called whom, from where to where, for what period of time, at what time of day, under what rate structure, and on whose equipment.

From a sales and use tax standpoint, these companies operate in an environment that is rapidly changing due to expanding tax bases and a lack of statutory clarity, and is often governed by case law crafted over a period of years in every possible court in the country. It is no wonder that assessments can be large and wield significant financial impact (or damage). Many tax laws were written when the technology was different; the providers were all facility-based and landlines were the predominant means of accomplishing voice-only transmission.

Today, there are no fewer than a dozen states imposing sales taxes on interstate telecommunications. The list is growing as one reads these words. However, the major challenge to the telecommunications tax department is in all of the other taxes, fees, and charges that are transactions-based, touching virtually every call. Forty states impose a variety of taxes, fees, and charges linked to telecommunications services. There are over 300 taxes imposed on over 675 bases. If you think handling sales and use tax reporting is a challenge, consider that a fully compliant, multistate telecommunications company probably reports tax on over 55,000 returns to nearly 11,000 jurisdictions annually. It is not unusual for the taxes and fees on an average telecommunications statement to exceed 20% on a combined basis. Some of the names associated with the various imposts are:

— Federal Universal Service Fund Tax

— State Universal Service Fund Tax

— Federal Telecommunications Excise Tax

— Public Utility Commission Fee

— Poison Control Fee

— Number Portability Fee

— E-911 Fee

— Infrastructure Maintenance Fee

— Deaf Surcharge

There is something very ironic about calling the most recent law change in the industry the Telecommunications Reform Act of 1996.

• *Sales*

Determining taxable sales by telecommunications providers requires the taxpayer to be able to accurately interpret a code's definitions for telecommunication, definitions often outdated based on current state-of-the-art businesses. One must be able to identify the service address for the purpose of billing. However, the service address may be different from the place of call origin or terminus. Each of these locations can have a direct bearing on the taxability of the service. The taxpayer has to understand proper tax application, if any, on leases of equipment, provision of installation, repair, listing, call waiting, answering or other services, separate charges for intercompany billings, or resale considerations. If the company that provides basic telephone services or uses these services also provides a range of other services, e.g., cellular, mobile radio, paging, alarm monitoring, dedicated circuits, pay telephone, hotel, hospital or university service, etc., it is likely that such revenue may be taxable. The greatest difficulty in this mixed-bag world of telecommunications is understanding where a taxable service begins or ends, or what jurisdictions tax the service.

In recent years, case law has been established by *Goldberg v. Sweet*, 488 U.S. 252 (1989), which was the precedent-setting case for the issue of taxation of interstate telecommunications services. In *Goldberg,* the U.S. Supreme Court upheld the State of Illinois in taxing interstate telephone calls originating or terminating in Illinois, regardless of the number of other states through which the call might have passed. The case was judged in light of *Complete Auto Transit,* overcoming all of the four prongs in the test for commerce clause acceptability. The following issues are among those not addressed by the *Goldberg* decision:

(1) If a tax on interstate telecommunications does not offer a credit for taxes paid to other jurisdictions, would the tax be sustained?

(2) Would a similar tax be upheld if the billing or payment conditions were different from those in *Goldberg*?

(3) How would taxes on carriers, instead of a tax on the user, be viewed in light of this decision?

(4) How does this decision impact other industries having taxable interstate activities, e.g., cable television, news wire services, interactive tel-data services, etc.?

Perhaps one of the most important questions that a telecommunications operator must ask is whether the tax is really a sales tax at all, or really a gross receipts, user, or privilege tax masquerading as a sales tax. A second concern is whether the measure of the tax is the service alone or the service plus the various other billable and separately stated taxes, e.g., federal excise tax, 911 fee, local user of operator's tax, deaf and disabled fee, surcharges, and other amounts. In many cases, the only amount that will be taxed will be the intrastate component of the service and the repair, installation, and maintenance charges. Exemptions provided customers often parallel those allowed by the federal excise tax. Notwithstanding, telecommunications carriers should understand that the rules concerning resale and other exemptions may not always operate in parallel from tax to tax. User versus provider taxes treat exemptions very differently. If you are in the cellular telephone business, what are the issues associated with giving away or selling, at below cost, a telephone in exchange for a long-term contract?

In the last decade, a telecommunications product arrived on the scene that is truly stressing the industry, the prepaid telephone card. Simply stated, a telephone company sells time on its system at a discount to a labeler. That labeler markets a card to all buyers for use whenever and wherever the owner of the card might decide. The cardholder places a call to a special exchange that confirms the availability of time on the card allowing the call to be completed. Okay, tax wizards, where is the taxable moment here? Can we tax the sale of the card? If a call is made to or from a state that taxes telephone services, at what value is the sale measured? Is this double taxation on the same transaction, taxing the future use of the card at the time the card is sold and taxing the actual use of the service at the time the service is rendered? How does the telephone company know the retail price of the telephone call to compute tax, or does it matter? If you are in this industry, this problem is probably your nemesis. If you are not in this industry, pray that your current employer is not acquired by a telecommunications company or plan on learning a new language, a new set of tax laws, and a huge compliance chore.

• *Purchases*

Telecommunications carriers have the same problems that any service company has concerning purchases:

(1) What services are really resold for which a resale exemption certificate should be provided?

(2) As maintenance of a network is no small concern, what transactions may be viewed as nontaxable services provided by vendors?

(3) Does the operation of a telecommunications concern in the interstate commerce environment afford the purchaser any special tax opportunities in the purchasing process?

(4) Are purchases by an interstate carrier taxable when used in the operation of its business?

(5) Are there specific states where the location of equipment would offer special tax benefits?

(6) Does the purchase of parts of a network (cable, conduit, transmission towers, etc.) represent a tax opportunity based on a state's exemptions for a public utility?

Other special tax rules generally available to any taxpayer are probably available to telecommunications companies. Along with these opportunities are the same requirements that any purchaser must follow. Caution should be given to a presumption that a telephone company may be in the business of manufacturing telecommunications services and is therefore a manufacturer. Such a presumption could not be further from the truth and could create serious sales and use tax problems.

• *Special sales and use tax accounting issues*

There are no special tax accounting issues unique to the telecommunications industry, other than tracking the remarkable number of different taxes, fees, charges, etc. As with any industry, the capturing of sales (gross receipts, excise or other) taxes by the correct jurisdiction, rate and type of transaction is no small task. The greater the detail, the easier the reconciliation and reporting process.

Automating the tax accounting function is an absolute necessity in this industry. The volume of transactions is high, the types of taxes vary, and the issue of where a call originates and terminates can dictate using one tax or rate versus another. Certainly, this is an issue that could have been covered with equal ease in the section in this paragraph on sales; however, the burden often falls heaviest in the tax accounting department, due to the difficult tax return reconciliations required. Once properly automated, tax reporting becomes a mechanical process only occasionally disrupted by rate changes and the imposition of new laws. And, how do telephone companies, cellular companies, and beeper services address the issue of bad debt on their transactions? A very low rate of bad debt, involving millions of customers, can amount to more than pocket change, if not properly addressed.

The activity of legislative oversight is very important in this industry. Preemptive and pro-active legislative interaction with states and localities is a formidable, yet necessary, task.

• *Constitutional issues*

The telecommunications industry is likely to set precedents in the courts. This is because of the predominantly interstate character of the business, combined with the difficulty of establishing where the "sale" or "use" occurs. While *Goldberg* is the primary case law for this industry, what we know, see and understand about the capabilities of telecommunications today may bear little similarity to the business that will exist in 5 to 10 years (nor will the laws be the same). In the absence of tangible property (a telephone call is hardly tangible, considering how little credence the states pay to a spoken statement made to the purchaser who indicated a purchase was for resale), laws will be tailored to the industry or interpreted in the courts. Tax professionals in this industry will be on the cutting edge of sales taxation for years to come.

¶2207 Services

It is no secret that the service sector of our society is growing at a very rapid rate. The number of services available is increasing, along with the percentage of the corporate and individual populations participating in the service sector. The industries include, but are not limited to, banking, insurance and finance, health care, law, accounting, transportation, hospitality, personal care, consulting, and information. In reality, the list is much longer.

The final and broadest category that must be included is repair, the activity of making broken items work again. The thread of similarity that seems present in all of these sectors is the provision of the skill or activity by the provider for the customer, which may include the transfer of tangible personal property incidental to the performance of the service.

• *Sales*

Earlier in our discussion of measuring sales tax, this author was careful to note that the measure of tax may not exclude the amount attributable to labor. This is true if what is being acquired is the tangible personal property. However, if what is being acquired is the service of the provider, the amount of the "sale" valued by the labor component may be specifically excluded from taxable measure in many states. The concept recognized in the sales tax environment that answers the question of whether a sale is of a service or of tangible personal property is the "true object test"—that is, what is the true object of the transaction in question, the property acquired or the service provided.

At times, the distinction is very clear. Having one's teeth cleaned is a service. Nothing is given to the patient except the intangible feeling and knowledge that plaque was removed, along with some money from one's pocket for the service. Is having one's house cleaned any less of a service? What happens when the computer repair company repairs the computer?

Let's modify each of these activities and see the effect on the true object test. To the cleaning of one's teeth, add polishing, a gold filling (including a local anesthetic), and some x-rays. Do any of these items make the true object of the visit to the dentist anything less than dental service with the tangible property being provided incidental to that service? Taking the cleaning of one's house, does the true object of the arrangement with the cleaning service change if the floors are waxed, i.e., a layer of wax is supplied incidental to the service? If the computer repair company also provides a power supply and fan, a new RS232 cable, a new monitor and upgraded software, do we now have a sale of all of these parts or a service in which parts are supplied incidental to the service?

In considering the alternate options offered above, we have identified a simple service without much doubt and a service that includes the transfer of tangible personal property incidental to the service. As discussed at ¶401, state legislatures are changing their laws to define or enumerate taxable services that heretofore needed no definition because only tangible personal property was taxable. Perhaps the true object test is becoming less important as states include a greater number of services under the mantle of taxable transaction. Therefore, it is the responsibility of the tax professional to:

(1) question whether the service (in question) has been defined to be taxable, e.g., janitorial services in Texas,

(2) determine if regulatory consideration has been given to the service and, through that mechanism, is considered either taxable or exempt, and

(3) apply the true object test to determine if the intent of the purchaser was the service or the property.

The conclusion may not be easy to accept, but, in the absence of an opinion of tax counsel to the contrary, tax should be applied.

It is not uncommon for one's customer to believe that they have the certain answer on such an issue. In this situation, one may learn through the customer imparting that knowledge. This should be handled through a request for written advice. If the customer is able to "cite chapter and verse," independent confirmation can be achieved through one's personal review of the code section or regulation/rule. If the customer is relying on a private written opinion, it is advisable to acquire a copy of same, review it for its generic character (i.e., whether it applies to all similar situations, not just a specific fact pattern), and be certain that it is placed in the customer's file. The final insurance is to determine if the advice may be relied on by others, not only the party to whom it was addressed. A written confirmation of this reliability is highly desirable. Remember, an auditor can easily schedule a tax omission as "exempt sales overstated" if the transaction's exempt quality cannot be supported.

One must understand the rules related to services billed with or without parts (repair services), billed in conjunction with related transactions (transportation services), billed before or after the completion of the sale (installation), billed as a part of the selling price (finance or carrying charges), etc. While most of these issues are discussed in the context of the question, "what is included or excluded in determining taxable measure?", they are issues for service providers as well.

• *Purchases*

It is a broadly accepted rule that one providing a service is the consumer of supplies and materials used in the delivery of that service. A repair service that does not separately bill for parts delivered with the service is the consumer of those parts. Capital asset purchases are often taxable if they do not qualify for existing manufacturing exemptions. Other services may benefit from exemptions for their purchases by virtue of regulatory preemption, e.g., a common carrier or public utility. But, generally, purchases by service industry companies will be taxable.

• *Special sales and use tax accounting issues*

The most significant special tax problem for service providers exists for the provider who commingles taxable and resale property. If a manufacturer operates a repair facility for its products, the transfer of the parts from a resale inventory to a consumables inventory requires the appropriate tax accrual. This seems simple on the surface until one contemplates the parts crossing state lines. Equally confusing is the issue of parts being removed from a resale inventory and shipped to a field service representative in another state. Does the use tax on the conversion of resale to self-consumed property occur in the state in which the property was held for resale or the state in which the property will be consumed in the repair service?

• Constitutional issues

Can a repair service performed in state A on property being returned to state B be taxable in both states? The answer to this question can be surprising to the most experienced tax professional and does not appear to cause anyone enough discomfort to raise the specter of a federal challenge. From a case law standpoint, the majority of all activity is occurring at the state court level, where service providers in the information and data processing/telecommunications area are making court appearances. The challenges are often related to where the service is enjoyed versus where it is provided. The state courts have found in favor of both the taxpayers and the taxing authorities for differing reasons.

A second area of attention concerns software where the custom versus non-custom software issue is playing to large legal crowds. The software issue seems to be one that uses the courts to clarify statutory language.

A third and final area of interest is waste disposal. The question is whether waste disposal in conjunction with the transportation of waste is taxable.

One should be mindful that in all of these areas, the challenges are not moving beyond the state court level. The issue is generally a matter of definition within a given statute rather than a due process or Commerce Clause problem. Again, this author repeats a previously stated opinion shared by many attorneys in the tax environment: There are few challenges at the constitutional level that will be heard, let alone decided in favor of a taxpayer. *Quill* may not be the last, but there probably will be few others.

Chapter XXIII

Electronic Commerce, E-Business, and Other Mysteries of Cyberspace

¶2301 Introduction

If this chapter had been written in the fall of 2000, its significance would have been huge. In June 2001, only eight or nine months later, an industry that had a capitalization value in the six to seven trillion-dollar range had fallen on hard times. The implosion halved what was paper wealth and plunged many into financial disaster. Businesses we became comfortable calling the "dot-coms" of the millennium still exist, albeit in much smaller numbers. Many marvel that some of the well-known dot-coms remain in business today in the landscape of carnage, where nine out of ten dot-coms closed their doors and sent their minions scattering to the winds, like so many dandelion puff-balls blown into oblivion on a windy day. Those of us who eschewed this world of sudden wealth to continue in pursuit of our more mundane activities in traditional businesses still have our jobs. If we invested in the dot.coms, we are poorer but still employed.

As we take a deeper look into the issues of electronic commerce than we did in earlier editions of this book, we will discover a new vocabulary, some new and interesting questions, but very few conclusions that have been etched in stone. Electronic commerce is like the sales tax industry itself: change is assured.

¶2302 The Language and Business of E-Business

Electronic business (also known as e-business or e-commerce) is the industry that encompasses the world of commerce using electronic means, rather than traditional methods of buying and selling. It involves transacting business using computers (or other electronic devices) and the Internet. However, since the last edition of this book, an entirely new set of terms has been developed to describe the various forms of electronic commerce. The starting point is the dot-com, which is a company that sells its goods or services to customers that place their orders using the Internet. These companies are simply electronic business direct marketers. The predecessor to the electronic commerce industry is probably the direct mail marketing business, including the catalog merchants, beginning with such tried-and-true names as Sears, Montgomery Ward, Spiegel, etc. The transactions of electronic commerce link businesses and consumers (a.k.a. B2C) or businesses with other business (a.k.a. B2B).

There are several interesting variations on basic electronic commerce. The first is the consumer-to-consumer transaction that uses an intermediary, such as an electronic auction site. Individuals and businesses can sell their property to other individuals or businesses, using the auction site to facilitate the sales (by selling to the highest bidder). Secondly, businesses are using reverse auction sites to move excess inventories of goods and services (by looking for buyers making offers that are acceptable, but potentially less than the selling price for identical property or services sold directly without "competitive bidding"). Third, some sites are posting products for several sellers in large on-line catalogs. These might be characterized as indirect mass marketers. Entire industries (automotive, chemical, paper, etc.) are banding together to create malls to sell products of common interest on sites where the industry sellers offer products to be sold to the buyers.

A different part of the electronic commerce world is the world of content providers and digital sellers. The content providers offer information, relationships, contacts, research, and a long list of topical materials that may be free or involve a small service fee or subscription fee, resulting in the transfer of knowledge or the formation of relationships, often without a sale of property or services. The other area of content with a twist involves digital marketers that sell or provide software through the Internet. In the latter case, we are talking about licensed material that is delivered entirely on the Internet, without the intervention of external delivery or transfer of physical property.

The next category of Internet businesses are those that serve others on the Internet. The first in this group is the most obvious—the hosts. These companies include the actual Internet Service Providers, or ISPs. They operate the hardware and provide the connectivity that allows all of us to communicate throughout the World Wide Web. An ISP can be as simple as a local telephone company or an individual who owns a server that has a web address on the World Wide Web. The complex ISP may operate a giant server farm, enabling electronic mail communications, which serves individuals and businesses.

The second group of Internet service businesses are those that provide processing activities—the service intermediaries. These companies may bill, process invoices or clear payments, or provide linkage for their clients and their clients' customers. The sellers do not operate their own sites. Instead, they piggyback on the sites of the service intermediaries, outsourcing all but the task of physically shipping the product to the customer when the order has been processed.

Finally, one of the fastest growing electronic business segments is the one that is addressing the issue of bandwidth—those companies focused on the problem of getting more data to and through the Internet faster. These are ultimately infrastructure companies. They are part of the telecommunications, cable, and most recently, satellite industries. They sell compression technology to move large volumes of data faster down smaller electronic avenues or provide new methods of skirting existing avenues by using novel forms of connectivity. These are mostly the providers of solutions that require hardware (earth-bound or sky-based), either between Internet destinations or at the destinations themselves.

As we consider this overall list, we must remember this is a dynamic environment. New businesses and technologies will offer solutions with remarkable speed. They will arrive on the scene quickly and offer greater speed and facility in communications. When the fourth edition of this book was written, I suggested that "the life cycle for a computer is now under one year." Two-plus years later, the life cycle of a computer is probably down to six months, the cost of a computer has plummeted, and the way in which we connect to the Internet has experienced its own revolution. A personal digital appliance (PDA) now serves as a cellphone, an Internet computer terminal, a personal clipboard or filing system, a ticker for all forms of news, as well as a music source, global positioning satellite (GPS) device, and most recently a remote television. What is the next option we will see on a PDA?

¶2303 Historical Responses to a Quandary

The big tax question, especially for e-commerce, is "Where is the situs and event that marks a transaction for tax purposes?" Keeping in mind that a sales or use tax is imposed on a discrete event, we need to find the event to tax before we consider whether it is taxable. To understand this question requires a look at how our governments and courts have attempted to address this issue.

- In 1992, the *Quill* decision provided a bright line for considering the taxation of interstate activity. This decision, however, left room for politicians to take further action, which has been remarkably slow in coming, considering the size of the issue.

- Also in 1992, a commission was formed by Congress and asked to propose policy on taxation of interstate (remote) commerce. An initial moratorium was established with a narrow scope, pending the recommendation of the commission. Little was resolved, and the moratorium was extended until it expired on October 21, 2001, without much fanfare or a significant conclusion.

- In 1993 and 1994, the Direct Marketing Association, which is the organization of mostly mail order and direct mail marketing companies, struggled and failed to draw a line in the tax-nexus sand with the Federation of Tax Administrators.

- In 1997, 1998 and 1999, a group of trade, professional and governmental associations, largely headed by the National Tax Association, formed a commission to present its independent recommendations to the public. Many issues were addressed, but many were sidestepped, due to the conflicting views of the representatives.

- In 2000, the Streamlined Sales Tax Project (SSTP), a state collaborative effort, started deliberations to find a way to simplify the concepts of sales and use taxation and thereby facilitate a workable solution for taxing electronic commerce. This effort continues to suffer from vested-issue stubbornness. Some conclusions have been reached, but many questions remain unanswered. Alternative ideas have been floated by the National Conference of State Legislatures. Over 20 states are considering model act legislation relating to simplification. In ¶2305 below, additional discussion is included on the SSTP.

Where do we stand today, thirteen years after *Quill*? Everyone agrees that we have a problem with a possibility of solution in the foreseeable future. States and localities will fight to preserve main-street tax revenues, which are eroding as electronic commerce's share of sales revenue increases. Electronic businesses currently enjoy a taxation compliance holiday and a competitive price advantage, as the power struggle over taxing Internet activity remains in limbo. Main-street businesses complain bitterly about their disadvantaged position. States want to simplify the process (even considering a third-party provider to handle tax compliance), eliminating industry's arguments that compliance is a nightmare. Localities want to protect a tax revenue source if state rules trump local rules. The remaining players struggle to stay out of the fray. What will ultimately happen is anyone's guess. What we can discuss are the issues that seem central to the debate. Ultimately, it is probably Congress that will be required to legislate a way to address the inequities of *Quill*.

¶2304 Getting Down to E-Business Taxation

How does one determine where a sale or purchase takes place? States want their just tax on this ever-increasing piece of business. This is an issue of definition of activity. Is the activity included (defined) in the statute as an activity subject to tax? Is the activity actually taxable? States recognize how difficult it will be to get the purchaser to voluntarily pay use tax when an untaxed taxable purchase is made. Also, the recordkeeping for all of these individual transactions would be horrific. The second problem is determining a consistent method of taxing electronic commerce to avoid double taxation and problems with inter-state commerce. At ¶2305, there is a discussion of what the Streamlined Sales Tax Project is doing to address the issue of uniformity to promote simplicity and increased compliance, whether or not it is legally required.

Imagine the following transaction: An individual, Fred, is flying from his home in Georgia to visit Aunt Martha and Uncle Harry in Nevada. During the flight, Fred whips out his trusty laptop, plugs into the air phone, dials his Internet provider in Atlanta, is connected to a CD shop in Maine that has a web site that is hosted by a provider in Vermont. Fred orders one CD to be shipped to his mother in New Jersey. Prior to Fred's arrival in Nevada, a bank in North Carolina processes the credit card payment. Where is the tax situs for this transaction? Let's consider a few possibilities:

(1) We could impose sales tax on the Maine CD shop, on the presumption that the presence of Fred's instruction via computer constituted a sale in the state of Maine. Although the seller's web site was in Vermont, the final instructions were received in Maine and acted upon there. Also, the fact that Fred was crossing state lines at the time of the transaction makes it difficult to place him at a point where one could say that a sale occurred. Isn't there a problem here because the sale is really in inter-state commerce?

(2) New Jersey use tax collection responsibility could be imposed on the Maine CD shop, under the presumption that it knew where the property was to be shipped and no other purchase site could be determined. Isn't there a problem here, since the Maine CD shop may have no nexus

in New Jersey and, therefore, would be under no obligation to collect the use tax?

(3) Would it be possible to tax the sale at the location of the web site of the seller? This novel approach implies that the point of negotiation of the sale is where the customer and seller's computers finally lock horns in formulating the transaction. Those states that have many ISPs would love this idea. The U.S. Supreme Court, in *Oklahoma Tax Commission v. Jefferson Lines*, 115SCt 2018 (1995), would consider this an acceptable solution and tax the transaction at the web site. Unfortunately, the creativity of sellers would surely result in moving all web sites offshore or into states without a tax, thereby saving the seller compliance woes. With no sales subject to sales tax, all purchases would be subject to use tax, putting us back at the starting point. Therefore, this is an unlikely solution.

(4) Could each state through which an electronic signal passes tax a portion of the transaction? Again, the Court has considered this issue. In *Goldberg v. Sweet*, 109 SCt 582 (1989), the Court stated that the passage of electronic signals is not a substantial nexus, although the ultimate test had to do with origination and termination of a connection (call).

Currently, the battling parties are showing interest in suggestion (1), above. The concept is called the "base state system." The idea is that a transaction would be taxed in the state of the commercial domicile of the seller or where the highest value of service occurs. The highest value of service would likely be where the order is filled and the property is placed in the stream of commerce. Under this approach, there is one state, one tax and one rate for any transaction, regardless of where Fred, his mother, the airplane, a server, etc., is located.

In the sales tax world, it will take little time for one to conclude that the only way such an approach would be adopted is by federal legislation. This is clearly a Commerce Clause issue. This problem will have to be addressed separately from the perspective of all other taxes that could attach to an electronic commerce transaction or the income therefrom.

Again, who are the battling parties? First, the state governors and state legislatures are concerned with the revenue that might be lost if no tax is imposed on electronic commerce. Protection of the state's retail sales base would be the challenge. Secondly, the sellers want to minimize their burden of compliance. While they could accept reporting tax in their domicile states, it is at best a lesser of evils. There is little doubt that these sellers want to collect and report state use tax on behalf of their customers, not to mention local use tax. This has the smell of the direct mail marketing problem all over again. Thirdly, the local jurisdictions are concerned that someone might establish taxation on a state-rate-only basis, hanging the locals out to dry. Simply stated, the federal government is not going to focus below the state level.

In 1999 and again in early 2000, CCH surveyed all of the states to determine how they are actually addressing the taxation of Internet transactions. The results of this survey were published in *Sales and Use Taxation of E-Commerce*.[1] Most states responded, with the following exceptions:

- New York, Illinois, West Virginia, and Ohio did not respond because their policies and rules were still in formation;
- Nine states—Georgia, Indiana, Louisiana, Michigan, South Carolina, South Dakota, Tennessee, and Wisconsin—did not respond; and
- Alaska, Montana, Delaware, New Hampshire and Oregon have no sales tax and were not sent surveys.

CCH filled the void left by the non-responding states with editorial commentary on ways in which the states might respond, based on existing statutes. This is an excellent desk reference for E-commerce businesses.

The second major source of information on taxation of E-commerce is *Cybertaxation, The Taxation of E-Commerce*,[2] a comprehensive book by Karl Frieden, which examines the issues of sales taxation on E-commerce, as well as many other forms of taxation. This is a comprehensive, in-depth investigation into the topic. Tax professionals worldwide should consider this book an invaluable part of the complete tax library.

Because the Internet invites worldwide commerce, an Internet seller, content provider, service company, or bandwidth creator cannot simply avoid worldwide taxation issues. If one changed the scenario of Fred's transaction described above, so that Fred also purchased a gift for a cousin in Paris, what a full contingent of taxes would need to be considered, including value-added taxes, foreign and domestic income taxes, import duties, etc.; some taxes would be easier to address than others.

¶2305 Streamlined Sales Tax Project

A working commission, which was formed by a collaboration of states (not all), local jurisdictions (collectively by associations), industry (individually and collectively), and trade association representatives, has been meeting to develop uniformity in many aspects of the sales tax environment. The stated project mission of the SSTP is to "develop measures to design, test and implement a sales and use tax system that radically simplifies sales and use taxes." At the center of this goal would be the standardization of definitions, but not the manner in which the individual states will apply their tax rules to these definitions. For example, agreement was sought on how to define:

- classes of common products, e.g., food, clothing, etc.;
- tax bases, i.e., sales price, purchase price, etc.;
- bad debt;
- rounding; and
- sales sourcing—retail location, or ship-to or purchaser's address maintained for other purposes, or origin of seller's transaction.

---

[1] CCH INCORPORATED, 2000.   [2] CCH INCORPORATED, 2000.

The project also has looked at geographical issues (such as rating transactions by zip code), notification of change issues (including expectations for issuing rate change information), notification of boundary changes (such as expectations for posting changes to taxing geographies), and tax collection (including the use of certified service providers and automated systems). As we go to press, this is the status of the SSTP project.

The SSTP Steering Committee is comprised of state representatives from nine states, two serving as co-chairpersons. The states represented in the Steering Committee are: Florida, Kentucky, Missouri, New Jersey, Pennsylvania, South Dakota, Texas, Utah, and Wisconsin. The SSTP agreement becomes effective when 10 state legislatures adopt conforming legislation representing more than 20% of the US population. Late in 2003, the states of Arkansas, Indiana, Iowa, Kansas, Kentucky, Nebraska, North Carolina, Ohio, Oklahoma, South Dakota, Tennessee, Utah, Vermont, and West Virginia were supposedly in compliance with the SSTP agreement. This represented enough states and populace to meet the threshold. Additionally the states of Minnesota, Texas, Washington, and Wyoming are considered to be in "substantial compliance" representing an additional 11.7% of the US population. A state that has adopted the provisions of the SSTP into its tax statutes is deemed to be in compliance. However, the critical issue may be the effective date of the adopted provisions. For the above mentioned states, the effective dates vary as widely as July 1, 2003 to July 1, 2004.

Once the agreement is triggered, a governing board will be formulated, various advisory boards will be established, technology contracts will be developed and issued, and a host of other activities will take place. In the interim, other particularly messy unresolved issues must be addressed:

(1) How will bundled transactions be handled, i.e., those transactions having both taxable and non-taxable components? There is a large divergence in the way states are taxing services that are separated but integral to the sale of property.

(2) How will services be sourced? States that have local taxes that are origin-based are at the center of this discussion, e.g., Illinois, California, Texas, and Washington.

(3) What will be the disposition of digital property? The issue of taxing software rears its head in this context, e.g., load and leave, delivery via modem, custom or canned, maintenance, etc.

(4) How will the cost of collection be handled? Small taxpayers will bear a disproportionately large cost of tax collect as a function of the tax dollars collected compared to large taxpayers with the inverse condition.

When all of the other issues, the seemingly irreconcilable differences, are ironed out, the SSTP will move into the phase of being a voluntary program. The adopted statutory provisions will take effect as specified by legislative decree on a state by state basis, but an out-of-state seller's nexus status (obligation to collect as state's sales or use tax) cannot be changed without (literally) an act of

¶2305

Congress. And, to be sure, some amount of legal maneuvering will take place in the courts before all of the issues around *Quill* are put to bed.

So, with all of that said, where are we in the simplification process? We are closer than we were last decade when the first meetings of the "participating states" commenced discussion of SSTP. Is SSTP a done deal? In one sense, when all of the effective dates of the complying states have passed we can move forward to the next set of activities. And in the meantime, the Congress can debate the issue, filibuster, and perhaps even act, but this author is not holding his breath for a great breakthrough. The status of the SSTP/Internet moratorium act is discussed at the end of the ¶2308.

¶2306 Bricks and Mortar, Arise

One of the more interesting phenomena of the electronic commerce revolution is how, and to what extent, traditional business has embraced this new environment. There are several different models in development. At the simplest level, a traditional business adopts an E-business operation to compete with its electronic competitors. The most widely recognized example of this has been in the book business, where traditional book chain stores are morphing into dotcoms to fight Amazon.com.

A second form of adaptation consists of offering electronic delivery of hard products. The entertainment and media industries are making this leap. Sales are made directly or through others.

Embracing the electronic lifestyle is a third approach, which has been taken by some traditional companies. This process begins at the internal electronic mail level and progresses to the hosting of web sites for product and service presentation, customer service, and direct selling (almost as an afterthought in order to avoid ruffling the feathers of the existing channel vendors).

As mentioned at ¶2302, a fourth way that bricks-and-mortar companies are converting to e-commerce is through the use of electronic purchasing malls for entire industries, such as auto, paper, chemicals, etc. The electronic malls place vendors in a position of offering their products to many potential customers electronically from a single web site. We will continue to see more incursions by traditional businesses into the realm of electronic commerce because:

- It is less expensive—a web site does not need large physical stores and sales personnel to move product.

- It is more profitable—web selling at the same pricing structure generates greater profits for the same selling volume.

- It is doable—traditional businesses already have the infrastructure and financial resources to transition smoothly.

- It is possible—aspects of tax management are already in place; being digital means that sales data must be tracked differently but the systems are already (generally) in place.

However, with that said, bricks-and-mortar businesses still need to address the thorny issues of nexus, compliance, sourcing, etc., for their unrelated/related

¶2306

dot-coms. Drop shipment and shipping/handling matters are also challenging. Both the CCH MULTISTATE SALES TAX GUIDE and the Institute for Professionals in Taxation offer some guidance, providing charts and surveys covering these areas.

¶2307 The Intersection of Content and Conveyance

We can picture our brave new e-world in each of its various forms. We can consider the questions of taxability as we present the scenarios of sellers and buyers interacting to complete transactions. What is causing remarkable clouding of the issue is how the transactions are merging with transmission to raise some very puzzling tax issues. Every person, company, provider, collector, payor, processor, carrier, etc., participates in each transaction, but where one participant starts and stops its involvement is exceedingly difficult to identify. The percentage of an electronic transaction associated with its transmission is becoming increasingly significant. Our thought processes need to be expanded to reflect a different and complex paradigm. If you skipped ¶2206 on Telecommunications, you might want to flip back to it now. E-commerce is telecommunications. No e-business person can afford to ignore the intersection of content and conveyance.

¶2308 Dissension, Discord, and Disagreement

Where do we stand in the winter of 2004? What is the government doing or not doing? On November 28, 2001, President Bush signed a 2-year extension to the Internet Tax Freedom Act[3]. This Act suggests that states would be given authority to form a compact to jointly collect sales taxes from online vendors. The hidden "gotcha" provision required that this plan will only be implemented if at least 25 states participate in the compact, and only if Congress ratifies the compact. High-tech industry representatives noted the absence of two very important provisions in this new bill for which they lobbied heavily:

(1) that each state would have to impose the same Internet sales tax rate in all jurisdictions within its borders; and

(2) that state tax, similar to an income tax (Indiana Gross Receipts Tax, for example), that has a particularly strong impact on computer and software manufacturers, would have to be eliminated.

What agreement has been reached since November 2001? As more lines are drawn in the sand, I put my money on those who say a law change remains a long way off. I believe that consensus will be extremely difficult to reach. In the meantime, the extended Internet moratorium act expired in November 2003 and no new moratorium was passed, yet. SSTP and Internet moratorium legislation is sloshing around in Washington without action. Bills were presented to both the House and Senate in late September 2003 stating (among many things) that the Congress consents to the terms of the SSTP, excludes small businesses, mandates tax collection compensation to vendors, grants the SSTP governing board judicial review authority, establishs some minimum simplification rules, and warns the telecommunications industry to be ready for tax simplification by 2006.

---

[3] This Act, extended the moratorium until November 1, 2003. This moratorium prevents states from imposing taxes on Internet activities not already in place. This exemption does not impact the use tax liability imposed on purchasers of taxable property brought in from out of state for use in the purchaser's home state if the use tax was not collected by the seller..

Chapter XXIV
Is This Book Taxable?

¶2401 Introduction

The "acid test" in sales and use tax matters is found in live sales and purchase activity, permit registration, data collection, documentation, return preparation and the scrutiny of a compliance audit. While sales tax issues can be studied and discussed theoretically, the development and understanding of a specific set of transactions can produce useful awareness of the many nuances of this "taxing" profession. Therefore, consider the following real-life situation—is this book taxable?

As our scenario unfolds, one should recall the common statutory concepts presented in the foregoing chapters. While keeping those concepts in mind, we can employ decisiveness and tax candor in studying this "case." In this test case, one need not be concerned with the explicit issues of book authorship and publishing; however, the questions are real, the problems challenging and the exercise an introduction to the tax thought process.

What follows is a description of a generic situation, not necessarily the author's particular experience. There are many possible responses to the issues raised. Some answers are state specific; others, more universal. The proposed conclusions intentionally ignore the specific laws of a given state, but rather address the issues in a generic sense.

¶2402 Is This Book Taxable?

A publisher wants to cover a topic in a new book and contacts a specialist on that topic with whom the publisher negotiates an outside authorship and publishing agreement. The agreement provides that the author will prepare one complete manuscript to be delivered to the publisher on some future date. The manuscript will contain all of the material outlined in a proposal submitted by the author and accepted by the publisher. Following editorial review, the publisher will print, market and distribute the book, returning to the author a royalty measured by some percentage of the publisher's gross receipts on the sale of the book.

From issuing a "request for proposals" to receipt of the manuscript by the publisher, many activities will need tax consideration by both the author and the publisher.

(1) Are supplies used by the author subject to tax?

(2) Is the manuscript preparation a service or is the publisher paying for, through sharing the anticipated revenue stream with the author, the right to use or rent the author's ideas in the form of a manuscript?

(3) Is the manuscript itself considered tangible personal property and, therefore, subject to tax when it is delivered by the author (seller) to the

publisher (purchaser)? Is the manuscript tangible personal property purchased by the publisher for resale, or intangible property?

(4) If the transfer of the possession of the manuscript to the publisher results in no current consideration, when, if at all, does a sale occur?

(5) If the author hires the services of an independent editor, who is paid for editorial corrections and recommendations, are those services or elements of fabrication and are they taxable or nontaxable?

(6) If an otherwise taxable manuscript is transferred in a magnetic form, is a custom software exemption available?

(7) If an otherwise taxable manuscript is transferred in a telephonic form, i.e., by modem, is an exemption available?

The answer to the question, is this book taxable, will be found in considering three issues: (1) the taxability of the intangible content committed to a manuscript given to a publisher by the author; (2) the taxability of the tangible property represented by the actual book itself; and (3) the taxability of plant, equipment and supplies needed to publish the book.

Answers to most of these questions are based upon a state's posture toward taxing services. The "true object test," that is, the test to determine if the true purpose of the transaction was the property purchased or the acquisition of ideas expressed in a tangible form, is the first issue to address. Many states view the original manuscript delivered by the author to the publisher as tangible personal property merely incidental to the service of creating the manuscript itself. Accordingly, in many states, the manuscript is not taxable in its tangible form and, where no taxable sale occurs between the author and the publisher, all equipment and supplies used by the author probably are taxable.

However, as states reach out to tax services, the creative writing product may become taxable. If this occurs, the tax on a manuscript could be due on each royalty payment, whether in the form of an advance or an actual royalty paid to the author based on the publisher's sales receipts. Since only the advance is a known value, the timing of the tax liability would likely be determined by the advance itself. All other sales values could only be known, and the liabilities thereon established, after the book had been printed and distributed.

Would the infrequency of taxable sales (two or less per year in most states) render this transaction nontaxable? The fact that there are many payments does not turn a single sale into multiple sales; therefore, the occasional sales rule might apply.

Could the service (writing the manuscript) be viewed as a sale for resale? This is not likely as the manuscript itself is not a component part of the published book but only a method of providing the publisher the author's ideas in an easy (one would hope) to read form. However, if the transaction is a sale, then the supplies (paper and ink, or computer media) upon which the text of the book is placed could be purchased for resale. In a state offering a manufacturing aids exemption, scratch paper might be regarded as exempt. Where a manufacturing equipment exemption is allowed, a typewriter or computer could be considered nontaxable.

¶2402

Would the preparation of the manuscript on a computer diskette turn the manuscript into a piece of custom software? In nearly all states, software is only deemed to be "custom" if it is original program instructions. Use of "canned" word processing software would not appear to change the status of the transaction.

Can the transmission of the text by modem, where no tangible personal property changes hands, make a taxable manuscript nontaxable? In states taxing services, in general, and telephone services, in particular, the use of a modem would probably be immaterial. States exempting services would typically exempt "information" transferred by modem.

Would the use of outside editorial assistance be a taxable cost to the author? If the manuscript is taxable, the outside editorial service to modify the text would likely be a service purchased for resale.

Once the manuscript is in the hands of the publisher, there are a series of transactions which offer some interesting tax questions. The manuscript is given to (a) editorial personnel who review and polish it. It is (b) typeset, (c) supported with charts, diagrams and illustrations, (d) laid out, pasted up, and reduced to camera-ready art which is further (e) reduced to printing plates. The plates are (f) placed on a press with ink and paper, and out comes the printed word. The paper is (g) folded, cut, collated, covered and bound, and the manuscript is now a book, (h) placed in boxes and (i) shipped to a warehouse pending distribution. (See the descriptions of the activities below.) All of the activities which follow hereafter are sales-related issues we will address shortly.

The production of the book to this stage is clearly "manufacturing" in the view of every state. From a sales and use tax standpoint, the foregoing activities, performed by the publisher's facilities and personnel, are viewed differently than if the same process involved both the publisher and the publisher's contractors. Taking each of the steps in the production process, we can contrast the applicability of tax and draw some conclusions. In doing this analysis, we will assume a statute that does not tax services.

(a) *Editorial activities:* When performed by the publisher, these activities are part of the production process, adding value to the manuscript, and involve the consumption of some taxable supplies and materials. If the publisher were to contract with an outside editor, services of the editor generally would be nontaxable.

(b) *Typesetting:* Typesetting, performed by the publisher, which results in camera-ready galleys to be used for paste-up, is a service involving the internal consumption of taxable supplies. *Are galleys considered manufacturing aids?* Manufacturing aids often must come in direct contact with the product being produced for resale to qualify for such an exemption. This would not appear to be the case with typeset galleys. Typesetting services purchased by the publisher would likely be taxable as the "true object" of the transaction is the acquisition of the typeset galleys (tangible personal property) which will be used by the publisher in creating camera-ready art.

¶2402

(c) *Charts, diagrams and illustrations:* Again, as with typesetting, the rules for taxability seem to follow for this group of activities. Production of charts, diagrams and illustrations by the publisher would be part of the process of preparing the manuscript for publication, thereby involving the consumption of taxable supplies and materials used by the publisher's personnel. The outside purchase of these same services will likely be viewed as the purchase of taxable tangible personal property to be consumed by the publisher prior to the commencement of the manufacturing process itself.

(d) *Layout and paste-up into camera-ready art:* Camera-ready art, mechanicals, or art boards are the result of laying out and pasting up the galleys, charts, diagrams, illustrations, photographs, etc. This includes providing instructions to the camera operator describing the sizing, colors, art placement and tones of each page. As with typesetting and art production, these activities, performed by the publisher, consume taxable materials and supplies. Performed by outside contract, the publisher will likely find these services to be taxable as the purchase of taxable (or not) manufacturing aids.

(e) *Printing plates:* Printing plates, whether for a one or multi-color press run, are used to place the ink on the paper. Clearly, printing plates are manufacturing aids and should be viewed accordingly. Therefore, the materials purchased for their fabrication may be exempt as would their outright purchase from an outside supplier in a state that grants an exemption to manufacturing aids. However, printing plates could not be purchased for resale by a publisher for its own use. The plates are not resold. Modern computer technology is combining the steps in (b), (c), (d), and (e) above; however, the tax impact is not likely to be radically different when these activities are combined.

(f) *Paper and ink:* Whether purchased by the publisher to be used on the publisher's printing press or given to a contract printer, both paper and ink should be purchased for resale. Thinner or solvent would be a manufacturing aid as it evaporates rather than remaining with the finished product. The contract printer's service may also be purchased for resale.

(g) *Fold, cut, collate, cover and bind:* As with any step in manufacturing, performance by the publisher or a contractor notwithstanding, the activity itself and the supplies becoming part of the book (staples, glue, cardboard, etc.) may all be purchased for resale.

(h) *Boxing for shipment:* To determine the taxability of the box and labeling supplies, one must know the use of the packaging products. If the property is being shipped to the customer, most states would regard the box as nontaxable (a nonreturnable empty container to be purchased for resale and sold with its contents). However, if books are being shipped to the publisher's warehouse prior to delivery to customers, the same nonreturnable box may be taxable if the books are not sold to the customer in the same box. States have developed a variety of nuances to further confuse this issue, requiring the professional to use care in claiming a resale exemption for purchasing packaging materials.

(i) *Shipping:* Shipping prior to sale, that is, the cost of transportation of property from the publisher's printing plant to its warehouse, will be taxed or exempted based on the state's code. Shipping from a contract printer to the publisher's warehouse will be transportation in conjunction with the printer's resale sale to the publisher and, therefore, probably exempt from tax.

If we take a look at these first activities, we note that the tax cost to the publisher, when performing these activities in-house, may be far less than the tax cost of acquiring the same services from outside vendors. One can also recognize that, while tax should be an important cost variable for consideration, it should not blind one's vision of the bigger picture. Instead, the tax professional should assist management in understanding the purchase and production options along with their respective tax costs. Machinery and equipment exemptions should also be considered part of this same equation.

• *Compliance issues*

Finally, with the process of selling "this" book, all of the basic compliance issues surface in deciding if this book is taxable.

(1) In which states does our hypothetical company have nexus?

(2) What forms must be completed for registration?

(3) Is there a deposit required for taking out a seller's permit and who must sign it?

(4) Which customers or sales are subject to tax and what are the state and local tax rates?

(5) How frequently must the return be completed and filed?

(6) What certificates must be requested, what must they say, how frequently must they be replaced and how should they be maintained?

As we look back at this exercise, we find that one can substitute the word "book" for a wide variety of other products. Perhaps the activities of the author are really like a company's research and development activities. Pre-production activities are functions of design and tooling development. The printing plates are the tools and dies, the paper and ink are the raw materials and the solvents and thinners are the indirect materials. Most products are boxed and shipped. The lesson in this chapter to understand a company's products or services and how they are made from start to finish. It is just as likely that taxes are being underpaid as overpaid. There is no justification for either condition.

Finally, before we close, we should remember that our hypothetical book could be sold via the Internet in an electronic form. In other words, the customer can contact the seller and ask for the book to be downloaded and sent as an attachment to an e-mail. The book has no physical manifestation until the purchaser reproduces it on a local computer printer. Is our sale still taxable? In

¶2402

which states is it taxable? Who reports the tax? Our new electronic world adds convenience, to be sure, complexity, to be certain, and continued confusion, until our Congress or the states assert a policy that we must follow.

Glossary of Terms

Glossary Index

I. Definitions: Basic terms found in statutes

(1) **excise** (as in excise tax): an impost or duty levied on the manufacture, sale or consumption of commodities within a given geographical territory, or an extraction for license or permission to practice or conduct certain trades or occupations

(a) *International:* Value-added tax

(b) *Federal level:* manufacturer's, fuel, transportation, telecommunications, luxury, firearms, sporting goods, alcohol, etc.

(c) *State level:* fuel, tobacco, alcohol, gasoline, lodgings, etc.; sales, use, consumption, business and occupations, etc.

(d) *Local level:* sales, use, business license, transient or hotel bed, etc.

(2) **real property:** property fixed to the ground and improvements which become an integral part of same

(3) **tangible personal property:** depending upon the statute, property that can be held, smelled, touched, seen, or tasted, or which is otherwise perceptible to the human senses and is not real property

(4) **service:** an action performed by one party to, for, or on the property of another

(5) **computer software:** written or recorded instructions which direct the activities or processes of a computer

(6) **sale:** a transaction which results in the passage of title or possession or both from the seller to the buyer for consideration

(7) **use:** the exercise of any right or power over property which may be incidental to ownership of that property

(8) **measure:** the amount upon which the tax is based

(9) **retailer:** the party making the sale to ultimate consumers or a person engaged in the business of making sales at retail (in some states, also called a jobber or dealer)

(10) **wholesaler:** the party selling to retailers

(11) **vendor's discount:** that amount (as a percentage) of the tax due which the seller is allowed to keep as compensation for collecting the tax on behalf of the taxing authority

(12) **agent:** a person or company acting on behalf of a buyer or seller (however, in some states this term may be used interchangeably with the term "seller")

(13) **common carrier:** one that transports persons or property for others for a price without denying access to conveyance if an approved fare or charge is paid

(14) **sales price:** the total amount received for a sale less any deductions or allowances provided by statute (state specific)

(15) **purchase price:** the total amount less allowable deductions paid by a purchaser for property or services acquired (state specific); cost price and purchase price may be different when measuring use tax liability

(16) **conditional sale:** a sale involving the transfer of possession without transfer of ownership (held by the seller) until the entire sales price has been paid

(17) **occasional sale:** one in series of (typically) three or fewer transactions annually by someone not in the business of selling; often an infrequent sale of property, the type for which the seller was not required to hold a permit

(18) **FOB** (free on board or freight on board): an indicated location, e.g., shipping point, destination, warehouse, etc., where title to the property passes from one party to another: Note the FOB point does not indicate who is responsible for the cost of transportation, only who is liable for the property in event of damage or loss

(19) **place of sale:** location at which the sale is deemed to have taken place

(20) **gross receipts:** the total amount of money including the value of other consideration received from selling property or services

(21) **absorption:** the right of the seller not to pass tax on to the buyer

(22) **separation:** the requirement that the seller separately state (itemize) the tax

(23) **shifting:** the requirement that the seller shift the burden of the tax to the buyer

II. Definitions: Transacting business as a taxpayer

(24) **nexus:** connection, interconnection, tie or link (in sales tax, conditions which, when met, dictate that a party is required to register with a jurisdiction and follow the rules provided therein)—like pregnancy, it is hard to be a little pregnant

(25) **permit:** the grant of authority to act in a particular manner, i.e., the form issued to a registering taxpayer granting status to conduct business, in a particular fashion, within the issuing jurisdiction

(26) **certificate:** the document which, when given by a buyer to a seller, explains how tax should be handled in a given transaction—in some states the term certificate is synonymous with the term permit

(27) **direct pay authority:** a special type of permit authorizing a purchaser to purchase all property Free of-tax and self-assess use tax on that which is not subject to exemption

(28) **bracket system:** the chart provided by the taxing jurisdiction which specifies the actual tax due for a sale or purchase of a given value

(29) **reciprocity:** a concept often adopted and codified by many states forgiving tax due in its own jurisdiction when an equal or greater amount of the same (or possibly, different) tax has been paid on the same transaction in a second state

III. Definitions: The world of audits

(30) **statute of limitations:** the amount of time provided by law during which a right may be asserted or forfeited, e.g., tax can be assessed by an agency or refund be claimed by a taxpayer; assessment and refund rights are not always identical in a given state

(31) **waiver:** the relinquishment, either voluntary or intentional, of a right to act, e.g., that which keeps a period open for review (by the taxing jurisdiction)—evidenced by a form completed and signed by the taxpayer and the jurisdiction

(32) **assessment:** the amount of tax, interest and/or penalty due and collectable by a revenue agency

(33) **determination:** formal notification of assessment by the jurisdiction

(34) **jeopardy assessment:** the type of assessment filed by a jurisdiction that believes the taxpayer will not, cannot, or may not pay taxes due either timely or at all (often involves a lien filed in court)

(35) **grounds:** stated reasons protesting an assessment (also referred to in some states as the content which comprises the "petition for re-determination")

(36) **hearing:** the informal or formal meeting held with the auditor, audit supervisor, legal counsel, administrative law judge or representative of the taxing jurisdiction board or commission for the purpose of discussing or arguing the points and merits of a position (related to an assessment)

(37) **remedies:** the hierarchy of hearings and appeals to which the taxpayer is entitled in order to resolve a tax audit or gain relief or a decision in a tax matter

(38) **ruling:** a position or opinion of the taxing agency on a specific matter (generic or specific) best obtained in writing

IV. Definitions—Court cases

(39) **petitioner:** one who presents a petition or "takes an appeal from a judgment"

(40) **appellant:** one who requests that a higher court review the actions of the lower court

(41) **appellee:** usually the winner in the lower court against whom the appellant is making an appeal

(42) **pleading:** the framing of the issues by the plaintiff and defendant before the court

(43) **headnote:** comments found at the beginning of the case summarizing the significant facts and legal rules

(44) **holding:** declaration of the conclusion of law reached by the court as to the legal effect of the facts in the case

(45) **opinion:** expression of reasons why a certain decision or judgment was reached in a case (may be various if the justices or members of tribunal wish to be on record with particular views); also a view on an issue presented by appointed representatives of a taxing agency

(46) **remand:** send back from a higher to lower court

(47) **slip opinion:** decision of a court, tribunal, or magistrate published separately soon after it has been reached

CASE TABLE

References are to paragraph (¶) numbers.

Topical Index

References are to paragraph (¶) numbers.

References are to paragraph (¶) numbers.

References are to paragraph (¶) numbers.

References are to paragraph (¶) numbers.

References are to paragraph (¶) numbers.

References are to paragraph (¶) numbers.